Praise for *"Proof," Polic*

D0361599

"Understanding public policy—not just what it is, but how it is created—is essential knowledge for college leaders. Paul Lingenfelter's book provides new insights in how to construct evidence-based public policies based on solid research and evaluation."—**Michael N. Bastedo**, *Professor; Director, Center for the Study of Higher and Postsecondary Education, University of Michigan*

"Lingenfelter takes on the long-standing and highly problematic relationship among research, policy, and practice. He unmasks modern-day shibboleths about how performance management and randomized field trials are the new answers. While highly respectful of practitioner wisdom and judgment, he marks out clear limits here too. He argues persuasively that those engaged in the work of education must become active agents of its continuous improvement, and sketches out how policy makers can foster an environment where such systematic gathering and use of evidence is more likely to happen. This is a very wise book!"—**Anthony S. Bryk**, *President, Carnegie Foundation for the Advancement of Teaching*

"This book, whose author has been deeply involved in enacting and analyzing higher education policy in the United States for over two decades, makes an important contribution to our understanding of a key question: How do we know what policies actually work? This volume articulately describes the disconnect between academic researchers, who often pursue their own questions of interest, and the policy world, which is desperate for usable knowledge to help guide important decisions. Drawing on examples from education and other disciplines, this book helps us understand why this chasm exists and how it best can be bridged."—**Donald E. Heller**, *Dean, College of Education, Michigan State University*

"[The] problem of how to act effectively in the world knowing that there is never enough time or evidence to perfect one's decisions is as old as Aristotle and as contemporary as reforming the U.S. financial aid system for higher education.

"This book is richly informed both by Lingenfelter's extensive experience in scholarship, foundation leadership, and public affairs, and his exceptionally perceptive reading of a wide range of relevant literature. His writings range over problems of inference; of measurement; and of governmental, institutional, and individual decision making. He draws on examples in and out of education, in the United States and abroad. This is a fascinating, well argued, and in some ways personal book.

"You have in your hands a deeply informed and instructive book that is also a pleasure to read. I expect that you will enjoy and profit from it."
—*Michael S. McPherson*, *The Spencer Foundation*

"To improve educational outcomes, policy makers and practitioners need high-quality, relevant data and research that informs understanding of what works, for which students, and in what contexts. Lingenfelter illuminates the constructive tension among practitioners, policy makers, and researchers that is needed to design and answer important questions of educational improvement; cautions against ideological singularity in research methods and 'silver bullet' studies or solutions; and offers useful recommendations for ensuring that research is consequential."—*Laura W. Perna and Joni E. Finney*, *Graduate School of Education, The University of Pennsylvania; and coauthors of* The Attainment Agenda: State Policy Leadership in Higher Education

"Paul Lingenfelter has produced a 'must-read' for the layman and reflective fodder for the seasoned policy maker.

"This common sense and thorough walk through the development of assessment practice and policy, punctuated with diligent attention to research, should become required reading for educational policy makers.

"Few people could have written this book. Paul's wisdom and keen observations are clearly the result of a lifetime of learning and reflection from multiple experiences and schooled by his persistent quest for knowledge. That rich set of life's experiences come together to produce an outstanding contribution to education policy.

"Throughout the book Paul takes clear stances on controversial and perplexing issues and does not shy away from specific advice on the uses and role of assessment practice and policy."—*Gene Wilhoit*, *CEO, Center for Innovation in Education; former Executive Director of CCSSO; and former education commissioner in Kentucky and Arkansas*

"PROOF," POLICY, AND PRACTICE

"PROOF," POLICY, AND PRACTICE

Understanding the Role of Evidence in Improving Education

Paul E. Lingenfelter

Foreword by Michael S. McPherson

STERLING, VIRGINIA

Sty/us

COPYRIGHT © 2016 BY
Paul E. Lingenfelter

Published by Stylus Publishing, LLC.
22883 Quicksilver Drive
Sterling, Virginia 20166-2102

All rights reserved. No part of this book may be reprinted
or reproduced in any form or by any electronic, mechanical,
or other means, now known or hereafter invented, including
photocopying, recording, and information storage and
retrieval, without permission in writing from the publisher.

Library of Congress Cataloging-in-Publication Data
Names: Lingenfelter, Paul E., author.
Title: Proof, policy, and practice : understanding the role of
evidence in improving education /
Paul E. Lingenfelter.
Description: First edition. |
Sterling, Virginia : Stylus Publishing, LLC, 2016. |
Includes bibliographical references and index.
Identifiers: LCCN 2015022277|
    ISBN 9781579227500 (cloth : acid free paper) |
    ISBN 9781579227517 (pbk. : acid free paper) |
    ISBN 9781579227524 (library networkable e-edition) |
    ISBN 9781579227531 (consumer e-edition)
Subjects: LCSH: Education--Research--United States. |
Educational change--United States. |
Education and state--United States. |
School improvement programs--United States.
Classification: LCC LB1028.25.U6 L56 2016 |
DDC 371.2/07--dc23 LC record available at
http://lccn.loc.gov/2015022277

13-digit ISBN: 978-1-57922-750-0 (cloth)
13-digit ISBN: 978-1-57922-751-7 (paperback)
13-digit ISBN: 978-1-57922-752-4 (library networkable e-edition)
13-digit ISBN: 978-1-57922-753-1 (consumer e-edition)

Printed in the United States of America

All first editions printed on acid-free paper
that meets the American National Standards Institute
Z39-48 Standard.

Bulk Purchases

Quantity discounts are available for use in workshops and for
staff development.
Call 1-800-232-0223

First Edition, 2016

10 9 8 7 6 5 4 3 2 1

To Carol, our children, and our grandchildren.

CONTENTS

FIGURES AND TABLES

FOREWORD

Randomized control trials (RCTs) and a "what works" framework for policy innovation were greeted in the beginning of the new century as the latest "silver bullet" primed to yield rapid improvement in American education. The quite limited results to date have been a severe disappointment to many social scientists and some policy thinkers. To some degree, disappointed advocates of such policies have wanted to blame the education community for not "getting with the program"; that is, for failing to pay sufficient heed to the evidence that they are offered.

The fact is that the "what works" vision has encountered plenty of difficulties in its own terms. Thus, a lot of both time and money have been spent on trials that yield a "no decision" conclusion about whether they "work." Moreover, when an intervention has yielded a significant result in one place, the same intervention has often been found to yield a disappointing result in another place.

Some of this disappointment derives from scientific failures in the design and execution of experiments. Perhaps the most familiar flaw is the attempt to spot an effect without examining enough cases to detect the relatively small impact yielded by most successful interventions. Given the cost of field experiments, RCTs yield a lot of "million dollar maybes."

A bigger problem, however, may lie in an almost willfully naïve conception of how social science evidence can be effectively deployed to generate widespread improvement—to "scale up," as the jargon goes. Is the assumption that because an intervention worked with, say, middle-income seven-year-olds in a suburban district in the Northeast, we should believe the same intervention will have similar effects on disadvantaged nine-year-olds in an inner city in the South? Nothing in the theory behind RCTs should lead us to assume that results from one place will apply widely (what the jargon calls *external validity*), but it's awfully tempting to do so.

Moreover, since schooling interventions are very complex beasts, it's hard to know what implementing "the same intervention" even means. Consistent treatment is hard to achieve even when doctors are administering pills, but making two classrooms act alike is a lot harder. Thus, if trainers were brought in, what were their backgrounds? How much experience? Exactly what prior education? Does the number of minutes per day students are exposed to the treatment matter? How about class size, length of school year, attitudes of parents? A big problem is that RCTs can almost never tell you why something worked, for whom it will work, or under what conditions it will work. It's tough to know what the "active ingredients" in the recipe are. This makes it very hard to have confidence that a replicated intervention will have results like the original. The term *black box* could well have been invented with these kinds of trials in mind.

As the limitations of the naïve "what works" framework become more widely recognized in scientific and policy circles, several kinds of responses can be anticipated and to some extent have already been observed. The first approach is to go more deeply into the science and the analytics of randomized trials and find ways to redesign them to give better answers to the "why, for whom, and when" questions. There are important opportunities for progress on these lines, but the work is slow and expensive. Meanwhile, decision makers can't wait—they have to act.[1] The second, hardly novel, approach is to react to the limits of existing evidence and analysis by relying instead on gut instinct or traditional practice without any systematic attempts at measurement, assessment, or improvement.

The third approach is the one Paul Lingenfelter adopts in this volume. As I read this book, Lingenfelter has no desire to reject the use of measurement tools and analytic reasoning in the search for improvement at the levels of practice and policy, but neither is he willing to suppose that some scientific formula or impeccably designed experiment will relieve decision makers from the responsibility of judgment. This problem of how to act effectively in the world knowing that there is never enough time or evidence to perfect one's decisions is as old as Aristotle and as contemporary as reforming the U.S. financial aid system for higher education.

This book is richly informed by Lingenfelter's extensive experience in scholarship, foundation leadership, and public affairs as well as his exceptionally perceptive reading of a wide range of relevant literature. His writings range over problems of inference and measurement and of governmental, institutional, and individual decision making. He draws on examples in and out of education, in the United States and abroad. This is a fascinating, well argued, and, in some ways, personal book.

Humility, common sense, and patient reading and reflection—these are not the virtues most in evidence in American writing about education and social policy today. Far from it—it's hard to find any proposal for educational or social reform that doesn't promise "dramatic" or "transformative" change to be delivered in record time. Long experience of the resistance of complex organizations to abrupt and dramatic change puts little dent in such claims.

And the notion that well-wrought sentences and paragraphs—in contrast to bullet points and graphics—can play a productive role in advancing understanding runs up against the view that interruption-driven attention spans make patient analysis and exposition superfluous.

You have in your hands a deeply informed and instructive book that is also a pleasure to read. I expect that you will both enjoy and benefit from it.

Michael S. McPherson
The Spencer Foundation

Note

1. Valuable contributions include Granger, R. C., and Maynard, R. (2015). Unlocking the potential of the "What Works" approach to policymaking and practice: Improving impact evaluations. *American Journal of Evaluation*, 1–12 and Raudenbush, S., and Bloom, H. (2015, April). *Learning about and from variation in program impacts using multisite trials*. MDRC.

ACKNOWLEDGMENTS

Peter Drucker's *Adventures of a Bystander*[1] is the most charming, and among the most interesting autobiographies I've ever read. The central focus is not his life but the interesting people he met including, among others, Sigmund Freud; Henry Luce; Buckminster Fuller; Alfred Sloan; and two teachers, Miss Elsa and Miss Sophy.

My adventures and achievements are considerably more modest than Drucker's, but this book is largely about the people I've met, the authors I've read, and what they have taught me. Many of them are cited in the text. The book also reflects what I've failed to learn, have still to learn, and mistakenly think I've learned. That, of course, is not their fault.

I cannot name them all, but I especially wish to thank:

- My graduate school teachers at Michigan State University and the University of Michigan, who taught me about research methods, tests and measurements, public policy, and organizational theory, especially Marvin W. Peterson and James (Jerry) L. Miller Jr.
- Gerald Burkhouse, my first professional boss, who introduced me to Theory X and Theory Y, guided my first experience in supervising others, and assigned me the task of surveying the opinions of students living in Bursley Residence Hall at the University of Michigan. He personified continuous improvement, respect for data, and supportive supervision and accountability.
- Donald E. Stokes, who hired me when dean of the graduate school at the University of Michigan, gave me an opportunity to learn about research across the disciplines, and shared a pre-publication draft of his final and perhaps most influential book, *Pasteur's Quadrant: Basic Science and Technological Innovation.*[2] Thanks to the Brookings Institution for permission to use the key illustration from *Pasteur's Quadrant.*
- Richard D. Wagner, initially a source for my dissertation research and my boss for 11 years at the Illinois Board of Higher Education, who taught and continues to teach me about the practical and ethical dimensions of public policy and political behavior.
- Jack Corbally, James Furman, Adele Simmons, and Victor Rabinowitch, who, for 15 years, gave me the opportunity to learn from

the world-class scientists and educators whose work was supported by the John D. and Catherine T. MacArthur Foundation.

- Two especially helpful friends from the MacArthur time: Tom Cook, who introduced me to the profession of program evaluation; and Bob Rose, my colleague who suggested I read *Consilience* by E. O. Wilson.[3]
- All my staff colleagues and the members of the association of State Higher Education Executive Officers who supported and encouraged my writing and advanced my education. They are too numerous to mention by name.
- Colleagues at the State Higher Education Policy Center in Boulder, Colorado: David Longanecker, Dennis Jones, and especially Peter Ewell, who read and commented on several chapters.
- Mike McPherson at the Spencer Foundation, who gave me an office for a month and access to his staff and library early in the project. Mike's work exemplifies the productive, useful educational researcher.
- Tony Bryk, now president of the Carnegie Foundation for the Advancement of Teaching and Learning, whose professional contributions inspired much of this book and who was particularly helpful in providing feedback on Chapter 5. I am grateful to Harvard Education Press for permission to use the illustrations in this chapter.
- Colleagues at the National Institute for Learning Outcomes Assessment (NILOA), George Kuh, Stan Ikenberry, and Natasha Jankowski, who offered encouragement and helpful suggestions.
- John von Knorring, my publisher at Stylus, who encouraged me to write, patiently waited 4 years for me to get around to it, and provided helpful comments on every chapter.

Finally, deepest thanks to my wife Carol, who, for the 50 years after our first date, has contributed love, support, patience, helpful feedback, and her professional knowledge as an accomplished social work practitioner and teacher. Her practical wisdom and professional knowledge appear without citation in many places of this book. She has enriched my life in countless ways.

Paul E. Lingenfelter
April 2015

Notes

1. Drucker, P. F. (1978). *Adventures of a bystander*. New York, NY: Harper & Row.

2. Stokes, D. E. (1997). *Pasteur's quadrant: Basic science and technological innovation*. Washington, DC: Brookings Institution Press.

3. Wilson, E. O. (1999). *Consilience: The unity of knowledge*. New York, NY: Random House Digital.

INTRODUCTION

Curiosity and caring drive inquiry. Scholars want to understand, to know, and most of them want their scholarship to have an impact in the world.

Policy makers and practitioners also are curious and caring, although, for them, perhaps caring may have a higher priority. They have problems to solve, and they are curious about better ways to solve them.

An influential strain in the American scientific tradition put curiosity and caring about practical matters at opposite ends of a continuum. Vannevar Bush, the intellectual giant who shaped American science policy after World War II, argued that basic research and research to solve practical problems are different enterprises, perhaps even enterprises in tension. While advocating investments in research and development along a continuum from basic research through applied research to practical development, Bush considered basic research, free inquiry unconstrained by the pursuit of any practical application, to be the pinnacle of scholarly activity. He considered the pursuit of useful knowledge a lesser discipline, which should not be permitted to contaminate basic research.

In *Pasteur's Quadrant: Basic Science and Technological Innovation,* a half century later, Donald Stokes[1] argued that inquiry can simultaneously be driven by curiosity and caring, and that different pathways can lead to both fundamental understanding and practical utility. Thomas Edison, a tinkerer without peer, had no patience for theoretical inquiry, but inadvertently advanced fundamental understanding while relentlessly pursuing practical, valuable discoveries. For Louis Pasteur, the pursuit of fundamental understanding was driven by his obsession with finding solutions to the problem of disease.

The dialogue between Bush and Stokes has obvious implications for science policy, and it also leads to other fundamental questions: (a) What constitutes knowledge? (b) What are the characteristics of useful knowledge? (c) How can knowledge be employed to improve policy and practice? (d) How can knowledge be widely disseminated and effectively employed?

Although scholarship with relevance to policy and practice clearly abounds, neither the producers nor the consumers of scholarship seem satisfied with their relationship. The disrespect is mutual. The words *academic*

1

and *theoretical* often convey derision among policy makers and practitioners. For many academics, *political* is equated with *irrational* and *self-serving*. Harry Truman reputedly longed to find a one-armed economist who would not say "on the other hand." And an economist once suggested that politicians use data as a drunk uses a lamppost—for support, not illumination.

Beneath the jokes lie serious issues. Researchers, policy makers, and practitioners generally share a sincere interest in improving the human condition. Academics may be tempted to fault irrationality, ideology, or ignorance for the failure of research to inform policy and practice more powerfully, but policy makers and practitioners have learned that academics rarely can tell them "what works," that is, a practice or method that will reliably yield desirable results. Every self-respecting researcher wants to make important contributions. Nobody is really happy when the collection and analysis of empirical data on policy and practice is not respected, accessible, and put to good use.

Scholars must decide how to employ their talents: What questions are important and accessible? What methods will be fruitful? Policy makers and practitioners must make choices about the problems confronting them: What information is relevant? What knowledge is valid and useful? Which of many alternative strategies and interventions might be helpful? How can they find what they need?

My interest in such questions began in graduate school when I studied higher education, public policy, and research methods. At that time rational analysis (Planning, Programming, and Budgeting System, or PPBS) was a hot topic in government and experimental research for evaluating social policy was a fairly new idea. The aspiration of these approaches, never quite realized, was to make policy and practice more rational, more "evidence based" (a catchphrase that emerged later.) But I also studied organizations from the perspective of open systems theory, which leads one to appreciate complexity. I learned the principle of *equifinality*, a word that has always made me chuckle. In academic language, it means that in a complex, open system, the same result can occur through different pathways. In ordinary language: There is more than one way to skin a cat.

After graduate school at the Illinois Board of Higher Education, I worked for 11 years with colleagues to develop data systems and budgeting procedures that reflected the conceptual framework, data requirements, and aspirations of PPBS. We knew then that robust, definitive cost-benefit analysis among different programs was a chimera, but we still believed that better information on how resources were allocated and the cost of different programs could be used with common sense to help higher education leaders and state policy makers do a more effective job. That belief has been validated over time, even though the information available has not always been usefully employed by decision makers.

At the MacArthur Foundation where I worked for the next 15 years I was introduced to the thinking of many leading scientists through the Foundation's programs and research networks in mental health and human development, economics, population, international affairs, and education. I had a chance to meet scientists interested in chaos theory who were mounting ambitious efforts at the Santa Fe Institute to find predictability in the complex, adaptive systems of nature and human society. These experiences gave me opportunities to meet outstanding scholars and listen to freewheeling conversations as they wrestled with tough questions. My respect for these men and women deepened, but I soon realized that the dream of crisp, scientific solutions to most tough human problems is entirely unrealistic.

I then spent 13 years at the State Higher Education Executive Officers association, again working more directly on issues of practice and policy. My colleagues and I wrestled with how to make "accountability" a constructive force, not a finger-pointing exercise. We watched our K–12 colleagues struggle with No Child Left Behind,[2] a well-meaning but ultimately ineffectual strategy to improve educational opportunities for disadvantaged children. We participated in ambitious strategies to help states benchmark their performance in higher education to the leading states. We helped design and promote the utilization of common education data standards. We observed the development of Common Core State Standards in English Language Arts and Mathematics, and decided to encourage and support their utilization in improving college readiness and college success. We worked to promote the use of data to track student participation and mobility in higher education in order to know the true rate of graduation and better understand how to increase student success. And as somewhat skeptical colleagues, we collaborated in an international feasibility study to assess postsecondary student learning.

In the career just summarized, I've observed many efforts to improve policy and practice through the use of research and evidence. These efforts have made progress, but the progress achieved often falls substantially short of aspirations. Some seriously doubt whether evidence and research can lead to meaningful improvements in policy and practice. I am more optimistic. But seeking to understand what evidence and research can and cannot do and how they can become more useful is a worthwhile endeavor.

I've tried to address these gaps in knowledge by writing something between a comprehensive scholarly treatment of the topic (which is beyond my capabilities) and an account of my experience as a policy professional. I've drawn on the scholarly literature that I've found most helpful in understanding the issues and making sense of my experience, and I've illustrated conceptual and practical problems from my experience and my reading.

Most of the examples and situations I describe are drawn from education, but I've also drawn on social work, medicine, social welfare, and other fields of policy and practice where I've found useful material. The fundamental challenges and opportunities of using evidence and research are similar across all these fields, and they are similar in many settings—classrooms, schools and colleges, organizations of many kinds, and the executive and legislative branches of government.

As I close this introduction, let me define some terms, provide an indication of how my thinking has evolved, and suggest where the argument of the book is heading.

By *policy*, I mean actions taken collectively by social groups, governments, or organizations to achieve a purpose. Policy can be laws, regulations, procedures, the allocation of financial resources, or the granting of discretional authority or authority limited by rules to individuals (e.g., executives, police officers, or professionals) with particular responsibilities. Policy is an expression of power: the power of an individual in a monarchy, dictatorship, or sole proprietorship; or the shared, collective power in democratic governments, organizations, or corporations. Policy seeks to achieve an end or ends by taking actions that affect communities of people. Policy is not self-executing, however. It can fail for many reasons, including poor design and active or passive resistance by the people it seeks to influence or govern.

By *practice*, I mean actions taken by individuals to achieve a purpose. In this context I am focusing on professionals in education and other complex professions. Although such professionals typically work in an environment of organizational and governmental policies that may shape, support, or constrain their practice, they function somewhat autonomously as individuals delivering professional services.

(Steven Hodas, a long-time observer and participant in New York City schools, suggests that policy and practice reflect differences in white-collar and blue-collar culture, corporate management and labor, with sharp differences in expectations about the role and effectiveness of policy and strategies for getting things done in practice.[3] His observations are a useful lens for interpreting much of this book.)

In the term *research and evidence*, I include all the forms and tools of *professional social inquiry*, a term employed by Charles Lindblom and David Cohen in their book *Useful Knowledge*.[4] (A more complete version of their definition appears in Chapter 1.) I acknowledge all forms of quantitative and qualitative inquiry, ranging from observation and description to experimental research, as research; and I acknowledge all kinds of observations, ranging from descriptive narrative to precise measurement, as evidence.

The baseball movie *Moneyball*[5] provides a now-popular depiction of the difference between qualitative and quantitative research. In the movie, the professional scouts are qualitative researchers. They evaluate players based on their experience (and sometimes prejudices) in ways that are subtly ridiculed by the movie script. The nerdy quantitative analyst crunches many numbers on player performance (fielding, on-base percentage, batting with runners on base, etc.) and evaluates each player's value in terms of contract cost and likely production. In the movie and in actual life, of course, the low-budget Oakland Athletics did surprisingly well, and the field of sports statistics received a huge boost.

Moneyball is an entertaining movie and it makes a good point, but it is not the entire story. Although the sport of baseball is exceptionally well-designed for statistical analysis, the rest of life is not so well ordered. Policy makers and practitioners need both "hard" quantitative data and sophisticated qualitative research and analysis. As a gifted qualitative researcher once reminded her hard-scientist colleagues on the MacArthur Foundation Board, there are different ways of knowing.

Different kinds of research and evidence have different capabilities. To "know" how minority, low-income, poorly educated parents experience enrolling their children in a school staffed by teachers unfamiliar with their life challenges and culture takes skill in establishing relationships, interviewing, and observation. To "know" why it was difficult for a successful school superintendent in New York City to replicate his success in San Diego takes similar skills, along with particular knowledge of both settings to understand why certain capabilities would work in one and not another.[6] Qualitative research skills are essential for understanding complex, difficult to measure human attributes, relationships, and experience.

Despite its importance, qualitative research is unavoidably subjective and limited. One rarely finds commonly accepted scales for measuring qualitative observations, even though certain professions have developed procedures and guidelines for disciplined observation and the triangulation of evidence. Qualitative researchers seek to create compelling, persuasive narratives explaining why the world works as it does, and they often succeed. But qualitative research has difficulty in generalizing across settings, and without objective measurement it is quite difficult to demonstrate "improvement" of any kind.

Quantitative research, however, relies heavily on measurement and seeks to draw persuasive inferences about cause and effect. To some, "evidence" is not evidence unless it comes in the form of objective numerical data. In the extreme form of this view, evidence is not valid unless it is measurable and the independent causal effects of an intervention on an outcome are "proven" through rigorously controlled experimental research. At the opposite epistemological extreme, the critics of quantitative research argue that *all* observations, including "measured" phenomena are subjective, unavoidably biased by the perceptual filters of individuals and human culture. I understand the argument of unavoidable subjectivity, but taken to an extreme it goes far too far philosophically and practically. If the extreme version of the argument were true, people could learn nothing with confidence about the world, and it would not be possible to take any actions or learn anything that might systematically improve policy and practice.

The effective use of research and evidence in policy and practice requires an appreciation of complexity, context, and human agency. The sciences of physics, chemistry, and biology have made enormously important contributions to human life, but the simple application of the scientific method does not and cannot explain variation in human outcomes; nor can it improve policy and practice. Success in baseball might be improved, but it cannot be guaranteed by quantitative analysis. Policy and practice in education, economics, social welfare, and medicine are infinitely more complex than baseball.

As the reader will learn from the first two chapters of this book, I value scientific rigor but I do not strongly advocate the "gold standard"— experimental research with random assignment to treatment and control groups—as the highest, best form of evidence to improve policy and practice. Experimental research is poorly equipped to deal with many practical and policy conditions. Its contributions have not been successfully extended to very many domains of policy and practice beyond what Donald Berwick calls "conceptually neat" parts of medicine.[7] Perversely, the common experimental finding that in policy or practice "nothing works" leads to pessimism about the potential for achieving desirable outcomes. The problem is not that "nothing works," but that "what works" is rarely a replicable, easily testable intervention.

While acknowledging the difficulties, measurement—quantitative and, where necessary, systematic, qualitative expert ratings—is essential for improving policy and practice. The third and fourth chapters of the book consider the challenges of measurement; describe important initiatives that have made contributions, especially in education; and identify pitfalls and limitations of measurement. Measurement is an essential tool for both practitioners and policy makers. Despite some wishful thinking to the contrary, however, measurement and transparency are not, in themselves, interventions that can improve outcomes.

The fifth and sixth chapters of the book provide illustrative examples and consider the conditions under which research and evidence can usefully inform and improve policy and practice. The concluding seventh chapter briefly recapitulates the main arguments of the book and considers emerging practices and approaches that promise to help scholars, practitioners, and policy leaders become more successful in reaching their fundamental goals.

Notes

1. Stokes, D. E. (1997). *Pasteur's quadrant: Basic science and technological innovation.* Washington, DC: Brookings Institution.

2. No Child Left Behind (NCLB) Act of 2001, 20 U.S.C.A. § 6301 et seq.

3. Hodas, S. (2015, January 15). *Clash of cultures: Blue collar, white collar, and school reform.* Retrieved from http://www.crpe.org/thelens/clash-cultures-blue-collar-white-collar-and-school-reform

4. Lindblom, C. E., & Cohen, D. K. (1979). *Usable knowledge: Social science and social problem solving.* New Haven, CT: Yale University Press.

5. De Luca, M., Horovitz, R., & Pitt, B. (Producers), & Miller, M. (Director). (2011). *Moneyball* [Motion picture]. United States: Columbia Pictures.

6. Hubbard, L., Mehan, H., & Stein, M. K. (2006). *Reform as learning: School reform, organizational culture, and community politics in San Diego.* New York, NY: Routledge.

7. Berwick, D. M. (2008). The science of improvement. *Journal of the American Medical Association, 299*(10), 1182–1184.

I

PROOF AND POLICY

At the 1999 conference of the Association for Public Policy Analysis and Management (APPAM) a panel of distinguished researchers celebrated progress over the previous 20 years in using rigorous experimental and quasi-experimental methods to assess the effectiveness of programs or interventions in education and other areas of social policy.

Then a member of the audience stood and impolitely called for a "new kind of evaluation, a more sophisticated approach that will help build political and budget support for the programs we know work and help make them better." [Quotation paraphrased]

One panelist found the implications of these remarks "disturbing." Another, with more feeling, said it was "ideological" to resist the use of randomized assignment experiments in education and social policy.

For the panel, rigorously assembled empirical evidence, ideally using random assignment and experimental methods to demonstrate causality, constituted the only valid test of policy effectiveness. Those who resist or oppose such assessments may be suspected of avoiding accountability; foregoing opportunities to discover or develop really effective social programs; or, at worst, wasting vast sums of public resources in self-serving, ineffective programs.

The impolite questioner, working to solve difficult problems, believed her efforts are necessary, worthwhile, and effective, and that formal, scientific evaluations failed to demonstrate what she "knows." Such evaluations are costly, she said; they don't seem to help improve programs, and they seem to make it more, rather than less difficult to garner the necessary resources and wisdom to make social progress.

People not in the room might have raised uncomfortable questions for both the researchers and the program advocates. They might have asked the researchers, What benefits have accrued from 20 years (now more than 30) of using increasingly sophisticated research methods to improve policy and practice? What do we know for sure based on all your research? Or they might have asked the program advocates, Do you really want us to keep spending money on programs that can't demonstrate their value based on hard data? How do you know these are good programs?

I t seems like a long time ago now, but not much has changed. I have observed and participated in such debates for nearly a half century as a student, policy analyst, foundation executive, and educational association leader. It has always seemed sensible to use empirical evidence and rigorous analysis to guide decisions and improve performance. So why is it so difficult and progress so slow? What could make things better?

These are the questions that inspired this book. It is based on the work of scholars who have wrestled with these issues as well as the work of practitioners and policy makers struggling to solve problems and looking for help wherever it may be found. Drawing on the work of scholars I've found most helpful, this chapter will briefly consider the difficult conceptual and practical challenges involved in developing and applying knowledge to improve policy and practice.

Usable Knowledge in Everyday Life—The Modest Role of Science

According to its authors, Charles E. Lindblom and David K. Cohen, their small 1979 book *Usable Knowledge: Social Science and Social Problem Solving* was stimulated by "dissatisfaction with social science and social research as instruments of social problem solving."[1] As they observed, such dissatisfaction comes from both suppliers and users of social research.

Lindblom and Cohen approached the problem with a comprehensive view of social science and (especially Lindblom's) thoughtful previous work on the process of social problem solving. The essence of the challenge is captured in their observation:

> Seen as a whole, obstacles and potential for more useful social science pose profound questions about man as a problem solver, about knowledge and craft, about science, and about a complex social and political order in which knowledge and science are embedded and by which they are shaped.[2]

Lindblom and Cohen define *professional social inquiry* to include the work of seminal social theorists such as Adam Smith and Karl Marx, the several social sciences, classification, data collection and analysis, some (but not all) historical research, program evaluation, social commentary and criticism, mathematical modeling, consulting, and a variety of related intellectual activities. They wrote primarily to their colleagues, fellow practitioners of professional social inquiry (PSI).

Lindblom and Cohen suggest that PSI practitioners "greatly overestimate the amount and distinctiveness of the information and analysis they offer for social problem solving." *Ordinary knowledge* (which they define as "common sense, casual empiricism, or thoughtful speculation and analysis" with no particular debt to PSI) necessarily plays an important role in social problem solving. Even though the individual stocks vary and contain error as well as truth, every person uses ordinary knowledge to guide action. Direct observation, the most common source of ordinary knowledge, is the source of most of what we know. Through direct observation, for example, we know that "some public officials take bribes, wheat farmers will restrict production if paid to do so, children become angry when thwarted, and so on."[3]

Direct observation by thoughtful and gifted people trying to solve problems without the benefit of formal scientific analysis has also been the source of much of what is commonly considered *scientific knowledge*. The inventions that created the industrial revolution did not emerge from scientific research, but from the tinkering and experimentation of entrepreneurial engineers such as Thomas Edison without the benefit of theory or deep understanding of the physical world.[4]

Lindblom and Cohen observe:

> Despite the professional development of specialized investigative techniques, especially quantitative, most practitioners of professional social inquiry, including the most distinguished among them, inevitably rely heavily on the same ordinary techniques of speculation, definition, conceptualization, hypothesis formulation, and verification as are practiced by persons who are not social scientists or professional investigators of any kind.[5]

Social problems are "solved" (or, more accurately, "attacked") not typically by freestanding analytical work done by PSI practitioners or others, but through more complex processes involving interaction, social learning, and the generation and evolution of ordinary knowledge. Elections, markets, political debates over values and practical issues, even homeowners association meetings are examples of using ordinary knowledge and interaction to address problems. PSI sometimes plays a role in these processes, but often just a bit part.

The practitioners of PSI tend to resist accepting the relatively limited role for PSI in actual problem solving, even though observation of these processes is part of the ordinary knowledge they and most policy makers and practitioners share. Instead, they assert that policy is (or at least should be) constructed primarily or solely through a rational analytical process. In a wide-ranging review of scholarly commentary on the policy-making process, Lindblom and Cohen find numerous examples where PSI practitioners fail to recognize the role of interaction in problem solving, assume that policy is typically made by single "decision makers" employing rational analysis, and assert an authoritative role for PSI that exceeds the bounds of the possible.

In arguing that the potential of PSI to make significant contributions is bounded, Lindblom and Cohen write:

> First, PSI is costly, so much so that it cannot be used for most social problems nor pushed to conclusive answers on those issues on which it is used. Second, even if it were a free good, and thus available without constraint of manpower, materials, or money, it cannot achieve scientifically definitive or conclusive answers on certain kinds of questions. At core, both of these explanations trace to the complexity of the social world and, in the face of that complexity, man's limited cognitive capacity. To stretch that capacity is enormously costly, and even if it were stretched as far as imaginable, it could not handle certain kinds of questions.[6]

Lindblom and Cohen suggest that "authoritative" knowledge developed through PSI must come from one or both of two sources: (a) a high level of scientific conclusiveness; and (b) the extent to which the findings of PSI confirm or reinforce ordinary knowledge. Both conclusiveness and authoritativeness are a matter of degree, naturally, and to be fully authoritative in a practical sense, knowledge must lead to widespread acceptance and action. To the user, knowledge can be "authoritative" regardless of its source.

PSI practitioners typically aspire for their work to be independently authoritative, based entirely on scientific merit. But this aspiration is rarely, perhaps never, realized. One widely recognized obstacle to authoritative knowledge is irrational resistance to the findings of PSI. While the users, not the generators, of PSI may be rightly blamed for such resistance, this obstacle still presents a challenge for PSI practitioners in the conduct and presentation of their work. But irrational resistance is far from the only or even the most significant obstacle preventing PSI findings from being independently authoritative.

Other obstacles include:

1. [PSI] is not competent in sorting through the trade-offs among norms or values in conflict, such as the desirability of helping the needy on the one hand, and motivating initiative and effort on the other hand.
2. PSI rarely yields consistent findings, and more frequently provides variable or divergent, competing findings on difficult questions.

3. Conflicting definitions of the boundaries of social problems obstruct the construction of authoritative knowledge (e.g., is the failure of Johnny to read due to poverty, poor family support, poor teaching, inadequately supported schools, or some other factors?).

4. PSI knowledge becomes obsolete as human behavior and human communities change over time.[7]

For these reasons and more, Lindblom and Cohen conclude that PSI practitioners hope in vain to generate independently authoritative knowledge. This is not to say, however, that PSI cannot make significant contributions. It can collaborate with policy makers and practitioners engaged in interactive problem solving, and it can expand, refine, and sometimes disprove the ordinary knowledge held by those seeking to solve social problems. Many examples of the productive collaborations suggested by Lindblom and Cohen will be discussed in later chapters.

Scientific "Proof" From the Perspective of a "Hard" Scientist

What is authoritative knowledge? What kind of authentic evidence yields knowledge? What is *proof*? These fundamental questions are addressed differently from the perspective of the hard sciences.

In *Consilience: The Unity of Knowledge*,[8] the distinguished biologist Edward O. Wilson concisely summarizes the generally accepted view of the scientific method: "Science . . . is the *organized, systematic enterprise that gathers knowledge about the world and condenses the knowledge into testable laws and principles.*"[9] Wilson distinguishes science from pseudoscience by the following characteristics: (a) repeatability; (b) economy; (c) mensuration (using universally accepted scales); (d) heuristics (the stimulation of further discovery, which both extends and confirms the original discovery); and (e) consilience, the connection of discoveries (explanations) with other explanations in a consistent manner, which confirms both. Each of these characteristics warrants elaboration.

Repeatability is truly the "gold standard." Other scientists will find essentially the same results if they perform the same experiment under identical, or nearly identical, conditions. Repeatability is a much higher standard than *statistical significance*, in which statistical analysis is used to estimate the odds that the finding of an experiment was due to chance.

Parsimony is sometimes used for economy, Wilson's second criterion for science. Essentially, this means that science seeks to discover simple, clear relationships that apply to and can be useful in many situations. Such knowledge will have wide-ranging implications. Wilson writes, "The cutting edge of science is reductionism, the breaking apart of nature into its natural constituents."[10] Complexity is of interest to scientists as a challenge; that is, how the techniques of reductionism can burrow into nature's complexity and discover parsimonious principles or laws.

Wilson's third characteristic of science, consistent, universally accepted *mensuration*, is essential for scientific research. In the physical and biological sciences, research findings can be replicated and new studies can build on previous research, in part because there are generally accepted systems to measure results. Movement through space can be measured. Changes in the chemical composition of a compound can be measured. The amount of high-density and low-density cholesterol in the blood can be measured. Weight and temperature can be measured. In all these cases, universally accepted "yardsticks" have been developed.

The word *heuristic*, Wilson's fourth criterion for science, is rarely used by nonspecialists. "Theory" is a reasonable synonym for "heuristic," but not if it is used to mean a random, unproved hypothesis. A heuristic is not a "fact," but an informed idea about how the world works. In this context, it is based on facts that have been demonstrated through research. A heuristic based on research is an explanatory idea, or "theory" extending what has been learned to new ideas about relationships or treatments that might prove to be true. When these ideas are tested, they help build more fully developed explanatory models, or theories.

Wilson's fifth criterion for science, consilience, is also unfamiliar to most people. *Consilience* means that all the pieces fit together. The essential meaning of consilience is the same as the subtitle of Wilson's book, the unity of knowledge. Authentic knowledge does not contradict itself. Knowledge in physics cannot contradict knowledge in chemistry or biology. For Wilson, all science must move toward consilience, building on discovery after discovery, through repeated "proofs" based on universally accepted measures; and through heuristics leading to new discoveries, more powerful "theories," and deeper, authentic knowledge.[11]

Most social scientists, policy makers, and practitioners will acknowledge that these five elements of "real science" are comparatively rare in their world. Wilson suggests rather emphatically that their absence is the reason the social and behavioral sciences have failed to make significant progress.[12]

The biggest gap, according to Wilson, is the absence of consilience. Medical science is built on a foundation of molecular and cell biology, and medical scientists "pursue elements of health and illness all the way to the level of biophysical chemistry."[13] Social science, although admittedly *hypercomplex*, to use Wilson's term, does not have a similar foundation of a shared theory with the concomitant base of scientific knowledge on which to make progress. Instead, according to Wilson, social scientists espouse competing theories of human behavior; they defend the cacophony by suggesting it is creative and constructive; they do not share language across disciplines, even though they use precise language within disciplines; and they are divided by political ideology. Wilson spares none of the social sciences from his critique (including economics, perhaps the most rigorous among them), and urges research that crosses the boundary between the biological and social sciences and builds on emerging work in cognitive neuroscience, human behavioral genetics, evolutionary biology, and environmental science.

At the end of his critique of the social sciences, Wilson recognizes the daunting technical problems facing the social sciences and acknowledges that at least some philosophers of science have concluded that constructing a robust bridge between the natural and social sciences is impossible. Resisting such pessimism, Wilson insists that authentic science must pursue consilience. He asserts that progress in the social sciences can come only by building and crossing the bridge between the natural and social sciences toward the construction of unified knowledge.

Can We Find Proof in Policy and Practice?

One has to admire Wilson's courageous determination to pursue consilience in the social realm and his optimism that a bridge between the natural and social sciences is feasible. But Lindblom and Cohen's restrained ambition seems more realistic. The core problem is not that social scientists are more ideological, less courageous, or less brilliant than other scientists; to be clear, Wilson makes no ad hominem attacks, and he respects the talent and commitment of social scientists. The core problem is that social scientists are working on what Wilson acknowledges are hypercomplex systems of biological organisms (human beings) whose behavior is shaped by varied, complex social environments. Furthermore, humans have the ability to make choices and take actions; this ability, combined with the inherent complexity of the organisms and their environments, creates insurmountable (or, for the courageous Wilsonian optimist, *nearly* insurmountable) problems for the techniques of scientific reductionism. Complexity compounded by agency is formidable.

In her book *Unsimple Truths: Science, Complexity, and Policy*, philosopher of science Sandra Mitchell argues that a new approach to epistemology, more flexible than scientific reductionism, is needed. She writes:

> Similarly, traditional philosophical analyses of the cleanest, clearest cases of causal interactions . . . are difficult if not impossible to apply to the messy, murky causal relations that are displayed by genes and phenotypes,

human interventions on the global climate, or the multi-level feedback-laden phenomena studied in modern psychiatry. A revised and expanded epistemology is required to face the challenge of understanding these complex behaviors. . . . How are complex structures different from simple ones? What types of complexity are there? How do the answers to these questions bear on our understanding of nature, how we come to know it, and how we should base our actions and policies on that knowledge? . . . The complexity of complex structures impels us to modify our conception of the character of usable knowledge claims beyond the narrow domain of universal, exceptionless laws. Exceptions are the rule and limitations are to be expected in the laws that describe many complex behaviors. We will see that the traditional notions of controlled experimentation as the best scientific method for ascertaining causal structures can fail to accommodate robust, dynamic behaviors. Both the search for "the" scientific method and for some small set of fundamental laws that explain everything, everywhere, must be replaced by a more pragmatic and pluralistic approach to scientific practice.[14]

Mitchell argues that, just as twentieth-century physics challenged the simplicity of Newtonian physics, abundant evidence of biological and human diversity, emerging from the interactions of organisms with their environment, requires an expanded approach to epistemology. In her words, such an expanded approach incorporates:

- *pluralism*, integrating multiple explanations and models at many levels of analysis instead of always expecting a single, bottom-level reductive explanation;
- *pragmatism* in place of absolutism, which recognizes there are many ways to accurately, if partially, represent the nature of nature, including various degrees of generality and levels of abstraction, and acknowledges which representation "works" best is dependent, in part, on our interests and abilities; and
- the essentially *dynamic and evolving character of knowledge* in place of static universalism, which feature requires us to find new means of investigating nature and a reconfiguration of policy strategies for acting on the knowledge we obtain.[15]

Mitchell supports the argument for an expanded epistemology with examples drawn from molecular biology, evolutionary biology, social dynamics within biological systems, and the interactions between genetic predispositions and environmental stress associated with mental illness. In arguing for a more flexible epistemology, she writes, "Reductionism becomes the enemy only when it is promoted as the only game in town. Pluralism in explanatory strategies recognizes the diversity of causal structures that populate our world."[16]

Mitchell is clear that science must still be empirical. Observing the inevitable and salutary emergence of an increasing diversity of scientific theories and models, she writes, "I do not believe that any actual scientific practice supports 'anything goes' pluralism or provides reason to abandon the belief in well-confirmed scientific theories as representative of the world. Empirical test remains the arbiter of scientific worth."[17]

After describing various options of scientific pluralism proposed by others, she argues for *integrative pluralism,* an approach that examines the interrelationships of causal structures at each level of complex systems, considering the roles of contingent and interacting factors. (Although there is no evident connection in their thinking, Mitchell's description of integrative pluralism is consistent with the "realistic evaluation" approach of Pawson and Tilley[18] described in the following chapter.)

In concluding her argument, Mitchell writes,

> Unfortunately, this leaves a picture of science as having substantially greater challenges than the one painted by a thoroughgoing reductionist approach. On my view, there is no privileged level to which all explanations must be directed: there are multiple levels of causes. The reality of the successes and failures in contemporary sciences of explanations of complex natural systems allows us no other conclusion.[19]

Warren Weaver's 1948 essay "Science and Complexity" analyzed the problem of complexity with an illuminating metaphor. Before the twentieth century, most of the significant advances in science were achieved by isolating the causal effects of one factor on another, simple two-variable problems, such as a billiard ball moving on a table. Weaver notes that relatively simple scientific insights about the physical world in this era brought us, for example, the telephone and radio, the automobile, the turbine, the diesel engine, and the modern hydroelectric plant.[20]

Analyzing the behavior of two or three billiard balls on a table is also possible, Weaver noted, but the increase in analytical difficulty is surprisingly great. When there are 10 or 15 balls on the table at once, "the problem becomes unmanageable, not because there is any theoretical difficulty, but just because the actual labor of dealing in specific detail with so many variables turns out to be impracticable." Interestingly, as Weaver observed, the problem would be easier if there were millions of balls on a massive table in a disorganized, random pattern because one can use statistical techniques to answer certain kinds of questions with useful precision: On average, how far do balls move before hitting another ball? How many impacts per second do balls have? And so on. The analysis of many variables in disorganized complexity can be quite fruitful and practical, as it has been in the analysis of the physical universe (e.g., the movement of molecules) and in the assessment of risk as done by the insurance industry.[21]

What About the Potential of Big Data?

The "big data" movement currently receiving great attention has achieved benefits from the analysis of disorganized complexity that likely exceed anything Weaver could have imagined. In *Big Data: A Revolution That Will Transform How We Live, Work, and Think*, Viktor Mayer-Schönberger and Kenneth Cukier describe compelling examples of how massive databases of information have been used to predict human behavior, estimate risk, and solve a surprisingly diverse range of human problems.[22]

The predictive power of correlations found in large data sets is the driver of big data's contributions. The opening example in the book discusses a paper in *Nature* that documents how engineers at Google were able to predict the spread of H1N1 flu in specific geographic regions by looking at the search terms entered by users on the Internet. They did not develop a theory based on terms people might use if feeling ill; rather, they ran 450 million mathematical models to find a combination of 45 search terms that had a strong correlation with official flu statistics nationwide. A model developed using data from 2007 and 2008 predicted the spread of flu in 2009 considerably faster than the CDC could document it based on clinical reports.[23] (Donald Stokes, the distinguished political scientist for whom I worked, once described factor analysis as "seizing your data by the throat and demanding: Speak to me!")

As explained by Mayer-Schönberger and Cukier, the analysis of massive data sets does not require careful attention to the quality and consistency of data definitions and collection procedures, nor is it necessary to understand why relationships occur among variables. So long as reasonably strong correlations can be found, people can benefit from knowing *what* relationships exist, without understanding the reasons *why* they exist. One exuberant advocate of big data, editor-in-chief of *Wired* magazine Chris Anderson, suggested in a 2008 editorial "the data deluge makes the scientific method obsolete." He backpedaled in the face of a vigorous response, but Anderson's point is that massive amounts of data, in some cases *all* the data, make it possible to draw significant and useful inferences about relationships without hypothesis testing or causal theories.[24]

The analysis of data is being used for purposes ranging as widely as predicting where manhole covers are likely to explode in New York City, targeting marketing on customers most likely to buy, and identifying likely terrorists. The movie *Moneyball*[25] depicts how the more sophisticated analysis of data on baseball players performance helped the Oakland Athletics achieve a winning season and deepen the fascination with and use of statistical analysis in professional sports.

Mayer-Schönberger and Cukier conclude their analysis of the current and potential uses of big data with a thoughtful discussion of implications, limitations, and risks. The correlations generated from data analysis may yield useful information about the probability of future behavior, but they neither determine nor future behavior predict with sufficient accuracy to justify taking certain kinds of actions concerning individuals. Should people likely to commit a crime be incarcerated as a preventative measure? The policy dilemmas involved in the insurance industry provide other examples of this problem. To what extent should individuals bear the full cost of their *probable* future? Should homes in risky locations or people with established illness be uninsurable?[26]

Although understanding correlations and predictive relationships is enormously helpful in policy and practice, the objective most often is not simply to predict but to shape the future, to intervene in ways that enhance social and individual well-being. This requires addressing questions involving *organized complexity* that, as Weaver indicated, are far more difficult to solve than the simple two-, three-, or four-variable problems solved in the nineteenth century. Analyzing organized complexity is also more difficult than the problems involving millions of variables and cases analyzed by big data without any systematic organizational interference. The biological sciences and the social sciences, to a much greater degree, must deal with many variables, with variable patterns of organization and organisms, and with the relationships and interactions between organisms and their organized environment.[27]

The difficulty of dealing with organized complexity is evident when comparing research in the medical sciences with work in chemistry and physics. "Authoritative knowledge" is much more elusive in medicine, even though we have made huge advances in understanding the biochemical basis of human life and health. In the social sciences, the climb is steeper yet.

Challenges in Applying Scientific Knowledge to Practice

Even the most robust findings of normal scientific knowledge often do not translate very well into the domains of social policy and practice. The gap between scholar and practitioner is not simply one of understanding or training. Donald Schön[28] suggests three reasons why practitioners in the everyday world of organizations often find it difficult to use the results of what he calls *normal social science.*

- First, knowledge is represented differently for the scientist and the practitioner. The scientist is seeking "controlling laws" across many situations, whereas the practitioner is seeking knowledge about a particular situation with a unique set of conditions. The "precise, quantitative, probabilistic, abstract, and complex" ways that research-ers represent knowledge cannot be readily translated to the practice setting.

  Many policy analysts have had the experience of eagerly digging into a research article on an important issue just to find that statistically significant results, at best, account for 5% to 10% of the variance in the sample population. The practitioner or policy maker seeking to improve student learning, for example, may be able to make use of such knowledge to deal with a particular situation, but not with a high degree of confidence in its efficacy.

- Second, practitioners face a gap in the valid application of social science. How can a practitioner know, Schön asks, that "general causal relationships among variables, established in a research context, will hold at a particular time in a particular practice setting?"[29] In practice, it is rarely possible to know and give proper weight to all the factors involved in assessing the applicability of general causal relationships established through research. The pressures, time constraints, and confusion of actual organizational practice make it difficult to carry out such strategies.

- Third, Schön argues that a gap between discovery and production thwarts the efforts of practitioners to implement strategies of action. In ordinary organizational life, people often inadvertently behave in ways that sabotage their expressed intentions, even when they have a clear goal and a strategy for reaching it. He maintains that it is rare for researchers to take this tendency into account in their efforts to discover and promulgate useful inventions.

This critique of "normal" policy analysis and program evaluation is not a challenge on epistemological or scientific grounds but on grounds of utility and performance. Objective reality exists. Hard data are important and useful; however, in social policy and practice, science faces obstacles far more formi-dable than it faces in dealing with the physical or even the biological world.[30]

This point was brought forcefully to my attention in 1985 when I accepted a job with the title of director of program evaluation at the

John D. and Catherine T. MacArthur Foundation. The board of directors then included several world-class scientists: Jonas Salk, who created the first polio vaccine; Jerry Wiesner, former president of MIT and John F. Kennedy's science adviser; and Murray Gell-Mann, Nobel Prize laureate in physics. There were no shrinking violets in this group, but Gell-Mann in particular forthrightly and directly expressed his views. When we met, he told me, "You can't evaluate what we do, it's impossible!"

I imagine he was thinking of cost-benefit analysis or formal evaluation based on quantitative indicators, expecting that my new job would turn out to be both annoying and totally unproductive. I mumbled something to assure him I would not attempt the impossible but would try, nevertheless, to make a contribution and not be annoying.

It is easier to not be annoying than to make a contribution when working on problems in complex systems with many contingencies, interacting variables, and uncertain causal relationships. When quantitative data are relevant and available, formal analysis and even scientific experimentation may be quite useful. But when formal research or quantitative evaluation is impossible, qualitative description and analysis, systemic data collection and inquiry, and the observations and judgment of well-chosen experts *can* make a contribution. Even when quantitative information is available, qualitative description and analysis of context is essential to make sense of quantitative indicators.

During my time at MacArthur we evaluated programs by making explicit the assumptions and theories undergirding our program strategies, assembling available evidence and opinion on how they were working, and inviting external expert advisers to help us make sense of that evidence and opinion. Nothing about the effectiveness or ineffectiveness of MacArthur Foundation program strategies was ever "proved" through program evaluation, but qualitative information and relevant quantitative data helped inform and shape the decisions made by the staff and the board.

Research for Fundamental Understanding and Research for Use

An influential viewpoint in the philosophy of science (greatly advanced by Vannevar Bush's *Science, the Endless Frontier*[31] after World War II) has maintained that basic research and applied research are fundamentally different enterprises. Accordingly, concerns for practical application should not shape in any way decision making in the pursuit of knowledge. This view is held even while asserting that the advancement of fundamental knowledge has frequently, perhaps even inevitably, led to beneficial uses. Bush's view is no longer unchallenged doctrine, but the relationship between the search for useful knowledge and fundamental understanding bears further examination.

In *Pasteur's Quadrant: Basic Science and Technological Innovation*, Donald Stokes challenged the view that basic science and applied science are inherently in conflict. Drawing on numerous examples in the history of science and technology, he argues that the motivation to understand and the motivation to solve problems often exists simultaneously. Inquiry, regardless of motivation, has the potential to advance both utility and fundamental understanding. Stokes's insights are helpful in understanding and reconciling the perspective of E. O. Wilson as compared to that of Lindblom and Cohen.[32]

Stokes's four quadrants of scientific research are illustrated in Figure 1.1.[33] The work of physicist Nils Bohr is an example of research motivated by the search for fundamental understanding with no concern for utility. Thomas Edison's research is in the diagonally opposite quadrant, motivated only by utility with no concern for fundamental understanding. Louis Pasteur's work (and I would suggest that of E. O. Wilson, especially as he thinks about the social sciences) is motivated by a search for fundamental understanding as well as considerations of utility.

The fourth quadrant, motived by simple curiosity or the desire to organize information about particular things, seeks neither utility nor fundamental understanding. Stokes did not assign any researchers to the quadrant, because work of this type tends to drift into the other quadrants. Stokes suggests that the initial motives of Roger Tory Peterson (*Peterson Field Guide to Birds of North America*)[34] and Charles Darwin (*On the Origin of Species*)[35] were neither fundamental insight nor use, but Darwin's work, especially, led to fundamental understanding.

Figure 1.1 Stokes's Quadrant Model of Scientific Research

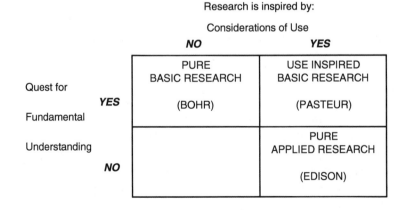

Research is inspired by:

Considerations of Use

	NO	YES
Quest for **YES** Fundamental	PURE BASIC RESEARCH (BOHR)	USE INSPIRED BASIC RESEARCH (PASTEUR)
Understanding **NO**		PURE APPLIED RESEARCH (EDISON)

Utility Without Proof: Scholarship for Policy and Practice

The withering criticism of E. O. Wilson; the measured caution and counsel of Lindblom and Cohen; and the daunting challenges described by Warren Weaver, Sandra Mitchell, and Don Schön confront efforts to inform policy and practice through systematic research and analysis.

If proof is the object, it is difficult to be very optimistic that science will, in the foreseeable future, develop proven approaches for solving problems of social policy and practice. A quixotic search for proof is the first of many pitfalls to be avoided by researchers seeking to be *useful* to policy makers and practitioners. The following chapters will explore other pitfalls as well as promising pathways.

Notes

1. Lindblom, C. E., & Cohen, D. K. (1979). *Usable knowledge: Social science and social problem solving*. New Haven, CT: Yale University Press.

2. Ibid., pp. 2–3.

3. Ibid., pp. 12–13.

4. Weaver, W. (1948). Science and complexity. *American Scientist, 36*(4), 536–544. See also: Stokes, D. E. (1997). *Pasteur's quadrant: Basic science and technological innovation*. Washington, DC: Brookings Institution Press.

5. Lindblom & Cohen, p. 15.

6. Ibid., p. 40.

7. Ibid., pp. 40–53.

8. Wilson, E. O. (1999). *Consilience: The unity of knowledge*. New York, NY: Random House Digital.

9. Ibid., p. 53.

10. Ibid.

11. Ibid.

12. Ibid., pp. 181–209.

13. Ibid., p. 182.

14. Mitchell, S. D. (2009). *Unsimple truths: Science, complexity, and policy*. Chicago, IL: University of Chicago Press, p. 3.

15. Ibid., p. 13.

16. Ibid., p. 107.

17. Ibid., p. 108.

18. Pawson, R., & Tilley, N. (1997). *Realistic evaluation*. London, England: SAGE Publications.

19. Ibid., p. 115.

20. Weaver, p. 536.

21. Ibid., pp. 537–538.

22. Mayer-Schönberger, V., & Cukier, K. (2013). *Big data: A revolution that will transform how we live, work, and think*. New York, NY: Houghton Mifflin Harcourt.

23. Ibid., pp. 1–3.

24. Ibid., pp. 70–71.

25. De Luca, M., Horovitz, R., & Pitt, B. (Producers), & Miller, M. (Director). (2011). *Moneyball* [Motion picture]. United States: Columbia Pictures.

26. Mayer-Schönberger, & Cukier, pp. 150–197.

27. Weaver, pp. 539–540.

28. Schön, D. A. (1995). Causality and causal inference in the study of organizations. In R. F. Goodmann & W. R. Fisher (Eds.), *Rethinking knowledge: Reflections across the disciplines* (69–100). Albany, NY: SUNY Press.

29. Ibid., pp. 72–73.

30. The preceding material was originally published in Lingenfelter, P. E. (2011, May). Evidence and impact: How scholarship can improve policy and practice. *Change Magazine, 43*(3). doi:10.1080/00091383.2011.569260

31. Bush, V. (1945). Science, the endless frontier: A report to the president (Report OCLC 1594001). Retrieved from https://www.nsf.gov/od/lpa/nsf50/vbush1945.htm#transmittal

32. Stokes, D. E. (1997). *Pasteur's quadrant: Basic science and technological innovation.* Washington, DC: Brookings Institution Press.

33. Ibid., p. 73.

34. Peterson, R. T. (2008). *Peterson field guide to birds of North America.* Boston, MA: Houghton Mifflin Harcourt.

35. Darwin, C. (1859). *On the Origin of Species by Means of Natural Selection, or the Preservation of Favoured Races in the Struggle for Life.* Retrieved from https://en.wikisource.org/wiki/On_the_Origin_of_Species_(1859)

2

EXPERIMENTATION AND
PROGRAM EVALUATION

[We are] committed to the experiment: as the only means for settling disputes regarding educational practice, as the only way of verifying educational improvements, and as the only way of establishing a cumulative tradition in which improvements can be introduced without the danger of a faddish discard of old wisdom in favor of inferior novelties.[1]

—Donald T. Campbell and Julian C. Stanley, 1963

Every educated person knows that the experimental method, following carefully established and replicable procedures, is used by natural scientists to establish a law or principle about the way the world works.[2] Using techniques that are similar to those used in the science of discovery, the natural science–based, problem-solving professions of medicine and engineering have also used the experimental method to determine whether a human action or intervention can solve a problem or cure an illness. The results of experimentation in the physical sciences are normally quite convincing and robust. Although usually less definitive, experimental results in the more complex biological and medical sciences are often quite impressive.

The social sciences and the professions of economics, psychotherapy, social work, education, and counseling also have used scientific techniques and experimentation to evaluate the effectiveness of human actions, or interventions to solve problems. In these fields, a significant body of opinion claims that experimentation is the only way to prove the effectiveness of a social intervention. But those claims are disputed, and the record of achievement is more sketchy. This chapter will consider these claims and the evidence and argumentation that supports and challenges them.

Evidence-Based Policy Using the Experimental Method

The mission statement of the Coalition for Evidence-Based Policy, a Washington, DC, advocacy group, nicely sums up the perspective of those who advocate systematic, experimental, program evaluation to guide social policy and practice:

> The Coalition seeks to increase government effectiveness through the use of rigorous evidence about what works. In the field of medicine, public policies based on scientifically-rigorous evidence have produced extraordinary advances in health over the past 50 years. By contrast, in most areas of social policy—such as education, poverty reduction, and crime prevention—government programs often are implemented with little regard to evidence, costing billions of dollars yet failing to address critical social problems. However, rigorous studies have identified a few highly-effective program models and strategies ("interventions"), suggesting that a concerted government effort to build the number of these proven interventions, and spur their widespread use, could bring rapid progress to social policy similar to that which transformed medicine.
>
> The Coalition advocates many types of research to identify the most promising social interventions. However, a central theme of our advocacy, consistent with the recommendation of a recent National Academy of Sciences report, is that evidence of effectiveness generally cannot be considered definitive without ultimate confirmation in well-conducted randomized controlled trials.[3]

The National Academy of Sciences report cited by the Coalition offers the following recommendation on criteria for establishing strong evidence of effectiveness:

> Federal and state agencies should prioritize the use of evidence-based programs and promote the rigorous evaluation of prevention and promotion programs in a variety of settings in order to increase the knowledge base of what works, for whom, and under what conditions. The definition of evidence-based should be determined by applying established scientific criteria.
>
> In applying scientific criteria, the agencies should consider the following standards:
>
> Evidence for efficacy or effectiveness of prevention and promotion programs should be based on designs that provide significant confidence in the results. The highest level of confidence is provided by multiple, well-conducted randomized experimental trials, and their combined inferences should be used in most cases. Single trials that randomize individuals,

places (e.g., schools), or time (e.g., wait-list or some times-series designs), can all contribute to this type of strong evidence for examining intervention impact.

When evaluations with such experimental designs are not available, evidence for efficacy or effectiveness cannot be considered definitive, even if based on the next strongest designs, including those with at least one matched comparison. Designs that have no control group (e.g., pre-post comparisons) are even weaker.

Programs that have widespread community support as meeting community needs should be subject to experimental evaluations before being considered evidence-based.

Priority should be given to programs with evidence of effectiveness in real-world environments, reasonable cost, and manuals or other materials available to guide implementation with a high level of fidelity.[4]

These statements are just two of a multitude asserting that randomized clinical trials are the best, strongest kind of evidence on which to base policy. Although the potential contributions of other experimental designs are acknowledged, they are relegated to an inferior, "not definitive" status.

Over the past four decades, the commitment to using experimental research for addressing social problems has been most persistently and visibly pursued by MDRC, a nonprofit research organization founded by the Ford Foundation and several federal agencies in 1974. MDRC now has an annual budget of more than $70 million, a highly prestigious board and respected staff of experts, and a long track record of carefully designed and executed studies of social and educational programs focused on alleviating poverty and advancing economic opportunity. A wide range of topics have been explored by MDRC: K–12 and higher education, afterschool programs, job retention and advancement, welfare reform, and prisoner reentry, among others.[5]

In another example, in 2002 the federal government established the What Works Clearinghouse in the Institute of Education Science. The Clearinghouse has energetically assembled teams of social scientists to review and evaluate research on the effectiveness of different educational practices and instructional materials and approaches. Its website offers practice guides on 17 instructional topics, and evaluations of the effectiveness of more than 500 instructional interventions or approaches.

The idea of using the medical research model of randomized clinical trials to evaluate policy and practice has gained many adherents. Before examining the contributions of experimental evaluation to policy and practice and its critics, it may be useful to revisit the seminal work of Donald T. Campbell and Julian C. Stanley.

Campbell and Stanley on Experimental and Quasi-Experimental Research

The classic guidebook for experimental social science research was written in 1963 by Donald T. Campbell and Julian C. Stanley and published as a chapter in an AERA handbook edited by N. L. Gage.[6] The chapter was later published separately as *Experimental and Quasi-Experimental Designs for Research* (1966). (The book had gone through six printings in 4 years when I bought my copy in 1970, and it is still published and widely cited.)

Campbell and Stanley make their commitment to experimental research clear in the quotation that heads this chapter. After acknowledging their debt to the Fisher (1925, 1935)[7] tradition of scientific experimental research, Campbell and Stanley stipulate that achieving rigorous control over the treatment and experimental conditions as envisioned by Fisher is more difficult when doing experimental research in social situations (e.g., education). They then demonstrate enormous discipline in identifying the pitfalls of social science research and ingenuity in designing rigorous experiments and "quasi-experiments" to overcome them.

Without question, Campbell and Stanley were committed to experimental rigor and hoped that scientific methods would be increasingly used for the evaluation and improvement of policy and practice. That said, they counsel the researcher who wishes to take research from the laboratory into the field to temper aspirations. They urge researchers to consider the task to be "probing," or testing theories, not "proving" them:

> In a very fundamental sense, experimental results never "confirm" or "prove" a theory—rather the successful theory is tested and escapes being disconfirmed. . . . *The notion that experiments never "confirm" a theory, while correct, so goes against our attitudes and experiences as scientists as to be almost intolerable* [emphasis added]. Particularly does this emphasis seem unsatisfactory vis-à-vis the elegant and striking confirmations encountered in physics and chemistry, where the experimental data may fit in minute detail over numerous points of measurement a complex curve predicted by the theory.[8]

As demonstrated by the assertions of the Coalition for Evidence-Based Policy, the scruples of Campbell and Stanley in avoiding the word "proof" *have* turned out to be intolerable and unsustainable in the common culture. Despite their cautionary counsel to researchers, the idea that experimental methods can identify proven solutions to social problems has been irresistible. The quest for proof is deeply embedded in the way we have come to think about the scientific method, and many researchers, policy makers, practitioners, and entrepreneurs continue to search for proven interventions.

Experimental Program Evaluation, Evaluated

In 1963, when Campbell and Stanley constructed a guidebook for doing experimental and quasi-experimental research, they were optimistic that such research could make significant contributions. Their optimism seemed justified. Without question, the tight logic of experimental research is persuasive. The power of these ideas is evident in the level of scientific acceptance they enjoy, in the enormous number of experimental research studies undertaken over the past half century, and in the widespread credibility of the experimental method among the public.

One cannot review the work of MDRC scientists and legions of other experimental program evaluators without being impressed by their intelligence, integrity, rigor, and work ethic. These studies are complicated, difficult to design, and difficult to implement. But after 50 years, it is difficult not to be disappointed with the performance of experimental research in helping policy makers and practitioners discover and implement proven solutions to social problems. Hundreds of studies apparently have not produced enough definitive evidence of program effectiveness to significantly improve policy or practice. Is the problem that nothing (or practically nothing) works? Is the problem that we haven't done enough research, or not enough good research? The websites of two well-known collections of experimental research, the What Works Clearinghouse of the Institute for Education Science and MDRC, were examined as part of an effort to explore these questions.

The What Works Clearinghouse

The What Works Clearinghouse (WWC) reports examining 7,712 studies of educational interventions. Of those studies, only 184 were deemed to meet the WWC standards without reservations (essentially randomized clinical trials with adequate samples and controls) and only 170 met WWC standards with reservations (the strongest quasi-experimental studies would fit into this category). A total of 1,048 studies were eligible for review but deemed not to meet WWC standards with or without reservations, and 5,550 studies were ineligible for further review after initial screening. Studies can be considered ineligible for review for several reasons, including the study design, sampling, or not being directly focused on the effects of an intervention.[9]

The WWC website provides impressive tools for examining its database, but it is evident that very few studies of interventions meet the standards proposed for experimental research, and the evidence generated from these studies rarely provides robust guidance for policy makers and practitioners.

In the area of literacy (the topic on which the greatest amount of research has been reviewed), for example, 5,964 studies were examined on 75 different interventions. Because the interventions were sometimes examined on more than one dimension of literacy or for different grade levels, 139 ratings of effectiveness were generated. Only 160 of the 5,964 studies met standards, with another 104 studies meeting standards with reservations. Only 12 interventions out of 139 are rated as having positive effects, with another 66 having "potentially positive" effects, but the body of evidence for three out of four of these ratings is judged to be "small." In evaluating the effectiveness of an intervention, WWC considers: (a) the quality of the research, (b) the statistical significance of the findings, (c) the size of the difference between the mean scores of participants in the treatment and control groups, and (d) the consistency of findings among studies.

In another example, dropout prevention, a smaller number (19) of interventions were examined, but the general pattern was similar. Most of these interventions were examined on two dimensions, persistence in school and completing school, so a total of 35 ratings were generated. Only a few of many studies meet the WWC standards of evidence (25 of 181), so the body of robust evidence is weak. Only 2 interventions are considered to have positive effects; 15 are considered to have potentially positive effects; 17 have no discernable effect; and 1 has "mixed effect." Of the 35 ratings, the body of evidence was considered "small" for 27 ratings, and "medium to large" for only 8 ratings.[10]

It is unsurprising that the WWC staff report that the greatest utilization of its website is not to explore the ratings of interventions but to download the practice guides, which suggest ways that teachers might improve their instruction in various areas. About 16,000 downloads of practice guides occur each month.[11] The practice guides cover 19 different topical areas and seek to guide practitioners by indicating the extent of research evidence supporting each recommendation.[12] A close look at just one practice guide, however, suggests some of the problems that can occur when research is used in this way.

In order to teach elementary students to be effective writers, the practice guide on that topic makes four sensible recommendations and rates the robustness of available evidence supporting the recommendation. Table 2.1 summarizes these recommendations.

This reader (and writer) found it difficult to understand exactly what was meant by recommendation 2, "Teach students to use the writing process for a variety of purposes." The other three recommendations describe a fairly crisp intervention, and it is reasonably easy to imagine a teacher attempting to follow the recommendation. But the intervention described for this recommendation seems formless.

After examining the descriptions of the research study and the recommendations in greater depth, it became obvious that the vague wording of

TABLE 2.1
Effectiveness of Approaches for Teaching Writing

Recommendation	Level of Evidence
1. Provide daily time for students to write.	Minimal
2. Teach students to use the writing process for a variety of purposes.	Strong
3. Teach students to become fluent with handwriting, spelling, sentence construction, typing, and word processing.	Moderate
4. Create an engaged community of writers.	Minimal

the recommendation actually refers to very complex, substantial approaches to teaching writing. The research examined instructional approaches that deconstruct the writing process for various purposes, help students learn systematic approaches for various purposes, help students emulate effective writing by example, and provide extensive coaching and feedback.

It is unsurprising that such complex and multifaceted instruction improved student writing because writing is complex and multifaceted. But such instruction is not a simple "intervention" that can be easily replicated. The other interventions *are* relatively simple, and although they are all likely to be helpful in improving the acquisition of writing skill, standing alone, it is unsurprising that they fail to generate impressive results in experimental studies.

MDRC

A look at the work of MDRC, a leading organization providing experimental research on social policy, further illustrates the gap between the expansive rhetoric advocating experimental designs to evaluate social policy and the way things really work on the ground.

At the end of 2013, MDRC published a summary of the top 10 (out of 40) most popular publications of the past year.[13] Four of these top 10 publications involved experimental studies on the effects of: (a) small public high schools on graduation rates in New York City; (b) accelerated study for developmental education students in New York community colleges; (c) Success for All, a whole-school reading reform program; and (d) cash payments provided to low-income families to achieve specific health, education, and employment goals. Most of these studies reported some positive effects, and they all offered observations on what particular factors seem to be effective or associated with positive outcomes.

Three of the most popular publications described new program designs in which MDRC is helping to develop demonstration projects: (a) a social impact bond, seeking to finance social improvements with private capital pledges, conditional on positive results; (b) a strategy to distribute student financial aid to college students like a paycheck over the course of a term as a means to encourage sustained academic effort; and (c) a program to improve the earnings and job security of low-income people by aligning training, placement, and postemployment guidance with employer needs.

Two of the most popular publications reviewed past research on interventions where a considerable amount of previous work has been done. One of these examined subsidized employment as a means of helping hard-to-employ people weather bad economic times and gain durable employment. It reviewed the mixed (mostly judged to be ineffective) record of previous efforts and described emerging efforts to try different models. The second study was a meta-analysis of the impact of family involvement on educational achievement of children ages 3 to 8.

The study of family involvement on education achievement reviewed 95 studies to determine the effects of family actions on the literacy, mathematics, and social-emotional skills of children. Similar to the foregoing review of studies in the What Works Clearinghouse, this review found that

> only a limited number of intervention studies have used rigorous, experimental designs. . . . Although some use randomized control trials (RCTs), the vast majority of individual intervention studies (even RCTs) do not provide enough information to fully determine any analytic or methodological weaknesses, such as not using an intent-to-treat analysis or not reporting on intervention implementation or study design flaws (that might result, for example, in differential attrition). Nevertheless, these studies do provide useful guidance when determining the future directions of family involvement research.[14]

The final report in MDRC's top 10 studies of 2013 is an MDRC working paper on research methodology, *A Conceptual Framework for Studying the Sources of Variation in Program Effects*, by Michael J. Weiss, Howard S. Bloom, and Thomas Brock. The abstract of this 50-page paper begins:

> Evaluations of public programs in many fields reveal that (1) different types of programs (or different versions of the same program) vary in their effectiveness, (2) a program that is effective for one group of people might not be effective for other groups of people, and (3) a program that is effective in one set of circumstances may not be effective in other circumstances. This paper presents a conceptual framework for research on such variation in program effects and the sources of this variation.[15]

The full paper is a very sophisticated analysis of the factors that produce variation in the effects of social programs that, except for the failure to question directly a high degree of faith in the utility of the experimental method, might have been written by a critic of MDRC.

One cannot help being impressed by the persistent commitment of MDRC to addressing the problems of poverty and expanding educational attainment as well as by the enormous intelligence, integrity, and discipline with which this organization pursues its mission. Observing its work over many years, I have often found interesting and insightful research on the challenges of addressing social problems but few findings that offer clear, persuasive evidence of the effectiveness of an intervention and anything other than highly qualified counsel for policy makers and practitioners. My observations on the top 10 most popular studies of 2013 are consistent with other observations over many years:

- The four reports evaluating interventions are competently done and yield interesting, potentially useful, but qualified insights, like most such studies.
- The three papers on emerging interventions demonstrate the unremitting drive of MDRC to find ways of improving outcomes (although in my judgment only one of the interventions, student aid distributed like a paycheck, is likely to be easily implemented in multiple settings and become potentially effective).
- The two studies reviewing research on subsidized employment and the effects of family involvement on educational outcomes demonstrate, in the first instance, the admirable commitment of MDRC to developing better ways of addressing a difficult problem despite many studies demonstrating the limited effectiveness of earlier approaches; and in the second instance, the difficulty of doing evaluative research on complex processes and the disappointing contributions of meta-analysis.
- MDRC's paper on the variation of program effects nicely summarizes what should be learned from its substantial experience employing experimental designs to evaluate social programs; that is, this tool rarely produces conclusive evidence about the overall effectiveness of a social program because of variation in the interventions, in the people treated, in the context of the intervention, and last, in the studies themselves.

Why Isn't Experimentation More Conclusive and Productive?

Unlike well-established scientific laws, medical and social practice interventions are never 100% effective, whether the intervention is a pill, a treatment regimen, an instructional technique, or a program to rehabilitate criminals. Commonly experimental evaluations estimate the "effect" of the intervention, and use statistical techniques to measure the size of the effect and the likelihood that it is genuine, rather than occurring due to chance variation. Often when a study involves many subjects a relatively small, perhaps unimportant measured effect may be statistically significant.

Warren Weaver's essay "Science and Complexity," discussed in Chapter 1, helps explain both the variation in the effectiveness of interventions and why human interventions to solve problems have difficulty achieving a high level of consistent effectiveness. Despite similarities among them, every human, every organization, and every social environment is constructed and organized in a unique way. The organization of complexity presents formidable analytical problems to the scientific method because the number of causal factors and potential interactions among them is enormous.[16]

Interventions based on the laws of physical science often approach absolute effectiveness because the systems and mechanisms involved are fundamentally simple. Some interventions in the medical sciences (e.g., vaccinations) achieve high levels of effectiveness where the cause of the disease can be isolated to a single factor. In these cases, widespread implementation has been achieved with great benefit to society as a whole. Even so, a few people with certain characteristics experience complications and should not be vaccinated.[17]

As complexity increases, however, the ability to achieve a high level of effectiveness in solving problems or achieving desirable results through human intervention decreases rapidly. The more numerous and complex the causal factors involved in the problem to be solved or the disease to be cured, the less likely a single intervention can yield satisfactory results. And the more complex the intervention, the less likely it can be delivered with uniform fidelity and yield consistent levels of effectiveness.

These issues are quite familiar to a substantial group of social scientists who have worked to evaluate and measure program impact and infer causation for more than a half century. A vigorous dialogue sponsored by the Evaluation Center of Western Michigan University between two leaders in this field, Tom Cook and Michael Scriven, offers a good overview of some of the advantages and limitations of randomized control trials (RCTs) for any reader who wants to dig more deeply into the technical and philosophical arguments of evaluation practitioners.[18]

Both Cook and Scriven are critical of approaches to program evaluation that sidestep external, empirical evidence, and they both agree that RCTs are a legitimate and strong basis for causal inference. Michael Scriven, however, argues RCTs do not deserve to be *the* standard, to the exclusion of other approaches because: (a) RCTs can rarely completely exclude alternative explanations for their results; and (b) methods for inferring causation other than RCTs can yield comparable levels of certainty.[19] Such methods, according to Scriven, include direct observation verified by multiple witnesses; the scientific claims of forensic science, such as autopsy reports; causal claims based on indirect evidence, such as the assertion that, the movement of tectonic plates created the Sierra Nevada; rigorous quasi-experimental designs; and highly disciplined case studies. Scriven notes much of science is based not on experimental research but on the analysis of a body of evidence of different kinds that establishes a result beyond reasonable doubt. This is, of course, the same standard used for a criminal trial.

Cook, a leading researcher using experimental evaluations (and a colleague of Donald Campbell), does not dispute Scriven's claim that other methods can be used to infer causation, but he argues that randomized experiments remain "the best single arrow in the evaluator's causal quiver."[20] Cook's comments in this dialogue and his publications (see especially "Post-Positivist Critical Multiplism")[21] demonstrate his aversion to overclaiming the power of any technique and his openness to criticism. He also believes that different methods are more appropriate for different problems. But for questions where a randomized experiment is an appropriate method, Cook steadfastly maintains it is the best option for examining causal impact and a necessary tool for disproving false claims of effectiveness.

Cook and Scriven are two of a number of influential voices in the field of program evaluation. A excellent overview of the contributions of other leading voices, including Donald Campbell, Peter Rossi, Carol Weiss, Robert Stake, Joseph Wholey, and Lee Cronbach can be found in *Foundations of Program Evaluation: Theories of Practice* by William Shadish, Thomas Cook, and Laura Leviton.[22]

A Brief Overview of Professional Program Evaluation

Although evaluative activity can be traced far back into history, the current profession of program evaluation traces its beginning to the 1960s. During that era, Robert McNamara introduced the Planning, Programming, and Budgeting System (PPBS) into the Department of Defense, under the intellectual leadership of Charles J. Hitch, an economist and operations researcher. The core idea of PPBS was to allocate budget resources according to program objectives, plans, and cost-benefit analysis. Both existing programs and potential program options were to be evaluated. On August 25, 1965, President Johnson announced that PPBS was to be adopted and applied in every other department and agency of the federal government.[23]

Full-bore PPBS proved to be highly controversial and unworkable in the federal government.[24] It wasn't easy to do PPBS in the Department of Defense, even with its relatively straightforward objectives, operational procedures, and constrained options. Imposing the planning and evaluation techniques of PPBS on annual budgeting for the full range of federal programs and priorities turned out to be wildly unrealistic. In the Nixon administration PPBS was officially abandoned, even in the Department of Defense. Cost-benefit analysis and program evaluation gained traction, however, despite the overreaching aspirations for their application in PPBS.

But the "pull-back position" (program evaluation without mandatory connections to the budgeting process) didn't turn out to be a simple task either. Shadish, Cook, and Leviton[25] outline three stages of the theoretical development for the field. An unavoidably superficial summary of their excellent overview follows.

In stage 1, "Bringing Truth to Social Problem Solving," Shadish and colleagues cite the contributions of Michael S. Scriven and Donald T. Campbell. Scriven, a logician and philosopher by training, provided much of the language and conceptual framework for the profession, including terms such as *summative* and *formative evaluation*. He argues that program evaluation is fundamentally about identifying criteria of merit, setting standards, and assessing performance through objective, empirical observation. As discussed earlier, Donald T. Campbell, a psychologist, is widely acknowledged for his leadership in experimental methods to assess causal impact. Thomas D. Cook, a frequent collaborator with Campbell, is also well known for his contributions to methodology and experimental program evaluation. As seen previously, Scriven and Cook sometimes disagree about what constitutes valid, persuasive evidence, but the fundamental objective of evaluation they emphasize is the same, assessing value and making valid causal inferences.

In stage 2, "Generating Alternatives, Emphasizing Use and Pragmatism," Shadish and colleagues discuss the work of Carol H. Weiss, Joseph S. Wholey, and Robert E. Stake. Carol Weiss, a sociologist, and Wholey, a program evaluator working within the federal government, found themselves looking for other ways to inform policy when experience demonstrated that finding "truth" to bring to social problem solving turns out to be complicated and difficult. Weiss recognized that evaluation occurs in a political context and itself is a political activity. Her work emphasized working with policy makers and stakeholders and using multiple methods, experimental designs, quasi-experimental designs, description, case studies, and so on to help them gain insight about policy and program design and operations in order to guide decisions for improvement.

Wholey began his career as an operations research analyst in the Department of Defense in the Kennedy administration and then moved to the Department of Health, Education, and Welfare (HEW) where he was responsible for program evaluation in the Johnson administration. He later worked at the Urban Institute and for HEW again in the Carter administration. Wholey, like Weiss, employed multiple methods, but the point of his work is not primarily to enlighten policy makers, but to improve program performance. He recognized that broad-scale evaluations of complex, multifaceted programs are impossible, but such programs can be improved through targeted evaluation and management interventions. His evaluation for "use" focused on questions of interest to policy makers and managers, and sought to develop evidence that they would find credible, convincing, and useful in improving governmental services.

Robert E. Stake, like Weiss and Wholey, recognized that research to establish causal relationships has limited utility to stakeholders. Rather than embracing multiple methods, including quantitative causal studies, he focused on observation and qualitative case studies as a means of serving the stakeholders who seek assistance. The term *responsive evaluation* is used to describe his approach of holistic description and analysis of practice. Without imposing external value judgments, he worked to help practitioners understand the facts and dynamics of their situation and discover possible ways to improve their practice. Stakes's approach of open inquiry without preconceptions has been widely acknowledged as an important means of understanding context and acquiring insights that otherwise would likely be missed.

Qualitative evaluation is sometimes linked with constructivist epistemology, which holds that the external world exists independently and human knowledge consists only of the subjective ways we construct reality from our experiences. From this viewpoint, the premises of the scientific method, including notions of demonstrable causation, are not necessarily valid. Rather, it is most important to understand the perceptions, experiences, and constructed realities of the people involved in a program and served by it. Yvonna S. Lincoln and Egon G. Guba writing together, and Michael Quinn Patton are prominent leaders employing this perspective. Qualitative evaluators have designed and used disciplined, sometimes quite elaborate approaches for collecting qualitative information from interviews, observation, and other direct and indirect methods. These techniques, of course, are also used by researchers who do not accept constructivist epistemology.

For stage 3, "Trying to Integrate the Past," Shadish and colleagues discuss the work of Lee J. Cronbach and Peter H. Rossi, two of many thought leaders who built on the work of both earlier stages. Cronbach's wide-ranging contributions include theoretical insights concerning the limits and appropriate use of experiments and other methods, and an emphasis on the diverse functions of evaluation in decision making and in society, which should be considered in program design. Cronbach especially emphasized the importance of "external validity," the difficult-to-achieve applicability of a finding to the broader world, not simply the population examined in an evaluation. Rossi, whose book *Evaluation: A Systematic Approach* (coauthored with Howard E. Freeman)[26] has been perhaps the most influential of his generation, elaborated a comprehensive approach to evaluation that considers issues of program design, monitors program performance, and assesses program utility. He included cost-benefit analysis in the assessment of utility, and suggested that the theory of a program design, *why* the program is expected to make a contribution, should be explicated and tested in evaluation. Rossi also developed the idea that evaluations should be tailored to the type of program in question, and suggested that expert judgment "connoisseurial assessment" is a legitimate tool in program evaluation.

In 1990, around the time Shadish, Cook, and Leviton published *Foundations of Program Evaluation,* Peter Senge's *The Fifth Discipline*[27] proposed strategies for organizations to improve through disciplined reflection, systems thinking, and group problem solving. *Schools That Learn: A Fifth Discipline Fieldbook for Educators, Parents, and Everyone Who Cares About Education*[28] was subsequently published to apply these ideas to improving education. Beverly Parsons's *Evaluative Inquiry: Using Evaluation to Promote Student Success* (2002) draws on the traditions of qualitative and quantitative evaluation and Senge's idea of a learning organization to propose strategies for schools to improve through self-directed evaluative inquiry.[29]

A Realist Approach for Evaluating Interventions

In the continuing evolution of the field of program evaluation, Ray Pawson and Nick Tilley have added an additional perspective, *realistic* evaluation.[30]

Like Cook and Scriven, Pawson and Tilley are critical of approaches to evaluation that sidestep or minimize the importance of objective external evidence, but like the stage 2 and 3 leaders described previously, they find experimental designs for program evaluation inadequate for guiding policy makers and practitioners. At the core of their approach, they claim that a profound weakness of experimental evaluation is its causal inference based on *succession*, or the observation of difference after treatment, rather than the *generation* of an effect. Let me try to explain this distinction in nontechnical language.

Essentially, experimental designs create equivalent groups (the treatment and the control group), administer the intervention to the treatment group, and then infer that any differences in results between the treatment and control group observed after (in succession to) the treatment were caused by the treatment. *How* the treatment caused (or generated) the effect is not illuminated by the experimental design. Succession as a basis for causal inference is rooted in David Hume's "view that causation is unobservable, [a perception of the mind] and that one can only make inferences on the basis of observable data."[31]

Pawson and Tilley argue that causation is "real," even if difficult to observe directly, and that mechanisms operating in society and in human beings both produce and change social conditions. The objective of evaluating a social program is to discover whether and how its theories about specific mechanisms actually work in changing social or individual conditions, when the program is delivered, in what ways, to which people, and under what circumstances. Succession is especially limited as a means of evaluating a social intervention because social interventions are not medical treatments like pills; they represent human interactions and human choices in varying contexts.

As Pawson writes:

> Medical treatments are tested using "placebos" and "double blinding," with the purpose of seeing if they work regardless of human volition. Social programmes, by contrast, *only work through human intentionality.* Social programmes are indubitably and unequivocally "theories." They are theories from the day they are born, when a policy maker conjectures, "if we present these people with these resources (material, social or cognitive) it may influence them to change their behavior."[32]

The Weiss, Bloom, and Brock MDRC paper cited earlier observed that the effects of social interventions vary among different interventions or types of intervention, for different groups of people, and under different circumstances. Pawson and Tilley argue that such variation is the reason that experimental research fails to offer clear guidance to practitioners and policy makers, and the reason meta-analysis fails to offer useful evaluations of policy and practice. Instead, they propose that the focus of program evaluation should be on the

theory behind each intervention and its effectiveness in particular situations—
the type of intervention, the way and by whom it is delivered, the different
types of people receiving the intervention, and the context of the situation.

In *Evidence-Based Policy: A Realist Perspective*,[33] Pawson uses the example of mentoring programs to illustrate the approach of realistic evaluation.
Mentoring programs have been created as a means of helping disengaged,
at-risk youth get on a pathway to productive self-sufficiency. A plausible
causal model of effective mentoring proposed by Pawson has four modes of
mentoring: (a) befriending, (b) direction setting, (c) coaching, and (d) sponsoring. In sequence, these modes (a) establish a relationship, (b) encourage
the young person to develop higher aspirations, (c) help the youth acquire
necessary knowledge and skills, and then (d) provide effective "sponsorship"
to move from education to employment.

All four of these stages are essential to achieve the program objective;
all four require somewhat different resources, abilities, and strategies for the
mentor; and different young people are likely to need different supports and
interventions at each stage. Realistic evaluation would articulate the program
theories related to each stage, examine the conditions necessary for the theories to work, and learn from the experience of attempted implementation.
Pawson reviews a series of published studies on youth mentoring programs
to illustrate how and why they have varied in success and failure in each of
these four stages. Randomized studies evaluating mentoring programs would
likely find all of them fall short of meeting their ultimate goal, while many
of them may have had significant success in several of these stages. A more
helpful evaluation would unpack the interactions between program and client in all of these ways.

Although Pawson and Tilley have persuasively argued the limitations of
experimental methods for guiding policy and practice, their examples of "realistic" evaluation also fail to achieve crisp, conclusive guidance for policy and
practice. The intellectual labor involved in comprehensive realistic evaluation is
perhaps even more arduous than that involved in creating and implementing a
good experimental design. Nevertheless, realistic evaluation avoids the unwarranted claims of authority and capability of experimental design proponents.
And it helps policy makers and practitioners reflect on their theories of change,
examine results, and improve. The hard truth is that for complex problems
nothing appears to offer what many policy makers and practitioners seem to
want—inexpensive, efficient, effective guidance for policy and practice.

Observations From the Case of Success for All

Success for All, a whole-school reading program focused on disadvantaged
students, has the distinction of being the only K–12 educational intervention

rated top tier for effectiveness by the Coalition for Evidence-Based Policy,[34] being rated for "positive effects" with an extent of evidence at the medium to large level by the What Works Clearinghouse,[35] as well as being widely recognized for effectiveness by other reform and policy bodies. It has received a U.S. Department of Education Investing in Innovation (i3) grant to support its expansion, and as part of that grant, it is the subject of a current MDRC evaluation mentioned earlier.

Success for All has been the beneficiary of consistent, talented, and dedicated leadership; substantial financial support; and extensive experience in developing effective approaches to reading instruction over a quarter century. In a personal interview, cofounder Robert Slavin expressed understandable satisfaction with the accomplishments of Success for All, gratitude for the endorsements and support it has received, along with measured frustration that the achievements of Success for All (and some other whole-school interventions created in the same period) have not achieved more widespread implementation at scale.[36] Reflecting on the experience of Success for All seems a useful exercise for putting the previous sections of this chapter in perspective.

First, Success for All is far from a parsimonious intervention. It is a complex, multifaceted program that includes guidelines for school leadership, curricular resources, highly structured prescriptions for instruction, continuous assessment systems, one-on-one tutoring for struggling children, formal strategies for dealing with nonacademic issues, extensive professional development for teachers and administrators, and a dedicated full-time facilitator.[37] The process by which it engages with a school requires strong evidence of buy-in, both financial support and evidence of teacher and administrator commitment to the program.

Success for All claims that every element of its program design is research based. After examining the program elements, one can easily imagine that most of the supporting research looks a lot like the techniques of "realistic" evaluation described by Pawson and Tilley: Researchers and instructors over time have tested theories about specific interventions or techniques in an effort to get better results for students and from the school system as a whole. Some of the research studies buttressing the design of Success for All have surely used experimental control groups, but the comprehensive design of the program reflects something much more elaborate—systems theory and the evaluation of specific interventions: How does the school as a social system work? What issues must be addressed? What resources must be employed? What techniques used in order to get the desired result of student success?

Donald Peurach's *Seeing Complexity in Public Education: Problems, Possibilities, and Success for All*[38] offers an unusually insightful analysis of Success for All based on a case study conducted over more than 10 years. His research identified multiple, interdependent systems of organized complexity (as described by Warren Weaver in Chapter 1) confronting the initiative: "its clients (students, teachers, and leaders in schools, districts, and states); its programs (its designs for improvement and supports for implementation); its own organization (especially its development, training, research, and executive operations); and the environments in which all operated."[39]

Each of these systems continuously presented problems for the Success for All Foundation (SFAF) to solve, and problems and interrelations among them grew, especially as it sought to scale up. Peurach observes:

> While every problem had a solution, every solution had a problem. . . . SFAF's attempts to match systems of problems with systems of solutions yielded systems of new challenges that greatly complicated its work. . . . The more SFAF did to support effective, large-scale, sustainable education reform, the more SFAF reproduced some of the most stubborn problems of U.S. educational reform within its own system. These problems included: misunderstandings of externally sponsored reform as either technocratic or bureaucratic (and not professional); implementation as rote and mechanical (and not flexible and adaptive); problems of incoherence, faddism, and distrust in schools; problems of program potential exceeding support for practice; and problems of fleeting environmental support.[40]

The main point of Peurach's analysis is that the challenges faced by Success for All are the inevitable challenges of all efforts to improve and solve problems in interrelated, complex educational systems. No crisp intervention, no "proven program," can solve a complex problem at scale, in different settings, and over time as situations change. This is not to say that improvement is impossible, but it suggests that continuing improvement requires constant analysis of problems and situations and continuous adaptation as circumstances change. The achievements of Success for All are due to the persistence of the SFAF community in problem solving under such circumstances, not in its discovery of a fixed solution. Peurach expresses the hope "that the story of SFAF and its analytic framework will motivate and enable continued learning among communities of educational reformers, and that their continued learning will bring a new vitality and richness to education reform."[41]

Perhaps in partial fulfillment of Peurach's hope, the first stage of the MDRC evaluation of Success for All's Investing in Innovation Grant importantly includes qualitative, descriptive research about the process of implementation, surveys of the reactions of teachers and administrators to the program, studies of implementation fidelity, and comparisons of similarities and differences in approaches between the experimental and control group schools. In the preface to the study, MDRC indicated:

> This fresh look at SFA [Success for All] will address important new questions about this much-studied initiative. As schools' approaches to reading instruction continue to evolve, does the SFA model remain substantially different from other reading programs used in the participating districts, or have the strategies used by those schools begun to look more like SFA? How do teachers and principals respond to SFA in a world of high-stakes testing and school accountability? Can schools implement SFA with the needed fidelity? And, finally, does SFA continue to produce better reading outcomes for students than other programs?[42]

The initial experimental results from the first-year program found a positive, statistically significant impact on one of two reading outcome measures (0.18 standard deviation in effect size) but no material difference in the scores between program and control group students on the second reading outcome measure. It is evident that the research agenda for this study is quite a bit broader than the "bottom line" program impact, which in this preliminary study at least is comparatively modest.[43]

A chapter on Success for All in *Research and Practice in Education* indicates that the intervention increasingly has begun to rely on teachers' understanding of the goals and concepts of the activities prescribed by the program, rather than simply complying faithfully with program instructions. This understanding, which is based on the knowledge and observations teachers engaged in the program, has provided more space for adaptation.[44]

It seems evident that the results achieved by Success for All are due to a combination of many factors: a thorough program design, an insistence on commitment from teachers and administrators, the substantial investments to assure discipline and fidelity in delivery, constant assessment of results, an openness to adaptation, and the search for further improvement.

Turning Gold Into Lead?

It is easy for me to agree with Tom Cook that experimental design is "the best single arrow in the causal evaluator's quiver."[45] As Cook wrote in a postscript to the Western Michigan University dialogue,

> The ultimate warrant for causal inference is not entirely tool-based, or even truth- or logic based. It is social. It has to do with acceptance of causal claims after intense critical scrutiny by a wide range of knowledgeable others, including those least likely to like a specific causal claim being made.[46]

So if the challenge is to persuade the deep skeptic, the nearly intractable opponent of investing in a particular social program, large positive effects from a randomized clinical trial are likely to be more effective than any other kind of evidence.

Unfortunately, given complex human beings, complex circumstances, and complex program interventions, compounded by the cost and difficulty of doing good experimental research on organized complexity, large positive effects from randomized clinical trials in social practice have been and continue to be quite rare. How large must an effect be before it overwhelms reluctance to make a change in policy and practice? It is evident that the effectiveness of Success for All, although impressive, has not been dramatic enough to lead to the universal adoption of the program. If it were easier to implement the intervention, or if it produced very large effects compared to other approaches, more teachers and administrators might be willing to subordinate themselves to the program design. Absent that kind of evidence, it is understandable that many practitioners and policy makers persist in pursuing different approaches.

It is hard to find any intervention that works dramatically well for the most difficult challenges, and only rarely do particular interventions work so much better than competing interventions that their superiority can be persuasively established through RCTs. Just as many (actually most) students learn to read in school given "normal" instruction, it is likely that many, perhaps most, thoughtfully designed interventions work for some people and some situations.

For complex, difficult problems such as teaching writing, the education of disadvantaged children, or mentoring disengaged youth, it is evident that fine-grained evidence and complex, multifaceted interventions are necessary. Such interventions are difficult to replicate with fidelity in different environments, and they often need to be adapted to the particular circumstances of a client or situation. Unless they are oversimplified, complex interventions also are difficult to evaluate accurately using experimental methods, and experimental evaluations standing alone provide little useful feedback. These are the reasons the MDRC study of Success for All cited earlier includes so many nonexperimental components along with its tests of program impact.

The weak track record of experimental research in identifying successful social interventions means that admitting only "gold standard" evidence in evaluating social programs has negative practical effects. Such a policy is likely to (a) fail to evaluate fully and fairly complex interventions addressing complex problems; (b) require an unrealistic, unproductive investment in experimental studies; and (c) preclude other approaches to evaluation and program improvement that can lead to more effective policy and practice. It risks becoming alchemy in reverse, turning gold into lead.

Even with these limitations, RCTs may still be "the best arrow in the evaluator's causal quiver" for the right kind of problems and interventions. What can they do best? RCTs are best suited for those social interventions and situations that are most like the medical problems where they have been most helpful. Such interventions and situations have the following characteristics:

1. The obstacle or challenge (often a virus or microbe, in the case of medicine) to the desired outcome can be readily identified and is not deeply interrelated to many other factors.
2. The clients to be affected by the intervention and the relevant circumstances in which they live are similar across different situations.
3. The intervention is relatively straightforward and easy to implement with fidelity in all the relevant situations.

A recent study intended to overcome obstacles preventing low-income families from applying for federal student financial assistance is a good example of such a study. Low- to moderate-income families with high school seniors who used H&R Block's assistance to file their income tax returns were also given information about eligibility and help filling out the FAFSA federal application for student financial aid. The provision of information alone had no discernable impact on applying for admission or attending college. But the provision of information plus help in completing the FAFSA form resulted in an eight percentage-point increase in college attendance among the high school senior sample.[47]

In this case the obstacle is clear and straightforward (a complex form is required to receive aid), all clients are affected by the obstacle in roughly the same way, and the treatment (efficient help in a convenient setting) is easy to implement with fidelity. It is highly likely that the effects found in this study could be replicated over and over again.

Although research using randomized clinical trials can make useful contributions to the evaluation of programs and interventions, their potential value decreases as the complexity of the problem or of the intervention increases. Because of their limitations, when experimental methods are employed to evaluate interventions for complex problems, they often become a stumbling block rather than a useful tool.

Notes

1. Campbell, D. L., & Stanley, J. C. (1963). *Experimental and quasi-experimental designs for research*. Chicago: Rand McNally, p. 2.

2. Experiments are not the only method employed by natural scientists, because experiments cannot address all questions. Astronomers, for example, cannot experiment with the stars. Much of scientific knowledge, like astronomy, is obtained from direct observation, measurement, and logical deduction, rather than experiments with control groups.

3. Coalition for Evidence-Based Policy. (2013, December 10). *Our mission.* Retrieved from http://coalition4evidence.org

4. National Research Council and Institute of Medicine. (2013, December 10). *Preventing mental, emotional, and behavioral disorders among young people: Progress and possibilities.* Retrieved from http://www.nap.edu/openbook.php?record_id=12480&page=373

5. MDRC. (2013, December 10). *About MRDC.* Retrieved from http://www.mdrc.org/about/about-mdrc-overview-0

6. Gage, N. L. (1963). *Handbook of research on teaching.* Chicago, IL: Rand McNally.

7. Fisher, R. A. (1925). *Statistical methods for research workers.* London, England: Oliver & Boyd.

Fisher, R. A. (1935). *The design of experiments.* London, England: Oliver & Boyd.

8. Campbell and Stanley, p. 35.

9. Institute of Education Sciences. (2014, January 08). *Find what works.* Retrieved from http://ies.ed.gov/ncee/wwc/findwhatworks.aspx

10. Analysis of data downloaded from What Works Clearinghouse Database (2014, January 08). Retrieved from http://ies.ed.gov/ncee/wwc/findwhatworks.aspx

11. Institute of Education Sciences (IES) staff (e-mail, November 18, 2013).

12. Institute of Education Sciences. (2015, July 03). Retrieved from http://ies.ed.gov/ncee/wwc/Publications_Reviews.aspx?f=All%20Publication%20and%20Product%20Types,3;#pubsearch

13. MDRC. (2014, January 8). Top 10 MDRC publications in 2013. Retrieved from http://www.mdrc.org/news/announcement/top-10-mdrc-publications-2013?utm_source=MDRC+Updates&utm_campaign=2e6b16edec-January_8_2014&utm_medium=email&utm_term=0_504d5ac165-2e6b16edec-34978901

14. Van Voorhis, F. L., Maier, M., Epstein, J. L., & Lloyd, C. M. (2014, January 8). *The impact of family involvement on the education of children ages 3 to 8: A focus on literacy and math achievement outcomes and social-emotional skills* (p. ES-2). Retrieved from http://www.mdrc.org/publication/impact-family-involvement-education-children-ages-3-8

15. Weiss, M. J., Bloom, H. S., & Brock, T. (2014, January 8). *A conceptual framework for studying the sources of variation in program effects.* Retrieved from http://www.mdrc.org/sites/default/files/a-conceptual_framework_for_studying_the_sources.pdf

16. As discussed in Chapter 5, Tony Bryk and his colleagues at the Carnegie Foundation for the Advancement of Teaching, inspired by the Pareto principle, suggest that

despite the complexity and unique aspects of each individual, a limited number of factors account for a large fraction of the variation in human experience and capabilities. Identifying such factors is a useful strategy in designing successful interventions.

17. Centers for Disease Control and Prevention. (2013, December 22). *Who should not get vaccinated with these vaccines?* Retrieved from http://www .cdc.gov/vaccines/vpd-vac/should-not-vacc.htm

18. Cook, T. D., Scriven, M., Coryn, C. L., & Evergreen, S. D. (2010). Contemporary thinking about causation in evaluation: A dialogue with Tom Cook and Michael Scriven. *American Journal of Evaluation, 31*(1), 105–117.

19. Ibid., p. 116.

20. Ibid., p. 110.

21. Cook, T. D. (1985). Post-positivist critical multiplism. In R. L. Shotland & M. M. Mark (Eds.), *Social science and social policy* (pp. 21–62). Beverly Hills, CA: SAGE Publications.

22. Shadish, W. R., Cook, T. D., & Leviton, L. C. (1991). *Foundations of program evaluation: Theories of practice.* Newbury Park, CA: SAGE Publications.

23. As implemented in the Department of Defense, PPBS became a highly elaborated, quantitative approach for weighing the costs and benefits of various options for achieving various defense goals. Hitch, who later became president of the University of California has written of Johnson's decision to apply PPBS to all of government, "I thought at the time that this was foolish—almost certain to lead to confusion, and likely to end up discrediting the management techniques it was trying to promote. Both happened."

Hitch said that the rest of government lacked the substantial body of research that supported PPBS in the Department, of Defense, and "most of the planning problems of most of the civilian departments . . . were far different from the military planning problems that had proved susceptible to systems analysts. The objectives were less clearly defined, or definable, and usually multiple; interdependencies with other problems, frequently the responsibility of other departments, were more complex; and the domestic political component was usually far greater. Hitch, C. J. (1996). Management problems of large organizations. *Operations Research, 44,* 257–264.

24. Wildavsky, A. (1969). Rescuing policy analysis from PPBS. *Public Administration Review, 29,* 189-202. Also Shick, A. (1969). Systems, politics, and systems budgeting. *Public Administration Review, 29,* 137–151.

25. Shadish et al.

26. Rossi, P. H., & Freeman, H. E. (1989). *Evaluation: A systematic approach.* (4th ed.). Newbury Park, CA: SAGE Publications.

27. Senge, P. (1990). *The fifth discipline.* New York, NY: Doubleday/Currency.

28. Senge, P., Cambron-McCage, N., Lucas, T., Smith, B., Dutton, J., & Kliner, A. (2000). *Schools that learn: A fifth discipline fieldbook for educators, parents, and everyone who cares about education.* New York, NY: Doubleday/Currency.

29. Parsons, B. A. (2002). *Evaluative inquiry: Using evaluation to promote student success.* Thousand Oaks, CA: Corwin Press.

30. Pawson, R., & Tilley, N. (1997). *Realistic evaluation.* London, England: SAGE Publications. On pages 1–29 Pawson and Tilley provide a brief, insightful summary of the field of evaluation from Campbell and Stanley to the turn of the twentieth century.

31. D. Hume, quoted in Pawson and Tilly, p. 35.

32. Pawson, R. (2002). Evidence and policy and naming and shaming. *Policy Studies, 23*(3/4), 211–230 (quote on p. 213).

33. Pawson, R. (2006). *Evidence-based policy: A realist perspective.* London: SAGE Publications.

34. Coalition for Evidence-Based Policy. (2014, January 14). *Top tier evidence: Success for All for grades K–2.* Retrieved from http://evidencebasedprograms.org/1366-2/success-forall

35. Institute of Education Sciences. (2014, January 14). *Find what works, literacy.* Retrieved from http://ies.ed.gov/ncee/wwc/FindWhatWorks.aspx

36. R. Slavin (personal interview with author, December 17, 2013).

37. These and subsequent descriptions of Success for All come from: Slavin, R.E., Madden, N. A., Chambers, B., & Haxby, B. (2009). *2 million children: Success for All.* Thousand Oaks, CA: Corwin Press.

38. Peurach, D. (2011). *Seeing complexity in public education: Problems, possibilities, and success for all.* Oxford Scholarship Online. New York: Oxford University Press, doi:10.1093/acprof:oso/9780199736539.001.0001

39. Ibid., p. 233.

40. Ibid., p. 237.

41. Ibid., p. 241.

42. Quint, J. C., Balu, R., DeLaurentis, M., Rappaport, S., Smith, T. J., & Zhu, P. (2013). *The Success for All model of school reform: Early findings from the Investing in Innovation (i3) scale-up.* Retrieved from http://www.mdrc.org/publication/success-all-model-school-reform

43. Ibid., p. ES-7.

44. Datnow, A., & Park, V. (2010). Success for All: Using tools to transport research-based practices to the classroom. In C. E. Coburn & M. K. Stein (Eds.), *Research and practice in education: Building alliances, bridging the divide* (pp. 77–91). Lanham, MD: Rowman & Littlefield.

45. Cook et al. p. 110.

46. Ibid., p. 115.

47. Bettinger, E. P., Long, B. T., Oreopoulos, P., & Sanbonmatsu, L. (2009). *The role of simplification and information in college decisions: Results from the H&R Block FAFSA experiment.* NBER Working Paper Series, 15361. Retrieved from http://www.nber.org/papers/w15361.pdf

3

MEASUREMENT

To do better, we must have a way to distinguish better from worse.[1]

—Alice Rivlin, 1971

A group of state superintendents from Southern states were meeting to discuss whether they should oppose or accept the publication of statewide scores from the National Assessment of Educational Progress (NAEP). The conversation was intense; most were certain that their states would be deeply embarrassed if the results were published, and they personally would feel the heat. Bill Clinton, then governor of Arkansas, was sitting on the side of the room without saying anything. Finally, one of the superintendents turned to him and asked, "Governor, what do you think?" Clinton responded, "Wouldn't it be better to know than not to know?"[2]

As E. O. Wilson asserts, mensuration using "universally accepted scales"[3] is a fundamental requirement for science. The absence of generally accepted (much less *universally* accepted) scales for measuring critically important social variables—outcomes, the nature and intensity of interventions, and relevant contextual conditions—is a formidable challenge for scholars seeking to improve the effectiveness of policy and practice. The story that opens this chapter illustrates just one reason measurement is challenging in policy and practice: Measurement is fraught with anxiety and political stress.

Political stress often generates avoidance and difficulty getting measures generally accepted, and there are other significant challenges. It is easier to measure temperature, weight, volume, chemical change, and other physical properties than it is to measure many of the important variables and outcomes in social policy or even in medicine. In social policy and medicine, some important variables or outcomes are easy or reasonably easy to measure (mortality, employment, wealth, income, infection or its absence, incarceration, and formal educational attainment); others are a bit more complicated (inflation, productivity, voluntary versus involuntary unemployment,

49

aptitude, learning of content, educational progress); and still others turn out to be quite difficult to measure (happiness, states of mental health or illness, problem-solving skill, creativity).

Despite the challenges, the importance of data and measurement in social policy and practice has been officially acknowledged since 1867 when Congress decreed "that there shall be established at the City of Washington, a department of education, for the purpose of collecting such statistics and facts as shall show the condition and progress of education in the several States and Territories."[4] The Bureau of Labor, forerunner for the Bureau of Labor Statistics (BLS), was established by Congress almost 20 years later in 1884.[5] The still primitive state of measurement in education, when contrasted to the wide acceptance and usage of BLS indicators for inflation, gross domestic product (GDP), unemployment, and so on, may indicate the comparative simplicity of economic life.

Political and civic leaders are increasingly and urgently calling for improving measurement in education. Governor Clinton's comment on the National Assessment of Educational Progress reflected the conviction of governors in the 1980s that better measurement was important for achieving educational improvement. Former secretary of education Margaret Spellings was fond of saying "You get what you measure," as she promoted the accountability provisions of the No Child Left Behind (NCLB) federal law. In the past dozen years, various philanthropies have invested tens of millions of dollars supporting the Data Quality Campaign and the development of Common Education Data Standards. And President Obama has proposed (and at this writing is seeking) to develop a rating system to assess the performance of colleges and universities in serving disadvantaged low-income students.[6]

The persistence and growing intensity of such efforts underscore the importance and potential power of measuring social policy outcomes. Substantial investments have been made in order to improve the quality, comprehensiveness, and utility of education measurement. Simultaneously, many have suggested that the tendency of policy makers to misuse and the public to misinterpret educational measures, especially testing data, has been quite harmful.

The issues of measurement quality, availability, utility, and proper use will be explored in this and the next chapter. This chapter will draw primarily on personal experience with four high-profile initiatives to improve the scope, quality, and utility of information to inform policy and practice:

1. Measuring Up, an effort to measure state-level performance in higher education and generate effective policy responses to improve performance
2. The Data Quality Campaign, State Longitudinal Data Systems, and Common Education Data Standards, all closely related initiatives to improve the availability and quality of educational data

3. Common Core State Standards for College and Career Readiness, an initiative to establish common learning objectives for K–12 education and to assess student achievement throughout elementary and secondary education in order to promote more widespread attainment

4. Assessing Higher Education Learning Outcomes (AHELO), a feasibility study launched by the Organization for Economic Cooperation and Development (OECD)

The contributions and challenges of psychometric testing play an important role in several of these narratives, but the measurement issues and the political and practical challenges of using data and measurement to good effect are considerably broader. In various ways the scholars, policy makers, policy analysts, and practitioners involved in these initiatives grappled with these fundamental questions:

1. What should be measured? What is important? What matters to policy and practice?
2. What data, collected with what definitions and procedures, and what combinations of data into metrics, will be credible and widely accepted?
3. What meaning can be legitimately derived from the information provided by the measures?
4. How should the information be used, by whom, and in what ways?

Measuring Up: State Performance in Postsecondary Education

Just before the beginning of the twenty-first century, Patrick Callan, who had previously served as a state higher education executive in California, Washington, and Montana, secured funding from several foundations to establish the National Center for Public Policy in Higher Education. Callan believed that American state policy makers and higher education leaders had become complacent about the performance and quality of higher education. The achievements of American higher education in the twentieth century, he argued, were inadequate to meet the demands of the emerging knowledge economy of the twenty-first century. Moreover, rapid educational progress in other countries was increasingly and seriously threatening the global competitiveness of the American workforce.

The mission of the National Center was to galvanize public awareness of these problems and to stimulate effective policy responses.[7] Measuring Up did not focus its attention on colleges and universities. Instead, it focused attention on the citizens of each state and how well they are served by public policies for postsecondary education. Moreover, in contrast to institutional quality and prestige rankings, it focused particular attention on those not well served. As noted by Peter Ewell, in social policy and practice, what we measure implicitly or explicitly reflects what we value.[8]

Measuring Up's Theory of Change

The National Center sought to use measurement as a tool to create interest in and awareness of higher education performance at the state policy level. Unlike some "report cards," it went beyond simply providing factual data to decision makers and the public—it sought to organize data into *information* that would help focus the attention of decision makers on particular issues. Dennis Jones's distinction between data and information and his insight that data must be organized in a way to provide *meaning* to decision makers undoubtedly influenced both the theory of Measuring Up and its strategy:

> The general properties of information are relevance, acceptability, time-liness, completeness, and accuracy—a set that overlaps to a considerable extent with the general properties of data—validity, accuracy, and reliabil-ity. But the properties of information are different from those of data in a cardinal respect: they are necessarily accessed relative to a group of users or a form of use; they cannot be stated in absolute terms. The properties of data are associated with measurement; the properties of measurement are associated with use, users, and context of use.[9]

The theory of Measuring Up was that policy makers, confronted with credible indicators of state performance on critical variables affecting the postsecondary educational attainment of its citizens, would use the policy levers at their disposal to generate improvement.

The Strategy and Its Implementation

Callan assembled a prestigious board of directors, a well-known group of advisers and expert consultants, and a strong staff. The strategy was to focus attention on the performance of individual states by grading the states in five areas: *preparation* for postsecondary education, *participation* in postsec-ondary education, *completion* of degrees and certificates, the *affordability* of postsecondary education, and the *benefits* states were receiving from post-secondary education. (In a sixth area, *student learning*, all states eventually received a grade of "incomplete" because no comparable data were available.)

Student learning was clearly the principal outcome sought by the National Center, but lacking comparable data, completion of degrees and certificates became the outcome variable measured. Preparation and affordability were identified as essential means to participation, which naturally is essential for completion. Logically, the states that perform poorly in preparation and affordability are likely to perform poorly on both participation and completion. At least one state demonstrated that it is possible to be well above average in participation but below average in completion.

After identifying these areas, the next challenge facing the National Center was to measure the policy relevant conditions for each area in all states in order to assign grades from *A* to *F*. Because no commonly accepted measures for any of these areas existed, the Center needed to cobble together relevant data from various sources into a set of indicators for each area, assign weights to the indicators, and construct a defensible overall score for each outcome area. The areas of performance remained unchanged during five editions of the *Measuring Up* report cards (2000, 2002, 2004, 2006, and 2008), but the data used to measure state performance evolved as better data became available.[10]

Within each grading category, the weighted indicator scores for all the states were used to identify the top-performing state, and the top-performing state's score was set to equal 100. The grades for each category were then set on an absolute scale: 93 and above equals *A*, 90–92 equals *A-*, 87–89 equals *B+*, 83–86 equals *B*, 80–82 equals *B-*, and so on, with *C* grades between 70 and 79, *D* grades between 60 and 69, and *F* grades below 60. (Due to the deterioration of affordability in all states between 2001 and 2004, in 2004 and later years, the National Center decided to use a 10-year-old benchmark for the top-performing state in affordability.) The indicators and weights used in *Measuring Up 2008* are summarized in Table 3.1.[11]

As described previously, the states were graded with reference to a standard, the highest performing state, not on a normalized curve, and the states generally varied considerably in their grades. Table 3.2 provides a distribution of the grades by state. Grades for Preparation were generally higher and varied somewhat less widely than for other areas: 23 states received an *A* or a *B* in 2008; no state received an *F* for preparation; and only 5 received a *D* grade. Grades for completion were similarly high, with 31 states receiving an *A* or a *B*, and only 3 states receiving a *D* or an *F*. Participation tilted in the opposition direction, with only 10 states receiving an *A* or a *B* and 18 states receiving a *D* or an *F*.

The *F* grades on affordability (only California received a *C*) reflected the nationwide deterioration of affordability from 1998 to 2008. As mentioned earlier, all states received an "Incomplete" on postsecondary student learning because no comparable data existed among states.

The inclusion of a grade for the benefits states receive from higher education is slightly anomalous because these benefits can accrue to a state

TABLE 3.1

Performance Indicators and Subindicators for *Measuring Up 2008*

PREPARATION

Indicators	Description	Weights
High school completion	18- to 24-year-olds with a high school credential	25%
K–12 course taking	Percentage of students taking math and science courses *	30%
K–12 student achievement	National assessments of student achievement and SAT/ACT and Advanced Placement test scores *	35%
Teacher quality	Seventh to twelfth graders taught by a teacher with a major in the subject area	10%

* These categories included three or more subindicators with weights adding to the total

PARTICIPATION

Indicators	Description	Weights
Young adults	Percentage of ninth graders graduating from high school in 4 years Percentage of 18- to 24-year-olds enrolled in college	66.67%
Working-age adults	Percentage of 25- to 49-year-olds enrolled in postsecondary education with no bachelor's degree or higher	33.3%

AFFORDABILITY

Indicators	Description	Weights
Family ability to pay (first-time, full-time undergraduates)	Percent of family income (average of all income groups) needed to pay for college expenses, minus financial aid for 2-year public, 4-year public, and 4-year private institutions weighted by enrollment in each sector	50%
Strategies for affordability	State investment in need-based financial aid as compared to the federal investment (20%) The share of income that the poorest families need to pay for tuition at the lowest price colleges (20%)	40%
Reliance on loans	Average loan amount that undergraduate students borrow each year	10%

COMPLETION

Indicators	Description	Weights
Persistence	First-year community college students returning their second year (10%) Freshmen at 4-year colleges returning the sophomore year (10%)	20%
Completion	First-time, full-time students completing a bachelor's degree in 6 years Certificates, degrees, diplomas at all colleges and universities per 100 undergraduate students Certificates, degrees, diplomas at all colleges and universities per 1,000 adults with no college degree (all three weighted equally)	80%

BENEFITS

Indicators	Description	Weights
Educational achievement	Adults (ages 25 to 64 years) with an associate's degree or higher (18.75%) Adults (ages 25 to 64 years) with a bachelor's degree or higher (18.75%)	37.5%
Economic benefits	Increase in total personal income as a result of the percentage of the population with some college (including an associate's degree), but not a bachelor's degree (18.75%) Increase in total personal income as a result of the percentage of the population holding a bachelor's degree (12.5%)	31.25%
Civic benefits	Residents voting in national elections (10.5%) Of those who itemize on federal income taxes, the percentage declaring charitable gifts (10.375%) Increase in volunteering as a result of a college education (10.375%)	31.25%

TABLE 3.2
Number of States Receiving Letter Grades in Each Grading
Area in *Measuring Up 2008*

	A	B	C	D	F
Preparation	5	18	21	5	0
Participation	2	8	22	15	3
Affordability	0	0	1	0	49
Completion	11	20	16	1	2
Benefits	5	15	19	10	1
Learning	0	0	0	0	0

from its ability to attract educated people from other states, regardless of the state's own educational performance. But the inclusion of a grade for benefits emphasizes that educational performance matters both to states and their individual citizens.

The National Center prepared the ground for Measuring Up by announcing its intentions and providing extensive information on its advisers and the underlying procedures used to develop the grades at a series of national conferences. It also launched parallel activities, such as its publication, *Cross Talk* (http://www.highereducation.org/crosstalk/back.shtml), which highlighted stories of state policy leadership, and other programs and publications to call attention to the need for policy leadership. It did not, however, relinquish control of the grading process to outside advisers, and it was very careful to release *Measuring Up 2000* and subsequent editions in a way that maximized national and state media coverage and avoided leaks before the release.

Testing the Theory of Change

The National Center's theory of change rested on two critical presuppositions: (a) that states and state policies play an important role in postsecondary education outcomes, and (b) that providing information on those outcomes and critical factors determining those outcomes would motivate state policy leaders to improve.

Direct observation of the states' roles (they determine characteristics and number of public institutions, their funding, their tuition policies, and the extent of state support for and regulation of nonpublic institutions) supports the first presupposition, but the extent to which state policy makers actually can influence the grades might be questioned. To explore this question, Alicia Cunningham and Jane Wellman[12] conducted an analysis of the relationships among the state grades and three clusters of external factors: (a) economic and demographic influences (labor force, income and income inequality, race and ethnicity, and population age distribution); (b) institutional design and structural influences (the number and type of postsecondary institutions in the state); and (c) influences from funding levels (the availability of resources to education K–12 through postsecondary).

Using stepwise regression procedures, the Cunningham-Wellman analysis found that various combinations of these external factors could predict (*R*-squared values) about 54% of the variance in preparation grades, 37% of the grades for participation, 50% of the grades for affordability, 64% of the grades for completion, and 53% of the grades for benefits. The high *R*-squared value for completion was generated by strong correlations with higher tuition levels and lower part-time study—both also associated with large numbers of enrollments in private, not-for-profit 4-year institutions.[13]

As Cunningham and Wellman note, the insights from such a statistical analysis are limited by the extensive interrelationships among the variables in their study and the impossibility of determining the direction of causality among them (e.g., To what extent is wealth in a state the cause or the effect of high levels of educational attainment?). Environmental factors undoubtedly constrain state policy makers, but a large portion of the variance in grades is *not explained* by such factors. Cunningham and Wellman write that their analysis "suggests that demographic influences are powerful, but that a good half of performance is associated with individual and institutional influences that are susceptible to change through decisions about system design and finance."[14] They also observe that leadership and other qualitative, less tangible factors likely play a role in state conditions.

Policy-Makers' Responses to Measuring Up

As the chief executive officer of the association of State Higher Education Executive Officers (SHEEO) from 2000 to 2013, I had the opportunity to judge the validity of the National Center's theory that better information would lead to action by state policy makers. Some state policy leaders were anxious about the prospect of state grades, and virtually all of them became engaged in understanding and, in some cases, questioning the methodology. The states with strong grades took pride in their achievements and pointed to the policies (e.g., strong student aid programs) that contributed to the results. States with weaker grades frequently used the grades to advocate for additional support or to mobilize strategies for improvement. Some of the states with weaker grades sought to influence the Center to change the grading system to provide credit for effort, without success. The Center did, however, in later editions of *Measuring Up* report change over time, documenting both improvement and deterioration in performance.

The Center did not presume that the grades would in themselves generate an active, engaged response from policy makers. It worked to assemble consulting teams to work with governors, legislators, and higher education leaders to craft improvement strategies; it buttressed the report with additional publications, and it worked to identify a new generation of young leaders who would understand the policy context and the current state of performance, and who would be likely to take an active role in pursuing improvements.

The development and publication of the performance measures highlighted some important policy issues that often were obscured. Some states, for example, showed above average levels of college enrollment for high school graduates—accompanied by very low rates of high school graduation. The variation among the states made it quite clear that where one lives in the United States has real consequences for the price of higher education and the probability of enrolling and completing a postsecondary credential.

On the whole, it seems reasonable to credit the Measuring Up project with considerable success in achieving the objective of increasing public visibility of higher education policy and generating public discussion and action. Naturally, it grew out of its time and the general national concern for improving education, so other initiatives and actors also contributed to the response to Measuring Up. Its campaign was especially buttressed by books such as Tom Friedman's *The World Is Flat*[15] and by OECD[16] reports showing that other countries are increasingly achieving higher levels of postsecondary attainment for younger citizens.

The leaders and staff of the Center were active participants in other higher education policy debates during this period. Its work undoubtedly influenced reports and initiatives by others, including a report on public accountability for student learning by the Business-Higher Education Forum;[17] the SHEEO sponsored National Commission on Accountability in Higher Education;[18] the Spellings Commission report, *A Test of Leadership*;[19] and a report by the National Conference of State Legislators, *Transforming Higher Education: National Imperative—State Responsibility.*[20] The National Center itself obtained funding and recruited a group of states to launch a pilot effort to assess student learning outcomes. This pilot test relied on existing professional and graduate admissions exams, Work Keys, an ACT assessment for community college vocational students, and the administration of the Collegiate Learning Assessment (CLA) to a sample of students.[21]

These successes, however, were accompanied by disappointments. Shortly after the publication of *Measuring Up 2000*, the economy fell into recession. The terrorist attacks of September 11, 2001, consumed much of the energy and focus of policy makers and citizens. Enrollments in postsecondary education began a growth spiral that would continue for a dozen years, but for three successive years state and local support stopped growing nationally (actually declined in some states), and tuition and fees grew rapidly to cover the funding gap.[22] State performance on Affordability declined so rapidly, that, as mentioned previously, the National Center changed its metrics for awarding grades. (This change clearly called attention to extraordinary price increases, but it reduced the insights generated by cross-state comparisons.) Policy conversations about higher education in the states and the nation become more numerous and intense, but distractions and constraints made it difficult for policy makers to focus on improvement strategies.

As a pathbreaking initiative to develop better measures of postsecondary educational outcomes and offer metrics that could guide improvement strategies, the National Center accomplished a good deal. Although the measures persist and are updated annually on the National Center for Higher Education Management Systems (NCHEMS) website (http://higheredinfo .org), the assignment of grades and the high visibility of Measuring Up has ended. Some hoped that Measuring Up would eventually evolve into robust, enduring indicators of performance that would play a permanent role in motivating and guiding public policy for higher education in the states. That might happen eventually, but the performance measures and the underlying data used by the National Center proved incapable of achieving such credibility and widespread utilization during its 10-year run. The National Center's work, however, as part of a larger educational reform movement, almost certainly contributed to the initiatives discussed in later sections of this chapter.

Data Quality, Data Standards, Data Systems

During the same period of the National Center's Measuring Up initiative, a number of U.S. educators and educational reformers focused explicitly on improving the quality and comprehensiveness of data and data systems as an essential condition of achieving educational improvement. One high-profile moment occurred in July 2005 when the National Governors Association (NGA) announced a compact of 45 states to begin using common procedures and standards for measuring and reporting the rate of high school graduation.

At that point different approaches employed by states and the federal government to calculate high school graduation rates produced general confusion. Some approaches counted only the number of students who announced their intention to "drop out" of high school as nongraduates. Other approaches compared ninth-grade enrollments to the graduating class

4 years later (the approach used by Postsecondary Education Opportunity and borrowed by the National Center for Measuring Up), which tended to decrease estimates of the cohort graduation rate due to the number of students who repeat the ninth grade.[23] Some states excluded special education students from the calculation, even though the academic potential of special education students covers a wide range and many graduate. Almost no approaches accounted for students who moved or transferred between schools.

Mark Warner, NGA chairman who was concurrently governor of Virginia, commented:

> Clearly, better data alone will not increase graduation rates or decrease dropout rates, but without better data states cannot adequately understand the nature of the challenge they confront. Knowing the scope of the problem, why students are leaving, and what their educational and personal needs are can help leaders target resources more effectively in support of those young people who are at-risk or who have already dropped out.[24]

So the call for better data, and more accurate measurement, was justified on the presumption that both state leaders and educators could be more effective if armed with better information.

The Data Quality Campaign (DQC), founded in 2005, the year of the NGA action on high school graduation data, defined the characteristics of an acceptable data system for K–12 education, urged states to implement such a system, and began annually reporting on the extent such systems have been created. The "10 Essential Elements" of the DQC state data system, the number of states implementing each element by 2011, and the number of states that had implemented the element in 2005 are displayed on Table 3.3.[25]

Table 3.3 documents enormous progress in achieving more widespread implementation of state data systems that meet the DQC criteria. DQC's persistent advocacy surely made a contribution, but the extent of its success has just as surely been amplified by hundreds of millions of federal dollars allocated to create state longitudinal data systems (SLDS) during the George W. Bush and Obama administrations.[26] DQC's 10 essential elements reflect an important shift in thinking about data systems that emerged in the early twenty-first century—a focus on student-level data rather than school-level data. As policy makers began asking more sophisticated questions about educational performance, it became evident that only data systems that monitored individual student information could address policy issues.

Peter Ewell from NCHEMS and Hans P. L'Orange from the State Higher Education Executive Officers prepared a companion paper to the

TABLE 3.3
Data Quality Campaign: Adoption of Essential Elements

	Data System Essential Element	# of States 2005	# of States 2011
1.	Statewide student identifier	37	52
2.	Student-level enrollment data	40	52
3.	Student-level test data	33	52
4.	Information on untested students	27	51
5.	Statewide teacher identifier with a teacher-student match	14	44
6.	Student-level course completion (transcript) data	8	41
7.	Student-level SAT, ACT, and Advanced Placement exam data	7	50
8.	Student-level graduation and dropout data	36	52
9.	Ability to match student-level P–12 and higher education data	12	49
10.	State data audit system	23	52

DQC essential elements for postsecondary education.[27] Similar to the DQC elements for K–12 systems, their 15 essential elements for postsecondary data systems focus on individual students, course-taking patterns, and student characteristics; but they also include information on student financial aid, persistence and graduation, essential privacy protections, and labor force participation.

Another component of this campaign has been the Common Education Data Standards (CEDS) initiative, led by the National Center for Education Statistics, working in cooperation with a large group of stakeholders ranging from early childhood education to the workforce community. The purpose of CEDS is to provide a "shared vocabulary for education data . . . voluntary, common data standards for a key set of education data elements to streamline the exchange, comparison, and understanding of data within and across P-20W institutions and sectors."[28] (P-20W refers to the continuum of preschool through postgraduate education and into the workforce.) CEDS was created to facilitate "interoperability" of data systems in schools, colleges, and the workforce.

The common education data standards reflect the complexity of education and its delivery systems. The development of education data standards has considered, for example, what data elements to include; the definition of the elements in ordinary language; a standard way of representing the elements in machine language; appropriate codes for various values of the element; the logical relationships among elements; connecting the data elements to individuals and to the institutions, schools, and workplaces serving them; and relating all these elements to the time events occurred and the time involved in various ongoing processes.

The CEDS website explicitly emphasizes that CEDS is not required by law and that the standards may be implemented partially or selectively over time, depending on the needs and priorities of schools and other data users and providers. But the scope of the project is enormous. A total of 1,349 data elements are currently included in CEDS version 4.0, beginning with "Ability Grouping Status" and ending with "Years of Teaching Experience." The word *assessment* is at the beginning of the name of 236 data elements in version 4.0 of the standards, beginning with "Assessment Academic Subject" and ending with "Assessment Type Administered to Children With Disabilities." Data elements vary widely, for example: "Allergy Type," "Blended Learning Model Type," "Professional Development Evaluation Score," and "Financial Account Name."

Certainly many, perhaps most, of the data elements of CEDS will not rise to a high level of policy relevance, even though consistent definitions and data conventions may have many operational benefits to schools and colleges. But common definitions and comparable data for elements such as courses taken, student grades, achievement test scores, time to graduation, receipt of financial assistance, intensity of postsecondary enrollment, and the rest will surely facilitate both more useful policy analysis and policy relevant research.

Unsurprisingly, the development of such detailed data sets, especially when the data includes information that can be linked to individual students, has stimulated concerns about data security and privacy. The Bill and Melinda Gates Foundation and the Carnegie Corporation of New York recently provided $100 million to establish InBloom, a nonprofit dedicated to target the needs of individual children and personalize learning through the use of data analysis and data systems. Initially, InBloom established partnerships with nine states educating more than 11 million K–12 students, but concerns about data security and the involvement of third-party vendors with student data have generated substantial controversy and prompted a number of school districts to withdraw from the relationship.[29]

The availability of comparable, well-documented data on individual students in large-scale databases is clearly an enormous resource for researchers, educators, and policy makers who seek to improve educational attainment. But the potential power of such data creates opportunity for abuse and misuse as well as benefit. Policy makers and society as a whole need standards for not only data definitions but also data handling and utilization. I will return to this topic.

Measuring Student Learning: Fundamental Concepts and Issues

The assessment of learning, or of the aptitude to learn, has been an industry of sorts since the nineteenth century, apparently inspired by the much older practice of imperial examinations in China. In 1895, according to George Madaus of the National Board on Testing and Public Policy, the "American Psychological Association (APA) appointed a committee to investigate the feasibility of standardizing mental and physical tests."[30] Quality assurance for the field reached a milestone when Oscar K. Buros published the *Mental Measurements Yearbook* in 1938. Buros continued updating the yearbook until his death in 1978, and others have continued the work since at the Buros Institute at the University of Nebraska. (*The Sixth Mental Measurements Yearbook* was central to my introduction to the field in 1968. The *Nineteenth Mental Measurements Yearbook* was published in 2014.)[31] Especially in the United States, the formal, standardized assessment of learning is a huge industry and a preoccupation for many educators and policy makers.

Despite more than a century of research and practice, the assessment of learning and aptitude remains a highly contentious and controversial practice. A thorough review of the issues related to standardized testing is far beyond the scope of this book (a Google search on the words "standardized testing" yielded 14,700,000 results), but the measurement of learning is so fundamental to educational policy a high level consideration of key issues is warranted here. I will focus especially on two recent initiatives to assess student learning, the Common Core State Standards for College and Career Readiness, and the Organization for Economic Cooperation and Development (OECD) feasibility study, Assessing Higher Education Learning Outcomes.

A grasp of seven concepts—reliability, validity, consequential validity, norm-referenced, criterion-referenced, domain, and sampling error—is essential for understanding the key issues in the measurement of student learning. Although these concepts are generally understood, a brief summary will be useful to set the stage for the discussion of policy issues.

Reliability simply means that the measuring instrument will yield consistent results if the measurement is repeated. Three different forms of reliability are: (a) test-retest reliability, when a test is given twice to the same person; (b) inter-rater reliability when several raters judge performance; and (c) internal consistency reliability, when different items within a test are designed to assess essentially the same ability or knowledge.

Validity means that the measuring instrument accurately measures what it is designed to measure. A thermometer that consistently reads 50 degrees regardless of the actual temperature would be reliable, but not valid. A thermometer that erratically measures temperature within 10 degrees of the actual temperature would be more valid than one stuck on 50 degrees, but less reliable. High levels of both validity and reliability are essential for a useful test.

Consequential validity, the utility of a measure for policy or practice, is the ultimate test of validity for policy and practice. In a classic article, Samuel Messick wrote, "the key issues of test validity are the meaning, relevance, and utility of scores, the import of value implications of scores as a basis for action, and the functional worth of scores in terms of the social consequences of their use."[32] Consequential validity may be present in data (especially informal, locally designed surveys) even if the psychometric reliability and validity of a measure is unverified or questionable. When information meets the test of credibility to a user and is a spur to adaptive behavior, it is more valuable than information which meets psychometric standards but is ignored. The chapter "Evidence of Student Learning: What Counts and What Matters for Improvement" by Pat Hutchings, Jillian Kinzie, and George D. Kuh in *Using Evidence of Student Learning to Improve Higher Education*[33] provides an especially useful discussion of the various types of evidence of learning that can be useful and the factors associated with productive use.

A *norm-referenced* test compares the performance of each test taker to the performance of all test takers, a random sample of all test takers, or test takers of a certain type (e.g., males, females, racial groups, etc). Typically, scores are reported in relation to the distribution of scores from all test takers in the comparison group, often in percentile terms or the equivalent. A score equaling the median score for all test takers will be reported as the fiftieth percentile, a score lower than received by 75% of test takers will be reported at the twenty-fifth percentile, and a score higher than received by all but 5% of test takers will be reported at the ninety-fifth percentile. The creators of a norm-referenced test usually seek to write questions of varying difficulty that will discriminate among test takers and create a wide distribution of scores that can be used to inform decisions such as admission to a selective college.

The validity of a norm-referenced test is often assessed by its ability to predict the performance of the test taker in subsequent activities. For example, what is the relationship between scores on a college entrance examination and college grades or college graduation? Numerous studies have examined the predictive validity of such exams, of high school GPA, of high school courses taken, and of these measures used in various combinations. Norm-referenced tests typically are "re-normed" periodically so that test results continue to discriminate among test takers, producing a "normal" distribution of test scores.

A *criterion-referenced* test examines the extent to which the test taker is able to demonstrate knowledge of content material or particular skills. A test of spelling ability is a simple criterion-referenced test; although performance is likely to vary among students, theoretically, all well-prepared and diligent students can score 100%. Criterion-referenced tests are designed primarily to assess mastery of knowledge or skill, not to rank students, but norms can be developed for any assessment. State achievement tests and the National Assessment of Educational Progress are criterion-referenced tests.

The validity of a criterion-referenced test is based on the judgments of experts in the subject matter of the test. The test designers seek to write questions that will assess different levels of mastery of the subject matter or skill on a scale that might range from minimal competency to a very high level of mastery. A panel of subject matter experts typically reviews each question and estimates the percentage of "minimally competent" test takers who will be able to answer it correctly. The aggregation of such judgments (often using the Angoff method, named for William H. Angoff, a distinguished research scientist at the Educational Testing Service) is used to establish *cut scores*, or gradations of mastery demonstrated by the assessment.[34]

Criterion-referenced tests have the advantage of being based on a defined set of learning objectives: In theory, average student performance on the same test will improve over time if there are improvements in instruction, student effort, and other factors positively related to performance. But they have the disadvantage of being based on judgment calls—possibly excellent judgment calls, but unavoidably arbitrary decisions about learning objectives, levels of mastery, and ways of measuring learning.

The gradations of mastery on criterion-referenced tests are often identified with descriptors such as are used for NAEP—basic, proficient, and advanced, reflecting different cut scores. This practice often leads to reporting of the percentage of students scoring in the categorical bands of achievement, such as "proficient" or "proficient or above." Sophisticated psychometricians tend to decry such categorical reporting practices for the following reasons: (a) large variations in scores typically occur in every category, and the differences between students close to the "line" between categories are usually much smaller than the differences within the categories; (b) the boundaries between categories are unavoidably arbitrary; (c) in high-stakes test environments, the reporting practices provide a strongly perverse incentive for teachers to invest in test-preparation instruction focused on students scoring just below a cut score, to the detriment of those scoring well above or below a cut score; and (d) these factors can produce misleading, deceptively large changes in test results between test administrations.

The *domain* of a test concerns the scope of the content and abilities included in the assessment. Spelling tests are commonly constructed to test the ability to accurately spell a limited number of words; if the number is manageable, the entire domain can be included on the test. More commonly, the subject matter domain of an assessment is enormously larger than could possibly be included on a test, and the questions involve more complex and difficult to measure skills than spelling. Questions on tests must be designed and selected to create a representative sample of the full domain, a challenging task. Questions also must be designed to measure a reasonably wide range of mastery within the domain.

For practical reasons, assessment often involves choosing a sample from a population of students as well as sampling the content of a domain. The practice of sampling is widespread and well accepted, so much so that the imprecision of measurements due to unavoidable (or worse, avoidable) sampling errors is sometimes ignored or given inadequate attention.

These technical matters are important in their own right, and they are also relevant when policy makers and practitioners consider the purposes for which assessments should be employed. In the argot of the program evaluation profession, assessments may be *summative*, designed to yield a summary judgment about capability or performance, or *formative*, designed to assist the student or client (and his or her instructors) in their efforts to develop or improve a capability. Theoretically, a single assessment might serve both purposes, but as a practical matter they are often at odds.

Another relevant dimension of learning assessment involves the design of questions and tasks presented to the test taker. Forced choice (multiple choice) questions have advantages: They can be easily and consistently scored, and they can be sharply focused on a particular ability or aspect of knowledge.[35] But sophisticated test-preparation coaches can help students guess the correct answer to multiple choice questions without a firm grasp of the content. Even worse, multiple choice assessments seem to foster didactic instruction ("drill and kill") that dampens rather than promotes student engagement.

Constructed-response questions, which require the respondent to write, reason, and calculate in order to develop the answer, avoid the disadvantages of multiple choice questions. But such questions are both harder to score and harder to score consistently, and they do not provide the sharp focus on specific content and skills available in multiple choice questions. In *The Flat World and Education: How America's Commitment to Equity Will Determine Our Future*, Linda Darling-Hammond outlines her view of the advantages of constructed-response questions and the negative consequences of excessive testing.[36]

In 1987 Peter Ewell, a leader in the postsecondary assessment movement, wrote a paper about managing what he considered the contradiction between the purposes of accountability and improvement. He then argued that assessment for accountability inevitably trumps assessment for improvement because accountability inspires defensive behavior that overrides adaptive, learning behavior. In a thoughtful essay published by the National Institute for Learning Outcomes Assessment (2009), Ewell revisits the issue and suggests that accountability and improvement remain unavoidably "in tension," but that the tension can and must be resolved.[37]

Daniel Koretz's *Measuring Up: What Educational Testing Really Tells Us* is an unusually readable and thoughtful analysis of these issues and concepts. His research documenting the effects of test preparation indicates that high-stakes testing leads to unsustainable score inflation and false evidence of improved learning.[38] Donald Campbell anticipated this issue long ago when writing "Campbell's Law": "The more any quantitative social indicator is used for social decision-making, the more subject it will be to corruption pressures and the more apt it will be to distort and corrupt the social processes it is intended to monitor."[39]

The persistent tension between assessment for improvement and assessment for accountability will be evident in the following two case discussions.

Common Core State Standards for College and Career Readiness

The Impetus for the Common Core

The reauthorization of the Elementary and Secondary Education Act in 2001, named the "No Child Left Behind Act," (NCLB) brought accountability for student learning in K–12 education to a new, higher level. It required states to establish their own standards with aligned state assessments in basic skills and to assess student learning for all students at selected grade levels at all schools. (Most states had standards and assessments, but their content and the ways they were employed varied widely.) Promoted by the George W. Bush administration, the law established consequences for schools failing to achieve "adequate yearly progress"[40] for students, and the consequences were designed to increase in rigor and severity if improvement fails to occur over a number of years. Various other requirements also were imposed in order to continue receiving Title I funding from the federal government.

NCLB passed Congress with bipartisan support, a reflection of wide and deep public interest in increasing educational attainment. But as states struggled to comply with its many requirements and definitions, the process of implementing the law proved to be cumbersome and contentious.[41]

In 2008, Gene Wilhoit, then executive director of the Council of Chief State School Officers (CCSSO), began working with the National Governors Association (NGA) to correct what he considered to be the most significant flaw in NCLB. In his words, "NCLB got it exactly backwards. It was flexible and permissive about the standards while being highly prescriptive on the regulations and process for dealing with inadequate performance."[42]

Wilhoit and many others had observed enormous disparities between certain state-level results on the National Assessment of Education Progress (NAEP) and what the states report as "proficient" or "adequate" educational attainment based on state standards and assessments. At issue was variability in both the rigor of state standards or learning objectives and the level of learning judged to be proficient on these criterion-referenced examinations. By having weaker standards and/or low cut scores that qualify for a proficiency rating, states mislead their citizens, teachers, and students on the actual level of educational attainment being generated in their schools. NCLB meant that states with higher standards put their schools and themselves at greater risk for federal sanctions. He concluded that educators need a clear and consistent set of standards or learning objectives to guide instruction and assess performance. The phrase "fewer, clearer, higher, evidence-based, and internationally benchmarked"[43] was used to describe the principles employed to develop the standards.

Development and Implementation Thus Far

CCSSO and NGA, with substantial support from private foundations, assembled an impressive group of experts to develop a set of common state standards for college and career readiness in mathematics and English/language arts. In addition to the standards for college and career readiness, they developed a progression of learning objectives for different grades of elementary and secondary education leading toward the knowledge and skill required for college and career readiness.

Standards Versus Learning Objectives: A Matter of Semantics

The common use of the word *standards* and the practice of states and K–12 educators to establish standards for practice and performance in elementary and secondary education is instinctively jarring to postsecondary educators. Postsecondary educators tend to emphasize the process of discovery and exploration in higher education, and consequently tend to resist "standardization" of any kind. The culture of K–12 education, however, while also valuing discovery and exploration, has been shaped by a social imperative to assure equality of opportunity and the attainment of fundamental knowledge and skill. Accordingly, standards for learning objectives, for teacher qualifications, for curriculum, for textbooks, and so on have been frequently established, often as a matter of law or regulation.

Postsecondary educators, of course, have standards as well, but they are less frequently placed into law and they often are not made explicit. A growing number of postsecondary academic leaders are convinced that clearer learning objectives and expectations will help improve instruction and student achievement. Accordingly, the desire to increase attainment and to assure academic quality has generated postsecondary movements similar to the Common Core state standards, but using words such as *learning objectives* and *qualifications framework*, or *qualifications profile*.[44]

The cultural differences reflected by these semantic differences make the working relationships between K–12 and postsecondary educators a bit more challenging, but bridging them in ways that better articulate the integrity of core values is likely to benefit both sectors.[45]

The release of the standards was accompanied by a strong communications effort to garner the support of states and educational leaders at every level. While CCSSO and NGA strongly emphasized the independent leadership of the states rather than the federal government in developing the standards, the Department of Education, led by Secretary Arne Duncan, announced that it would provide hundreds of millions in funding for two state consortiums to develop assessments for the standards. This de facto federal endorsement tended to dilute the legitimacy of state leadership in the minds of some critics.

By 2014, almost 5 years after the initial release of the Common Core Standards, efforts to use the standards to shape curriculum and to develop assessments to monitor progress and guide instruction had made considerable progress toward implementation. The Department of Defense Education Activity, 45 states, and four territories formally adopted the standards,[46] and several of the states not formally adopting the common standards have established similar standards and assessments of their own. The two assessment consortia supported by federal grants completed their principal assessment instruments for college and career readiness, and the first implementation of these assessments occurred in the 2014–2015 academic year.[47]

Both assessment consortia, Program to Assess Readiness for College and Career (PARCC) and Smarter Balanced, have worked to address the tension between the purposes of formative assessment, designed to give teachers and students information on learning gaps to promote attainment; and summative assessment, credible evidence of attainment and meaningful benchmarks along the learning progression envisioned by the standards through the elementary and secondary grades. Both have also sought to incorporate a mixture of constructed-response and fixed-response questions in their assessments. And both have struggled to do justice to the scope of the standards and to navigate the unavoidable trade-offs between summative/formative goals and fixed-choice/constructed-response questions.

In addition to the two federally funded assessment consortia, other for-profit and nonprofit test development firms are developing assessments geared to reflect the Common Core State Standards. They all are seeking to differentiate themselves on various technical approaches to testing, ease of administration, reporting, and cost, while claiming fidelity to the content of the standards for college and career readiness and the learning progressions of the Common Core.[48]

While the standards have received an enormous amount of support from educational, political, and business leaders, opposition is building as the implementation of assessments approaches. Some state and federal legislators are decrying the encroachment of a "national" or "virtually federal" system on the local control of schools, and some states are considering rescinding or have actually rescinded approval of the standards. (Some observers suggest that the "rejected" Common Core is still greatly influencing the content of state level alternatives.) Many are concerned about the high probability that a substantial percentage of high school graduates will be judged inadequately prepared for college and career by the assessments. Dennis Van Roekel, the president of National Education Association, which has supported the standards, recently asserted that the implementation has been "completely botched" in many states.[49] While reemphasizing his support of the initiative, Van Roekel claims that the implementation has not been given sufficient time or resources to be successful. It seems clear that the standards will not be implemented as rapidly or perhaps even as fully as their designers envisioned. But they are definitely shaping educational policy and practice in the United States.

Reflections on the Historical Context of the Common Core

The full development and implementation of the Common Core State Standards is beyond the scope of this book, although it surely will be the topic for many future book-length studies. (A Google search on the words "Common Core Standards" returned more than 60 million hits in a fraction of a second.) Instead, acknowledging my personal support for the standards,[50] I will focus here on the importance of this initiative in confronting fundamental measurement and educational improvement issues of relevance to policy makers and practitioners.

In the late 1950s, the launching of Sputnik by the former Soviet Union prompted a focus on educational attainment and investment that greatly benefited the baby boom generation and the nation. The principal objective initially was to expand the size of the system and to increase the nation's capability in science, technology, and foreign affairs. In 1965, Lyndon Johnson's War on Poverty expanded the focus to achieve more equitable educational attainment for low-income people and disadvantaged minorities. The first objective was achieved with unprecedented growth in postsecondary attainment by 1975. The second objective, more equitable educational attainment, has not yet been achieved. This failure has been a source of persistent frustration for 50 years.

By 1983, when the post–baby boom generation was in elementary and secondary school, the Reagan administration issued the report *A Nation at Risk*[51] that warned other nations were increasingly surpassing the United States in the education of its citizens. This report launched more than a quarter century of educational attainment initiatives in the United States that have been distinguished by a massive, generally unproductive investment of energy and resources. The failure of these investments to be productive is ironic because the importance of enabling every person to realize his or her educational potential is widely acknowledged, despite differences in political ideology and party affiliation.

Toward this objective, political leaders and educators have pursued an unremitting series of reforms—the new standards movement, school vouchers, charter schools, curricular reforms, testing regimes including the National Assessment of Educational Progress, teacher training and professional development reforms, financial reforms (and related court battles), NCLB, alternative teacher certification strategies, test-based performance assessments, and the rest. These efforts have yielded improvement, but significant, satisfactory progress is hard to find. One can more easily observe a lack of focus, a failure to persist with particular reform strategies, and unremitting conflict and debate in efforts to place or deflect blame or argue for competing "solutions."

At the substantial risk of oversimplifying a complex situation, let me advance a few generalizations to describe contrasting, polarized points of view in this political debate. One perspective argues that the lack of significant progress and the apparent loss of international competitiveness is due largely to the changing composition of the American school population (more economically disadvantaged students, more English language learners, etc.), growing economic inequality and poverty, inadequate investment in education, and misguided educational policies (excessive testing, turbulent leadership and shifting policies, attacks on public schools, unattractive pay and working conditions for teachers, etc.) that make the situation worse.

The opposing perspective argues that public education has been generously funded but has become a self-protecting monopoly, dominated by unions who resist accountability and make excessive demands and by broken bureaucratic systems for training teachers and leading schools. The failure of disadvantaged students to thrive in this environment is used by both sides to attack the other.

Sheer weariness, the passage of time, and inevitable changes (for better or worse) in the underlying conditions feeding this debate might eventually lead to a new consensus, or at least more restrained and open dialogue on educational policy and practice. But in the meantime, an enormous obstacle to common purpose and effective policy and practice is the absence of credible, consistent information on the outcomes of the educational process. It seems to me that the Common Core State Standards have the potential to address that gap.

Earlier in this chapter I described the complex, somewhat convoluted measures assembled by the National Center for Public Policy and Higher Education to measure preparation for postsecondary education and the extraordinary action of state governors to achieve a consistent measure of high school graduation. These efforts reflect a need similar to that addressed by the Common Core State Standards for College and Career Readiness. Without credible, widely accepted yardsticks for measuring both the extent and quality of educational attainment, it is difficult to imagine how practitioners and policy makers can become more effective in their work.

Even if all concede that reliable and valid outcome measures must be developed in order to improve policy and practice, the challenges of creating

---

Why Have Better Educational Measures Become Essential?

Over human history, more widespread educational attainment has gradually become increasingly necessary for individuals and societies. The economic and social benefits of learning became more apparent through the nineteenth and twentieth centuries, and educational attainment and supportive policies grew apace.

When equal access to college became an issue in the twentieth century, standardized college entrance examinations were invented to increase the fairness of college admissions. The primary objective of these norm-referenced exams was to predict success, not to increase student learning or the number of students who were "college ready." The presumption was that only a modest percentage of people were qualified for postsecondary education, so a *scholastic aptitude test* (the original name of the SAT exam) would help identify those able to handle the work. Examinations to help predict later academic achievement increased the efficiency of the admissions and instructional process.

In the twenty-first century, educational policy and practice based primarily on sorting and selecting no longer meet either social or individual needs. Nobody seriously believes that differences will disappear and every student will achieve the highest levels of knowledge and skill, but it has become an urgent objective of social policy to increase the number of people able to be productive in a knowledge-based economy. Educational attainment—knowledge and skill—has become as important as capital and natural resources in the world economy.

How to achieve widespread educational attainment is vigorously debated, but virtually all political and business leaders agree that it is needed. Early in his first term, on February 25, 2009, U.S. president Barack Obama called for every student to complete high school and then to complete at least 1 year of postsecondary education in order to realize his or her potential for becoming a productive member of society. Unlike many presidential proposals, this one has not attracted visible opposition. Learning at scale has become a consensus objective. It is difficult to imagine that it can be achieved without clear learning objectives, intentional instruction, and valid measurement.

such measures and using them appropriately will remain. The next case description further illustrates these challenges.

Assessing Higher Education Learning Outcomes (AHELO)

The Organization for Economic Cooperation and Development (OECD) has made significant contributions to policy conversations around the world through its comparative statistics and studies of a wide range of policy domains. Its comparative data on educational attainment and its Program for International Student Assessment (PISA) have attracted a good deal of policy attention in the United States.[52] Perhaps inspired by the amount of interest in and commentary on PISA data (which examines the skills of 15-year-olds in math, reading, and science), OECD in 2009 launched a feasibility study to assess higher education learning outcomes. According to its website:

> The purpose of this Feasibility Study is to see if it is practically and scientifically feasible to assess what students in higher education know and can do upon graduation.
>
> More than a ranking, the AHELO assessment aims to be direct evaluation of student performance at the global level and valid across diverse cultures, languages and different types of institutions.

A full scale AHELO would be a "low stakes" voluntary international comparative assessment designed to provide higher education institutions with feedback on the learning outcomes of their students and which they can use to foster improvement in student learning outcomes.[53]

The feasibility study included three assessments, one of generic skills, one for engineering, and one for economics. The generic skills assessment used the constructed response Collegiate Learning Assessment (CLA) as the foundational instrument for designing an examination to measure the general skills of critical thinking, problem solving, and writing. The examination for economics was developed by the Educational Testing Service (ETS) in the United States, and the engineering examination was developed by the Australian Council for Educational Research (ACER). ACER was responsible for the general management of the entire project, and it shared responsibility for the generic skills test with the Council for Aid to Education (CAE), the developers of the CLA.

The OECD staff actively and successfully recruited the participation of 17 countries (or jurisdictions within one of these countries) in the feasibility study. Each jurisdiction made substantial financial and in-kind commitments to the project.[54] Nine countries participated in the generic skills study, five participated in the economics study, and nine participated in the engineering study. Five countries participated in two or more strands. Participating countries included Abu Dhabi, Australia, Belgium, Canada, Colombia, Egypt, Finland, Italy, Japan, Korea, Kuwait, Mexico, the Netherlands, Norway, the Russian Federation, the Slovak Republic, and the United States. Three U.S. states participated, Connecticut, Missouri, and Pennsylvania. Charles S. Lenth, vice president of the State Higher Education Executive Officers provided project leadership in the United States, with support from the U.S. Department of Education and the Hewlett Foundation. The extent of international participation and the level of engagement of those participating clearly indicate a high level of interest in assessing and improving student learning.

The OECD website on AHELO provides links to a three-volume feasibility study report and substantial amounts of additional information on the project. Volume 2 of the feasibility study contains reports of the experience for individual countries, a discussion of general issues and conclusions, and a 40-page report of the independent Technical Advisory Group (TAG), which provided counsel and evaluative comment for the feasibility study.[55] Space does not permit a full discussion of the many lessons learned from this project, but the following paragraphs provide a few of my personal observations as a participant and observer of the initiative.

Can Postsecondary Knowledge and Skill Be Assessed on an International Scale?

The feasibility study sought to assess student learning in two disciplines and the general skills of problem solving, creative thinking, and writing. Although it was necessary to make strategic, somewhat arbitrary choices in the disciplinary assessments (e.g., what kind of engineering to assess and which aspects of economics to emphasize), the disciplinary assessments generally were considered to be useful and of acceptable quality. Whether it is practical and feasible to construct such assessments for the full panoply of higher education disciplines on an international scale is more doubtful.

The assessment of general skills across disciplines proved to be more challenging. The project found that differences in language and culture proved to be consequential problems in writing and translating general questions. Questions that worked well in some languages and cultures proved impossible to use in others. Also, it proved very difficult to achieve a consensus among psychometric experts on strategies for the assessment of general skills. Some were convinced that general skills are best addressed in a disciplinary context or in the context of closely related disciplines, rather than from a wide-open interdisciplinary perspective. And the trade-offs between fixed-response and constructed-response questions were persistent issues.

The feasibility study was, with a few exceptions, quite successful in managing the logistical challenges of administering examinations in 17 different countries using online technology. Clearly, if one can solve the problems of covering the relevant domains and of developing appropriate, cross-cultural assessments, it is feasible to administer the examinations and analyze the results on an international scale.

Can Student Performance Be Directly Assessed at a Global Level With Valid Results Across Diverse Cultures, Languages, and Different Types of Institution?

Focusing on two key parts of the question, "global level" and "valid," the AHELO feasibility study provides better evidence of the challenges of such an aspiration than of its feasibility. Although OECD envisioned drawing samples within a country's postsecondary sectors in later studies, the feasibility study did not attempt to draw a country-level sample for assessing student learning (as OECD does for PISA and its newly developed PIAAC assessment of adult competencies). Instead, individual institutions were asked to draw a sample of students nearing the completion of a 3- or 4-year degree program. In the feasibility study it was not possible to achieve consistent sampling procedures among institutions; some created a random sample, others used a convenience sample, and some gave the examinations to all students.

The project also experienced substantial differences among countries and institutions in the response rate for the examinations among students included in the sample. The median institutional response rates for the three examinations were: generic skills, 52.7%; economics, 74.1%; and engineering, 89.2%. The range for all three examinations, however, varied widely, from a low of 3.5% to 100%. The response rates were generally higher for the economics and engineering examinations, where the cohorts were smaller. Also, the response rate varied by the approach used for sampling; the average response rate was 89% for institutions using a census, 68% when a nonrandom selection method was employed, and 51% when students were randomly selected to take the test.[56]

In addition to sampling and response rate issues, a voluntary, low-stakes examination is likely to inspire variable levels of student effort. The AHELO project asked students to assess their own effort on a 4-point scale. For most countries, roughly 40% to 60% of students reported they had invested "close to or my best effort" in responding to the questions. Conversely, nearly half or more than half of students did not invest a high level of effort in the examination. In examining data from U.S. institutions two factors, student effort and academic ability, were virtually tied as the best independent predictors of test scores.

In addition to the challenges of dealing with a diversity of cultures and languages briefly discussed, these observations illustrate the challenges posed by differences among institutions and countries in responding to a global assessment. The differences in institutional culture and responses to assessments revealed by the AHELO feasibility study would likely be compounded by other differences, such as student selectivity, instructional goals and curricula, and instructional methods, apt to confound interinstitutional comparisons.

Can a "Low-Stakes" Voluntary International Comparative Assessment Provide Higher Education Institutions With Feedback They Can Use to Foster Improvement in Student Learning Outcomes?

Despite the difficulty of making valid, comparative inferences through the AHELO assessments, some countries and institutions report useful insights from the project. Some of the learning involved gaining new perspectives on the challenges and potential uses of assessing student learning; however, in several cases, a country was surprised to observe the substantial difficulty its students experienced in responding to constructed response questions. In response, these assessments have evidently fostered changes in instructional approaches in these countries.

To my mind, however, the AHELO project demonstrated the importance of achieving a good fit between measurement and utilization, considering both the purposes of the measurement and the capabilities and responsibilities of those who will use it. AHELO's avowed purpose was to develop a low-stakes international examination that could be used for the valid assessment of learning outcomes, useful to institutions for improving instruction and student achievement. Through the course of the feasibility study, a good deal was learned about the challenging dimensions of such a task: identifying appropriate boundaries for the domains of study; translating (without unacceptable loss of fidelity) content among languages and cultures; achieving consistent sampling and comparable, adequate response rates among participants; achieving the engagement and commitment of respondents to give a good effort; and more.

In addition to the challenges of managing such issues on a global scale, AHELO demonstrated the inherent difficulty faced by an international association of governments seeking to develop a tool for individual colleges and universities and their faculties in improving student learning. Essentially, OECD's avowed goal was to develop a fine-grained assessment to be used to improve practice at a very local level. No matter what was said, no matter how the task was approached, many observers viewed OECD's effort as ultimately destined to become an instrument of governmental accountability.

The division of responsibility between policy makers and practitioners, and the importance of measurements that are "fit" for their various purposes, is the subject of the next chapter.

Notes

1. Rivlin, A. M. (1971). *Systematic thinking for social action*. Washington, DC: Brookings Institution Press, p. 144.

2. As told at the Education Leaders Conference in Denver Colorado, 2002, by Roy Truby, EdD, former Chief State School Officer in West Virginia and former executive director of the National Assessment of Educational Progress. Confirmed in a personal e-mail from Truby, January 29, 2014.

3. Wilson, E. O. (1999). *Consilience: The unity of knowledge*. New York, NY: Random House Digital.

4. National Center for Education Statistics. (2014, February 8). In *Wikipedia*. Retrieved from http://en.wikipedia.org/wiki/National_Center_for_Education_Statistics

5. Bureau of Labor Statistics. (2014, February 12). In *Wikipedia*. Retrieved from http://en.wikipedia.org/wiki/Bureau_of_Labor_Statistics

6. Although there is wide disagreement about President Obama's proposal to rate colleges and universities, there is a consensus that the federal government needs to improve its data on higher education. See: Newman, J. (2014, February 14). What experts on college-rating system mean by "we need better data." *Chronicle of Higher Education*. Retrieved from http://chronicle.com/blogs/data/2014/02/14/what-experts-on-college-ratings-system-mean-by-we-need-better-data/

7. Measuring Up received inspiration and some technical advice from "Quality Counts," a K–12 state ranking developed by *Education Week* first published in 1997. "Quality Counts" continues as an annual publication.

8. Ewell, P. T. (2005). Power in numbers: The values in our metrics. *Change, 37*(4), 10–16.

9. Jones, D. P. (1982). *Data and information for executive decisions in higher education*. Boulder, CO: NCHEMS, pp. 23–24.

10. National Center for Public Policy and Higher Education. (2000). Measuring Up, 2000. *The State-by-State Report Card for Higher Education. San Jose, CA (subsequent)*

11. National Center for Public Policy and Higher Education. (2008) *Technical guide for Measuring up 2008. San Jose, CA.*

12. Cunningham, A. F., & Wellman, J. V. (2001, November). *Beneath the surface: A statistical analysis of the major variable associated with state grades in Measuring Up 2000*. Retrieved from National Center for Public Policy and Higher Education website: http://www.highereducation.org/reports/wellman/wellman.pdf

13. Ibid.

14. Ibid., p. 14.

15. Friedman, T. L. (2007). *The world is flat: A brief history of the twenty-first century*. New York, NY: Picador.

16. Organization for Economic Cooperation and Development. (2013, September 11). *United States country note—Education at a glance 2012:* OECD indicators. Retrieved from http://www.oecd.org/unitedstates/CN%20-%20United%20States.pdf

17. Business-Higher Education Forum. (2004). *Public accountability for student learning in higher education*. Retrieved from http://www.bhef.com/sites/g/files/g829556/f/report_2004_public_accountability.pdf

18. State Higher Education Executive Officers. (2005). *Accountability for better results: A national imperative for higher education*. Retrieved from http://www.sheeo.org/sites/default/files/publications/Accountability%20for%20Better%20Results.pdf

19. U.S. Department of Education. (2006). *A test of leadership: Charting the future of U.S. higher education*. Retrieved from http://www2.ed.gov/about/bdscomm/list/hiedfuture/reports/final-report.pdf

20. Bell, J. (2007). *Transforming higher education: National imperative—state responsibility*. Denver, CO: National Conference of State Legislatures.

21. National Forum on College Level Learning. (2014, February 17). *National forum on college level learning.* Retrieved from http://www.collegelevellearning.org

22. State Higher Education Executive Officers. (2014, February 14). *State higher education finance: SHEF.* Retrieved from http://www.sheeo.org/projects/shef——state-higher-education-finance

23. Mortensen, T. (2014, February 17). *Public high school graduation rates by state, 1981 to 2010.* Retrieved from http://www.postsecondary.org/spreadslist.asp

24. National Governors Association. (2005, July 16). *Governors sign compact on graduation rates.* Retrieved from http://www.nga.org/cms/home/news-room/news-releases/page_2005/col2-content/main-content-list/title_governors-sign-compact-on-high-school-graduation-rate-at-annual-meeting.html

25. Data Quality Campaign. (2014, February 12). *10 essential elements.* Retrieved from http://www.dataqualitycampaign.org/your-states-progress/10-essential-elements

26. By January 2014, all but three states had received grants to build state longitudinal data systems for education. Institute for Education Science. (2014, February 17). *Statewide longitudinal data systems grant program.* Retrieved from http://nces.ed.gov/programs/slds/stateinfo.asp

27. Ewell, P., & L'Orange H. P. (2009, Sept. 14). *The ideal state postsecondary data system: 15 essential characteristics and required functionality.* Retrieved from http://www.sheeo.org/sites/default/files/publications/ideal_data_system.pdf

28. Common Education Data Standards. (2014, February 19). *What is CEDS?* Retrieved from https://ceds.ed.gov/whatIsCEDS.aspx; for a list of the stakeholders advising the effort, see also https://ceds.ed.gov/stakeHolderGroup.aspx

29. Kamisar, B. (2014, January 8). InBloom sputters amid concerns about privacy of student data. *Education Week,* pp. 1, 13.

30. Madaus, G. (2001). *A brief history of attempts to monitor testing.* Retrieved from http://www.bc.edu/research/nbetpp/publications/v2n2.html

31. Buros Center for Testing. (2014, January 19). *Mental measurement yearbooks.* Retrieved from http://buros.org/mental-measurements-yearbook

32. Messick, S. (1990). Validity of test interpretation and use. *Educational Testing Service Research Report,* RR-90(11). Princeton, NJ: Educational Testing Service.

33. Hutchings, P., Kinzie, J., & Kuh, G. D. (2014). Evidence of student learning: What counts and what matters for improvement. In G. D. Kuh, S. O. Ikenberry, N. A. Jankowski, T. R. Cain, P. T. Ewell, P.Hutchings, & J. Kinzie (Eds.), *Using evidence of student learning to improve higher education* (pp. 52–83). San Francisco, CA: Jossey-Bass.

34. Standard-setting study. (n.d.). In *Wikipedia.* Retrieved from http://en.wikipedia.org/wiki/Standard-setting_study. See also procedures used for the National Assessment of Educational Progress: National Assessment of Educational Progress. (2014, February 20). *The setting of achievement levels.* Retrieved from http://nces.ed.gov/nationsreportcard/set-achievement-lvls.aspx

35. Koretz, D. (2008). *Measuring up: What educational testing really tells us.* Cambridge: Harvard University Press. For a thoughtful discussion of the advantages and limits of multiple choice questions, see pp. 35–45.

36. Darling-Hammond, L. (2010). *The flat world and education: How America's commitment to equity will determine our future.* New York, NY: Teachers College Press. See pp. 66–98, 282–285.

37. Ewell, P. T. (2009, November). *Assessment, accountability, and improvement: Revisiting the tension.* Retrieved from http://www.learningoutcomeassessment.org/documents/PeterEwell_005.pdf

38. Koretz, D. (2008). *Measuring up: What educational testing really tells us.* Cambridge, MA: Harvard University Press, pp. 235–259.

39. Campbell, D. T. (1975). Assessing the impact of planned social change. In G. M. Lyons (Ed.), *Social research and public policies: The Dartmouth OECD conference* (p. 35). Hanover: Public Affairs Center, Dartmouth College. As cited in Koretz, p. 237.

40. No Child Left Behind (NCLB) Act of 2001, 20 U.S.C.A. § 6301 et seq.

41. At this writing NCLB remains the law of the land, but its unpopularity and the inability of the Congress to agree on when and how to rewrite the law have led and permitted the Secretary of Education to make a large number of waivers that essentially gut its provisions. The conditions under which such waivers have been granted have been equally controversial, with critics suggesting the Secretary of Education is wielding undue power over local educational practices.

42. Gene Wilhoit, (personal conversation with the author, n.d.).

43. Common Core State Standards Initiative. (2015, July 6). *Standards-setting criteria.* Retrieved from http://www.corestandards.org/assets/Criteria.pdf

44. For examples, visit the website of the National Institute for Learning Outcomes Assessment (http://www.learningoutcomeassessment.org). View the publications of the former New Leadership Alliance for Student Learning and Accountability on the Council for Higher Education Accreditation website (http://www.chea.org/alliance_publications); and the current version of the Degree Qualifications Profile on the Lumina Foundation website (http://www.luminafoundation.org/dqp).

45. A slightly longer treatment of these issues can be found at: Lingenfelter, P. E. (2007, January 19). *K–12 and higher education: Cultural differences and consequences.* Retrieved from http://archive.sheeo.org/about/paulpres/AAC&U%20January%202007.pdf

46. Common Core State Standards Initiative. (2014, February 21). *In the states.* Retrieved from http://www.corestandards.org/in-the-states

47. Partnership for Assessment of Readiness for College and Careers. (2014, February 21). *About PARCC.* Retrieved from https://www.parcconline.org/about-parcc
Smarter Balanced Assessment Consortium. (2014, February 21). *Smarter balanced assessment consortium.* Retrieved from http://www.smarterbalanced.org/about

48. For one example, see a joint publication of ETS, Pearson, and the College Board: Lazer, S., Mazzeo, J., Twing, J. S., Way, W. D., Camara, W., & Sweeney, K. (2014, February 28). *Thoughts on an assessment of common core standards.* Retrieved from http://images.pearsonassessments.com/images/tmrs/tmrs_rg/ThoughtonaCommonCoreAssessmentSystem.pdf

49. Layton, L. (2014, February 9). Teachers union head calls for core "course correction." *Washington Post.* Retrieved from http://www.washingtonpost.com/ local/education/teachers-union-head-calls-for-core-course-correction/2014/02/19/ 0f6b2222-99b8-11e3-80ac-63a8ba7f7942_story.html

50. Lingenfelter, P. E. (2010, November 22). *Why SHEEO supports the common core state standards.* Retrieved from http://www.sheeo.org/sites/default/files/ 20101216-Why-SHEEO-supports-the-Common-Core-State-Standards.pdf.

51. National Commission on Excellence in Education (1983). *A nation at risk: An imperative for educational reform.* Retrieved from http://www2.ed.gov/pubs/ NatAtRisk/index.html

52. For a review of OECD resources in education, visit http://www.oecd.org/ pisa; and http://www.oecd.org/education/database.htm

53. Organization for Economic Cooperation and Development. (2014, February 25). *Testing student and university performance globally: OECD's AHELO.* Retrieved from http://www.oecd.org/edu/skills-beyond-school/testingstudentandun iversityperformancegloballyoecdsahelo.htm

54. Organization for Economic Cooperation and Development. (2014, February 28). *Countries participating in the AHELO feasibility study.* Retrieved from http:// www.oecd.org/edu/skills-beyond-school/countriesparticipatingintheahelofeasibility study.htm

55. Organization for Economic Cooperation and Development. (2014, January). *AHELO feasibility study report, Volume 2: Data analysis and national experiences.* Retrieved from http://www.oecd.org/edu/skills-beyond-school/AHELOFSReport-Volume2.pdf

56. Organization for Economic Cooperation and Development. (2014, January). *AHELO feasibility study report, Volume 1: Design and implementation* (pp. 161–163). Retrieved from http://www.oecd.org/edu/skills-beyond-school/ AHELOFSReportVolume1.pdf

4

MEASUREMENT: FIT FOR
WHICH PURPOSES?

"The idea is to use data as a flashlight, not a hammer."

—Aimee Guidera, executive director, Data Quality Campaign

"In higher education we measure with a micrometer, mark with chalk, and cut with an ax."

—Chuck Thomas, former National Center for
Higher Education Management Systems staff member

"Tell me how you will use my data to help me."

—Unidentified student discussing data privacy policies

Policy makers, practitioners, and scholars know instinctively that information is powerful. What is measured and how measurement is used, or might be used, often become highly charged political questions. Aimee Guidera's quote, while it promotes the benign and productive purposes of greater transparency and expansive data systems, implicitly acknowledges the unavoidable and frequently realized potential for data to be used unproductively as a hammer.

The potential for measurement to be abused for nonproductive purposes is not the only problem. As Chuck Thomas's wry comment suggests, initiatives to expand knowledge through measurement have sometimes generated precise indicators for uses that require very little precision. Measurement is often difficult and expensive. What should be measured, how it should be measured, and how measurements should be used are not trivial questions: Purpose matters.

Finally, measurement and data have many stakeholders and beneficiaries, whose interests may not be identical or even congruent. Who "owns" information when people are served by an institution or organization, the provider of service or the client? What are the rights of patients and students, and what are the rights of hospitals and schools? What rights does government have to information on education or health care when it is substantially underwriting the cost of service? What boundaries and guidelines should be established for data use?

Perhaps the most consequential and contentious aspect of these questions involves the relationships and the boundary between policy and practice. To what extent should law, regulation, and standardization shape practice? Which aspects of practice should be out of bounds for policy? What research, what data, what measures are necessary for effective policy and practice, and which are fit for which purposes? In this chapter, I will explore these practical and philosophical issues, first from the broad perspective of the educational data movement, and then consider how they apply to the data initiatives discussed in Chapter 3.

The Educational Data Movement

In his book *Assessing the Educational Data Movement*, Philip J. Piety[1] suggests that the educational data initiatives described in the previous chapter are being driven by a "sociotechnical revolution" that has given data collection and analysis a more prominent role in business practices. Data analytics have helped business leaders improve the effectiveness and efficiency of their operations and marketing strategies, and business leaders (and the private foundations they have created) quite naturally have become advocates and financial supporters for developing and using more robust data systems in education in order generate similar improvements. (The application of these ideas to health care will be considered in the next chapter.)

These educational data initiatives, and the concept of evidence-based policy and practice have attracted hundreds of millions of dollars in public and private investments and generated intense controversies over the use of data to evaluate schools and teachers. It might be too early to judge this nascent movement, but thus far it is hard to find compelling evidence that it has led to significant positive improvements in educational outcomes.

The No Child Left Behind (NCLB) initiative has left few if any visibly enthusiastic supporters, and it is hard to find persuasive evidence that its evidence-based accountability has improved student achievement. The What Works Clearinghouse has not assembled a very impressive set of demonstratively effective interventions (see Chapter 2). The Data Quality Campaign now publishes success stories on its website of how data have been used to improve educational outcomes, but these accounts tend to be the kind of anecdotal, nonsystematic evidence frequently derided by those advocating evidenced-based policy and practice.[2] As Piety, who has devoted considerable study to the movement observes, "the educational data movement is full of puzzles and seeming contradictions. None may be more significant than the lack of evidence of its own success."[3]

This is not to suggest that NCLB and the data movement have made no useful contributions. I believe they have. But although better data may be necessary, it clearly is not sufficient for improving educational outcomes. And it is becoming more and more evident that the underlying issues of legitimate use, fitness for purpose, rights to privacy, and data ownership remain unresolved.

The Controversial Postsecondary Student Unit-Record System

The political conflict in the United States over a federal student-level unit-record system in postsecondary education illustrates all of these issues. In 1997, the Department of Education created an Integrated Postsecondary Education Data System (IPEDS) survey of graduation rates to satisfy the requirements of the Student Right-to-Know legislation. The survey required institutions to report the percentage of their students enrolling for full-time study for the first time in higher education who graduate within 150% of the normal time to completion, 6 years in a 4-year institution and 3 years for a 2-year program.[4]

This carefully crafted compromise procedure was almost immediately derided for its omissions. Students who enrolled for part-time study and all transfer students were excluded from the calculation. Because the many students who transfer and graduate elsewhere show up as dropouts where they first enrolled, the graduation rates on a statewide or nationwide basis reported through this survey are substantially understated. A handful of adult-serving institutions have few if any students who meet the criteria for inclusion in the survey.

In the summer of 2004, three national associations, the American Council on Education (ACE), the American Association of State Colleges and Universities (AASCU), and the State Higher Education Executive Officers (SHEEO) association, wrote to John Boehner, chairman of the House Education and Workforce Committee, to recommend that the committee ask the Department of Education to do a feasibility study of a national student unit-record system in order to address these problems. The department subsequently completed such a study, and proposed a plan through which 40 data elements in four categories (demographic, enrollment, cost and financial assistance, and completion) collected on individual students could meet virtually all the existing requirements of the IPEDS survey, provide far superior information on graduation rates, and provide useful information on the relationship between the extent of student financial assistance from various sources and college enrollment and completion.

This proposal won the support of the National Commission on Accountability in Higher Education organized by SHEEO, the associations of public colleges and universities, and later secretary of education Margaret Spellings's Commission on the Future of Higher Education. But it quickly aroused the strong opposition of the National Association of Independent Colleges and Universities (NAICU). The President of the American Council on Education declined to sign the Spellings Commission report, in part because of its recommendation to create a student-level data system and the opposition of independent colleges and universities.

In a *Washington Post* op-ed titled "Big Brother on Campus" a private college president wrote:

> This proposal is a violation of the right to privacy that Americans hold dear. It is against the law. Moreover, there is a mountain of data already out there that can help us understand higher education and its efficacy. And, finally, implementation of such a database, which at its inception would hold "unit" record data on 17 million students, would be an unfunded mandate on institutions and add greatly to the expense of education.[5]

Supporters of the student unit-record system argued: (a) strong data security protections (as used in existing federal systems on employment, earnings, and tax records, as well as Department of Education surveys of individuals) would protect student privacy; (b) the important educational and policy questions to be informed by a student unit-record system can be answered in no other way; and (c) such a system would eventually be far more efficient, accurate, and powerful than the patchwork of systems currently used by institutions to aggregate data in order to respond to IPEDS surveys.

With the leadership of North Carolina congresswoman Virginia Foxx, the Higher Education Opportunity Act of 2008 (Sec. 113 Database of Student Information Prohibited) included a provision denying authority for the Department of Education to implement any data system "that tracks individual students over time." Ironically, the same section excepted from the prohibition the use of an existing student unit-record data system maintained by the National Student Clearinghouse in order to help institutions comply with the requirements of the federal guaranteed loan programs.[6] In the same act, Congress authorized funding for state unit-record data systems and eventually provided approximately $600 million in grants to the states for developing state-level unit-record systems that typically are far more complex and comprehensive than those the federal postsecondary system proposed in 2004.[7]

In 2014, the debate continues. Congresswoman Foxx now chairs the House Education and Labor Subcommittee on Higher Education and Workforce Training, and she shows no signs of changing her mind about a national student-level data system. Simultaneously, Senators Warner, Rubio, and Wyden are sponsoring legislation that would require the development of such a data system not greatly different from that proposed in 2004.[8] A recently published study by the New America Foundation revisited the political moves that occurred a decade earlier.[9] The persistence of this debate illustrates both the difficulty and the importance of finding feasible compromise solutions to the inherent conflicts among claims for data ownership, rights to privacy, and legitimate use.

Data Ownership and the Right to Privacy for Individuals and Institutions

Information and intellectual property are increasingly valuable and powerful. But they are far more difficult to "own" and control than money and physical property. In 2003 David Loshin, a leading writer in the information technology (IT) field, sorted through the dimensions of data ownership in three categories: value, responsibility, and psychology. The first two of these, value and responsibility, fall generally in the domain of IT managers who directly hold data and are responsible for the definition, quality, and security of data. They are also, of course, responsible for serving the user community through effective management. In meeting these responsibilities, IT managers add to and sustain the value of data.

The "psychological" dimensions of data ownership, according to Loshin, are more complex. These "owners" include those who create, consume, compile, fund, decode, package, or read data, as well as the subjects of the data who can claim privacy rights or image copyrights. Loshin suggested that the psychological ownership of data is "buoyed by an individual's aversion to accepting blame for failure versus a desire for claiming success. Data ownership is complicated because of 'turf' and 'fear.'"[10] Although Loshin wrote largely for a business audience, the issues of turf and fear seem to apply universally.

The use of educational data has been shaped by the Family Educational Rights and Privacy Act (FERPA), a 1974 federal law that establishes the conditions under which a school may release information on an individual student. Although generally schools may not release personally identifiable information about a student without consent, the law and related regulations establish a substantial list of exceptions, beginning with *directory information* over which there is no expectation of privacy.[11] The extent and practical application of those exceptions have been vigorously debated during the emergence of the educational data movement. Practices vary considerably among states, and restrictive interpretations of FERPA have inhibited data sharing for policy research, a primary objective of the Data Quality Campaign and others.

In 2011, the Department of Education established the position of chief privacy officer and issued revised guidance to clarify the interpretation of the law. These actions helped clarify legal issues and led to more secure data sharing and policy research, but multiple claims for the ownership of data and information still make it difficult to establish simple, straightforward privacy guidelines. Every student has an ownership claim to his or her academic record and other educational records, including test scores, disciplinary actions, and other sensitive material that might be used for purposes of personal advantage or disadvantage. The institution also has a claim of ownership, both because the records were produced jointly and because of the responsibilities it bears for guarding student data, assuring its accuracy, and validating claims of educational achievement.

The risk of unauthorized disclosure of student information was frequently mentioned as a reason for opposing a national student-level data system. Creating any new database increases such risk, but it is unlikely this concern was the most powerful motivation for opposing the proposal. Large amounts of sensitive personal data on individuals are held securely by numerous entities, including, of course, the federal government. The same Congress that prohibited the creation of a federal student-level database financed the creation of far more detailed state student-level data systems and exempted by indirect reference the continuing use of the student unit-record database held by the National Student Clearinghouse.

It is far more likely that *institutional privacy*, not student privacy, was and remains the primary factor motivating opposition to a national student-level data system. In addition to tracking the movement of students among institutions, the number of credits accumulated before graduation or withdrawal and accurate graduation rates for students attending multiple institutions, the proposed federal student-level data system would have provided information about institutional financial assistance to individuals, along with the amounts of assistance provided from state and federal sources.

Information about institutional student aid would have been helpful in evaluating the impact and effectiveness of student financial assistance generally. As the single largest source of student financial assistance, it is unsurprising that federal policy makers would be interested in obtaining it. Although some might argue that information about institutional student financial assistance should be fully transparent, it is easy to understand why private colleges and universities would be reluctant to share information on individual awards.

For better or worse, colleges and universities use the pricing mechanism like many other enterprises: Some customers are charged more and some are charged less for reasons related to market conditions and opportunities. Students with financial need or special abilities may receive discounts. Colleges with more capacity than enrollment demand manage their admissions and pricing policies to fill available spaces. Colleges with more enrollment demand than space manage admissions and pricing to attract a mix of students they believe will best serve the institution's mission, quality, and reputation.

The desire for institutional privacy is not limited to pricing, even though that may have been the most powerful factor in this conflict. Colleges and universities compete with each other for students, faculty, and reputation. Like individuals, colleges quite naturally want to maintain a degree of control over the information about them in the public domain. So it is unsurprising that private colleges especially would not welcome what might be perceived as invasive transparency.

Some argue that the right of consumers (and the public) for information trumps all privacy rights for institutions. But I would counter that the right of privacy for individuals and institutions should be tempered by the rights of others, and it is a legitimate issue for both.

So how might a line be drawn between legitimate and limited privacy rights? The examples included in the FERPA general guidance for students illustrate two underlying sets of principles. The first set of principles is the right of the data subject to assure the accuracy of the record and that the rules governing disclosure or nondisclosure are observed. Students have a right to view their records, to challenge their accuracy, and to hold the institution accountable for proper use and protection of the record. If the institution disagrees about a student complaint about accuracy or inappropriate disclosure, the student has a right to offer evidence for adjudication.

The second set of principles implicit in the FERPA guidelines is more nuanced. The general rule requires the student's written consent before the disclosure of educational records, but many exceptions apply. The general principle requiring written consent establishes a zone of privacy that can be violated only for justifiable causes, which are illustrated by the exceptions to the general principle.

Directory information such as name, address, terms of enrollment, and the rest can be disclosed without permission. Also, a student's record can be viewed by institutional staff with responsibilities for instruction, counseling, or administrative functions related to the student's education. A student's record can be disclosed in connection with applications for financial assistance, it can be disclosed to parents if the student is a dependent, it can be disclosed when there is a health or safety emergency, and it can be disclosed when there is a violation of the law. When a disclosure of information is justified for a particular purpose, only relevant information may be disclosed, not the entire record. Except when there is a violation of the law or others are placed at risk, all of these disclosures and the use of information may be justified as being in the best interests of the student.

While an analogy between individual rights and institutional rights to privacy could be pushed too far, there are similarities. Both function in public space, compete with others, and have a legitimate interest in putting the best foot forward. One could argue that institutions have no right to conceal relevant information from a legitimate authority, just as students have no right to deny access to their records to faculty and counselors at their institution. But just like individuals, it seems reasonable to grant institutions some protection from information being made available publicly in ways that could harm them in the competitive marketplace, except when others are placed at risk, the law has been violated, or their functional effectiveness is clearly outside the bounds of acceptable performance.

The fundamentally sound rationale of the educational data movement warrants continuing work to address the challenges posed by data ownership and privacy concerns. Individual privacy generally has been protected, with rare breaches most frequently occurring at inadequately protected local sites, rather than in connection with policy studies or large governmental or nongovernmental databases. Scrupulously careful uses of student-level data have produced important policy studies, such as the college completion reports of the National Student Clearinghouse.[12] And individual-level data, encrypted to assure privacy, have been shared to good effect among different data holders, such as K–12 schools, postsecondary institutions, and employment agencies in four Western states.[13] Eventually more such studies, and continued vigilance to assure data security, will increase the public's comfort with such research.

The matter of institutional privacy is more complex, in part because its legitimacy is not universally recognized. Consequently, many institutions, fearing unbounded intrusions into institutional data, have vigorously resisted efforts such as the proposed national student unit-record database. The practice in some states of grading K–12 schools *A* to *F* and the virtually irresistible impulse to turn data into ranking league tables doesn't help.

These obstacles to the effective use of institutionally held data to improve policy and practice can be overcome. In the face of continuing pressures for transparency, some American colleges and universities have taken up the challenge of developing and disclosing better data on key indicators, such as student completion. The data of the National Student Clearinghouse has been used to achieve this purpose as well as some of the other objectives of a national student unit-record system, through efforts such as the Student Achievement Measure (SAM) proposed by the Association of Public and Land-grant Universities (APLU). Such uses are growing. The data standards movement and advocacy for open data may eventually permit the use of administrative data sets at institutions to be used for studies of policy and practice that, with proper controls and agreements, could increase enlightenment without inappropriately violating either student or institutional privacy.

What about the rights of others to information that might be relevant to their decisions to employ, to enroll, or to purchase services? Such rights are legitimate and they apply to both students and institutions. Neither have an unqualified right to privacy, and one might argue that institutions have a weaker claim to privacy because they serve the broader public. An implicit, sometimes explicit theory of the educational data movement is that more transparency will serve the public by motivating educators to improve and giving parents and students information they need to avoid lower-quality providers. Also, because institutions accept governmental funds, one could argue there is a superior governmental interest in the use of these funds.

The responsible, effective use of transparency is a legitimate tool for both accountability and consumer information, but achieving responsible and effective transparency is not a simple matter.

Differentiating Policy and Practice

Although they play a role, the wariness and political turmoil over the use of data and information in policy and practice are not fundamentally caused by a distrust of empiricism or a perverse avoidance of accountability. The deeper concern is about misuse, especially misuse on a massive scale. One dimension of the concern is political, a desire to avoid the concentration of power. Examples of this dimension are the almost sacrosanct commitment to local control in American K–12 educational policy, the value placed on academic freedom and institutional autonomy in higher education, and the willingness of Congress to approve state student unit-record data systems while prohibiting a federal system. But the political dimension is simply a facet of a deeper, practical question: In order to improve human life, who should use information and data for what purposes, and how should they use it?

The words *policy* and *practice* often appear together, including in the title of this book. But policy and practice are not different aspects of the same thing. Each is consequentially relevant to the other, but the responsibilities, the work, the tools, and especially the capabilities of policy makers and practitioners are different. The effectiveness of both policy and practice depends on excellence in both domains and an appropriate and complementary division of labor between them.

The most crucial question involves the division of labor between policy and practice. Practitioners have the responsibility to deliver service, to achieve the goals of policy. Policy makers have responsibilities for influencing the total size of available resources and for allocating those resources among various purposes. Through the power of law and regulation that govern the use of public funds, policy makers also decide what mechanisms should be employed to govern the use of public resources in pursuit of policy objectives.

In the classic book *Politics, Economics, and Welfare*, Robert A. Dahl and Charles E. Lindblom[14] identified four broad mechanisms available to policy makers for achieving social objectives: (a) a price system (markets), (b) hierarchy (flexible command and control), (c) bureaucracy (less flexible rule-making with enforced compliance), and (d) polyarchy (debate and bargaining among decision makers at various levels). All four mechanisms have advantages and disadvantages on these dimensions—flexibility, focus, stability, efficiency, control, accountability, and adaptability—that Dahl and Lindblom analyze at length. To some extent all four mechanisms are employed individually and in combination by governments and other social organizations in order to achieve different purposes.

The division of labor between policy and practice is shaped by the choices policy makers make among these four mechanisms. If policy makers emphasize hierarchy and bureaucracy, they shrink the space available for practitioners to exercise judgment and discretion. If they emphasize markets and polyarchy, they create space for practitioners to exercise discretion and judgment. The "right" balance among these mechanisms naturally becomes a matter for debate and adjustment, ideally based on actual results more than ideological preferences. As a general rule (and in keeping with James Scott's analysis discussed later) most would agree that policy is more effective when it focuses on broad principles and the allocation of resources to priorities than when it becomes involved in finer-grained dimensions of practice and implementation.

History provides many examples in which policy makers and policy have overreached and failed in attempts to improve community life and shape practice. In his book *Seeing Like a State: How Certain Schemes to Improve the Human Condition Have Failed*, James C. Scott[15] brilliantly analyzes the circumstances in which well-meaning but misguided state initiatives have resulted in failure, sometimes with tragic consequences.

Scott argues that all states (and most human organizations) are naturally inclined to organize and simplify complex social and natural environments in order to achieve control, solve problems, and secure their own authority and power. For some purposes such efforts are essential, and they often have positive effects. For example, the organization of public life enables more efficient transportation, orderly ownership of land, effective sanitation, and better security, the means of sustaining the state through taxation.

But the failure to recognize and mitigate inevitable trade-offs between positive and negative effects of enforced organization can be a serious problem. Sometimes, as in the case of monocultural forestry and agriculture, unanticipated side effects lead to severe ecological damage. Scott terms this tendency of state behavior *thin simplification* and illustrates cases where it has led to failure with many examples from forestry, agriculture, and city planning.

The tendency to organize and simplify can be dangerously exaggerated by what Scott calls *high-modernist ideology*. In Scott's words, high-modernist ideology is

> a strong, one might even say muscle-bound, version of the self-confidence about scientific and technical progress, the expansion of production, the growing satisfaction of human needs, the mastery of nature (including human nature), and, above all, the rational design of social order commensurate with the scientific understanding of natural laws.[16]

Scott distinguishes high-modernist ideology from scientific practice because it is "uncritical, unskeptical, and thus unscientifically optimistic about the possibilities for the comprehensive planning of human settlement and production."[17] According to Scott, high-modernist ideology prizes order, control, and uniformity almost as a matter of aesthetics, and it tends to disrespect the "ordinary" knowledge of non-elites.

Scott suggests that thin simplification and high-modernist ideology are most dangerous when combined with an authoritarian state and a prostrate civil society unable to resist an authoritarian state. These factors were present in the egregious examples of state failure Scott cites, namely the Great Leap Forward in China, collectivization in Russia, and the compulsory creation of villages in Africa. Even in cases where authoritarianism does not make the scale of failure catastrophic, thin simplification and high-modernism have generated dozens of failed agricultural development projects in the Third World and failed designs for new cities, such as Brasilia.[18]

Although thin simplification and high-modernist ideology have been especially associated with authoritarian governments, Scott argues these tendencies shape the behavior of all governments as well as large-scale, market-driven capitalistic enterprises. The common problem is the imposition of rules and structures with only superficial understanding of context and the complex interactions inherent in natural and social processes. Failures in city planning have typically imposed an aesthetically attractive order that fails to take into account the movements and social processes that people employ in meeting the complex needs of daily life.[19] Misguided agriculture policies have implemented massive, orderly strategies that "solve" one or two problems of efficient production while failing to account for the structure of natural systems with its diversity and complex relationships among soil, topography, insects, water, and plants.

The imposition of rules and structures based on thin simplification is often accompanied by a failure to recognize and value the sometimes intuitive, adaptive knowledge of practitioners that is essential for functionality in complex environments and situations. Scott uses the Greek work *mētis* to describe such knowledge and offers numerous examples of its power and importance. One particularly telling example is the tactical use of work-to-rule actions by trade unionists wishing to gain leverage over management without actually striking. To employ this technique

> employees begin doing their jobs by meticulously observing every one of the rules and regulations and performing only the duties stated in their job descriptions, without using the subtle informal knowledge required to do almost any kind of productive work. The result, fully intended in this case, is that the work grinds to a halt, or at least to a snail's pace.[20]

While acknowledging that social organization is essential in a crowded world, Scott argues that *mētis* is essential for dealing with diversity and complexity. The rational structures and thin simplifications created by governments and organizational leaders to address human problems work most effectively only in partnership with practical knowledge.[21] Lacking a partnership with practical knowledge and skill, thin simplifications not only fail to solve human problems but also exacerbate them and create additional problems.

In a similar vein, Lee S. Shulman in *The Wisdom of Practice: Essays on Teaching, Learning, and Learning to Teach* takes the reader on a rich tour of *mētis* in teaching and learning. A summary of Shulman is far beyond my scope here, but two quotes from these essays are particularly relevant to this topic:

> [Just as the most common verbs in every language tend to be complex, irregular, and difficult to learn] the more central a concept, principle, or skill to any discipline or interdiscipline, the more likely it is to be irregular, ambiguous, elusive, puzzling, and resistant to simple propositional exposition or explanation. Thus, if we are to make less into more, we had better recognize that less is harder than more, less is more complex than more, less is more enigmatic or cryptic than more.[22]

And:

> What policymakers fail to understand is that there is an unavoidable constraint on any piece of research in any discipline. . . . To conduct a piece of research, scholars must necessarily narrow their scope, focus their view, and formulate a question far less complex than the form in which the world presents itself in practice.[23]

Policy and practice are neighbors. To be good neighbors, as Robert Frost suggested, they need good fences. Conversations over the fence, of course, are beneficial to both.

Data and Measurement Guidelines: For Policy, Public Use, and Practice

What guidelines should inform the use of data and measurement in policy and practice? Perhaps sharp boundaries cannot be drawn for every circumstance, but general guidelines are needed to reduce the contention over data availability and use, and to realize the potential of measurement to improve policy and practice.[24] The following questions are proposed as a basis for such guidelines.

First, what are the responsibilities and decision-making needs of the following key stakeholders: policy makers, the general public, and practitioners? Practitioners need detailed information on individuals, but policy makers and the general public do not need and should not have access to that information. Policy makers and the public do need research based on individual information. Rigorous privacy safeguards are necessary for such research, but the feasibility of such safeguards has been demonstrated. The continuing willingness and commitment of the policy and research community to observe both privacy and appropriate boundaries of inquiry can and should help create many more useful opportunities to learn from individual data in administrative and policy databases.

Second, are the uses of data and measurement well matched to the capabilities and the responsibilities of those with access to the information? Policy makers, as Scott's examples demonstrate, can do great harm if misguided policy is enforced at scale. Even when the power of policy is constrained by checks and balances in a democracy, overreaching attempts to solve problems for which policy tools are ill-suited are doomed to be ineffective and harmful. For example, while achieving only marginal gains toward its objectives, the overreaching measurement mandates and sanctions of No Child Left Behind consumed vast amounts of resources, energy, and political capital. As a general rule, policy should support effective practice, not attempt to create or manage it through direct interventions.

Excessive confidence in the capabilities of the public to use large amounts of information as a means of improving performance is another example of overreach. Highly focused, decision-relevant, robust indicators (e.g., automobile fuel efficiency estimates) can be quite useful to consumers, but a large, comprehensive collection and presentation of data and information is more likely to be confusing or generally ignored due to its indigestibility. As a general rule, the more extensive the information provided to the public as a tool for consumer choice the more likely information overload will reduce its impact on their decision making.

The distinction Dennis Jones makes between data and information is relevant here. As noted in Chapter 3, data exist independently from context but *information* does not. Information must be useful to a user and in the context of the user. It is not helpful to have information that is incomprehensible, irrelevant, or potentially misleading.[25]

Information, even from large databases, properly interpreted and presented to the public can be useful if the proper conditions for usability (including appropriate caveats) are achieved. But the practice of organizing information to create rankings, and especially to identify "failing schools," is fraught with potential for error and injustice. In *Hiding From Humanity: Disgust, Shame, and the Law*, Martha Nussbaum[26] argues that the tactic of shaming (with concomitant stigmatization) is virtually always disproportionately unjust. Ray Pawson, a British scholar, colorfully describes the use of transparency as a tool for changing behavior as "naming and shaming."

Naming and Shaming: An Ineffective Tool for Changing Behavior

The logic of naming and shaming is illustrated by Ray Pawson with this quotation:

> There is not a crime, there is not a dodge, there is not a trick, there is not a swindle, there is not a vice, which does not live by secrecy. Get these things out in the open, describe them, attack them, ridicule them in the press, and sooner or later public opinion will sweep them away.[27]

According to Pawson, the theory of all such initiatives contains four components:

1. identification: in which performance is measured and reported;
2. naming: through which the failing/deviant party is identified and disclosed publicly;
3. public sanction: through which the public responds to the disclosure; and
4. recipient response: through which desirable behavioral change follows the sanction.

The theory may fail to achieve its objectives if one or more of these shortcomings occur:

1. Culprits may be misidentified due to poor measures, inadequate monitoring, or other factors.
2. The disclosure may be poorly managed or poorly presented in ways that impair public understanding of the ratings or that generate disputes undermining the credibility of the information.
3. The sanctions may be misapplied, perhaps going beyond the intended shaming effects to yield humiliation, defamation, or deprivation; or falling short of the intended effects to yield stoicism, apathy, or sympathy.
4. The shamed culprits may respond in unintended ways, perhaps accepting the label, ignoring the label, or adopting perverse behaviors.

Pawson analyzed a number of naming and shaming strategies (a British car theft index, hospital report cards, Megan's Law to identify and publicize the location of sex offenders, and others) in order to examine whether and how they succeeded or failed. The British car theft index was most successful because the indicator was clear-cut, some of the major manufacturers chose to make vulnerability to theft a competitive issue, and consumer awareness was dramatically heightened when the insurance industry began charging extremely high premiums to insure high-risk cars. More commonly, however, naming and shaming strategies founder on one or more of the four shortcomings listed previously.

Rigorous use of data by practitioners for monitoring performance and improving quality, of course, is not naming and shaming. Successful examples of such uses will be discussed in Chapter 5.

Pawson finds that shaming strategies typically fail to achieve their intended purposes due to one or more of the factors identified in the previous text box.

Third, do the uses of data and measurement respect privacy rights?   As a general rule, with the permissible exceptions noted previously for FERPA compliance, only practitioners with responsibilities for serving individuals (and data administrators held to very high ethical standards for nondisclosure) should have the right to view individual data when the person is identifiable. As argued previously, organizations and institutions also have privacy rights, but they are limited by their responsibilities to the public and the public's right to consumer information.

McKinsey and Company's Global Institute recently published an essay urging governments to promote and facilitate open data on a worldwide basis. The article suggested many possible benefits from open data and also outlined the risks to individual privacy rights and organizational confidentially that must be managed.[28] The enthusiasm of the McKinsey authors has overtones of Scott's high-modernist ideology, but the potential benefits of more open data, with appropriate risk mitigation, are evident.

Fourth, are the data, the metrics developed from the data, and the uses of data and metrics accurate, reliable, valid, and fit for purpose?   In 1835, while writing *Democracy in America*, Alexis de Tocqueville explained his unwillingness to undertake the difficult task of comparing the social expenditure in France and the United States with the following observation:

> It would be dangerous to attempt this comparison; for when statistics are not based on computations that are strictly accurate, they mislead instead

of guiding aright. The mind is easily imposed upon by the affectation of exactitude which marks even the misstatements of statistics; and it adopts with confidence the errors which are appareled in the forms of mathematical truth.[29]

To be useful, social indicators should be robust, relevant to decision making, and appropriately qualified by the material contextual factors. The obligations to achieve and assure accuracy, reliability, and validity too often get short shrift where there is great demand and opportunity for measurement and analysis. The need to assure fitness for purpose raises the standard even higher. The potential for harm at scale is greatest when data and measurement are used for policy or when policy requires their use in practice. When there is intent to use measurement for policy, or even when there will be a temptation to use measurement to guide the use of state power, fitness for purpose is critically important. The proliferation of indicators and the aggregation of indicators to construct rankings of schools, hospitals, or communities (clearly an irresistible temptation) tend to degrade actual utility, except for the marketing of the highly ranked. As the number of indicators employed grows, generally less attention is paid to properly qualified inference and the quality of data.

Peter Ewell's article "Linking Performance Measures to Resource Allocation: Exploring Unmapped Terrain" offers a helpful framework for evaluating the utility of different types of data in the policy environment.[30] He suggests that properly contextualized "hard" data—unambiguous, robust, simple indicators of workload and performance—can appropriately guide policy decisions. More complex, fine-grained indicators (typically with a standard error of measurement) give a false sense of precision, which is a dangerous platform for policy actions. The importance of employing caution and multiple-perspectives when using data to make policy decisions is difficult to overemphasize.

Fitness for Purpose: Legitimate and Effective Uses of Measurement

In light of the data measurement guidelines discussed in the previous section, this chapter concludes by examining the four measurement initiatives described in Chapter 3: The Measuring Up project focused on postsecondary education; campaigns to establish more robust data standards and data systems; the Common Core State Standards for college and career readiness; and the OECD project, Assessing Higher Education Learning Outcomes (AHELO).

This discussion will focus principally on the four questions identified previously:

1. How does the initiative serve policy makers, the public, and practitioners? Is the division of labor between policy and practice clear and productive?
2. Are the uses of the data well suited to the capabilities of the users?
3. Are privacy rights an issue?
4. Are the data accurate, reliable, valid, and fit for purpose?

Measuring Up

Of all of the initiatives discussed in Chapter 3, Measuring Up most clearly focused its work on policy and on policy makers. The state is the unit of analysis for Measuring Up, and the logic of the measurements and the discussion of the results focus on state policy. State performance is the subject, measured by three statewide indicators of educational achievement (preparation, participation, and completion), one enabling indicator (affordability), and one outcome indicator (benefits). The clear focus on a few policy relevant metrics distinguishes Measuring Up from many other less sharply focused state-level "report cards."

Measuring Up offered policy makers a theory of the factors generating higher postsecondary educational attainment and indicators of state performance for each important factor in the theory: preparation, participation, completion, and affordability. The components of each factor are explicit and logically persuasive (e.g., preparation consists of high school completion rates, K–12 course taking, student achievement, and teacher quality). Because the state is the unit of analysis, Measuring Up implicitly encourages policy makers to focus on state policies that might contribute to improvement in each of the measured areas.

Table 4.1 provides examples of policy actions that could lead to improvement in the domains measured by this initiative. Most of these involve the allocation of resources to different purposes, but some involve standards or measures of performance that could be used to shape the allocation of resources.

Measuring Up deserves high marks for focusing on policy issues and for developing policy relevant measures and implicit, sometimes explicit theories of how policy changes could improve outcomes. Measuring Up also posed no threats to privacy, either for individuals or institutions due to its focus on state indicators.

Measuring Up was energetic and creative in devising multifaceted measures of preparation, participation, completion, and affordability. Its measures of participation and completion are fairly straightforward (noting, however,

TABLE 4.1

Policy Tools Relevant to the Policy Domains Measured by Measuring Up

Policy Area Measured	Potential Policy Tools for Improvement
Preparation	<ul><li>Course-taking requirements or incentives for the high school curriculum.</li><li>State standards and assessments of college readiness.</li><li>Policies and resources to address student preparation and shortcomings through effective remediation.</li><li>Teacher certification requirements.</li><li>Teacher compensation resources.</li><li>Resources for effective teacher professional development.</li><li>Resources for effective teacher preparation.</li><li>Resources and policies to support high school completion.</li></ul>
Participation	<ul><li>College application advocacy programs and other informational resources beginning in junior high school.</li><li>Student financial assistance based on financial need, with incentives for preparation and effort.</li><li>Resources and incentives for the educational reentry of adults.</li><li>Resources for institutions focused on serving nonparticipating populations.</li></ul>
Completion	<ul><li>Avoiding or changing funding approaches that reward enrollment without persistence.</li><li>Monitor completion rates, time to degree, and credits to degree; and provide incentives/resources for improvement or sanctions for persistently sub-par performance.</li></ul>
Affordability	<ul><li>Provide adequate direct state support to keep tuition at a level to encourage, not discourage, enrollment of all students who can benefit.</li><li>Establish or expand a state need-based grant program that covers tuition costs for low-income students. (Pell Grants and student work are barely adequate to cover nontuition costs.)</li></ul>

that completion data are now much improved through the National Student Clearinghouse studies). Completion and participation data have since helped energize the Complete College America[31] and the American College Application Campaign[32] initiatives. Both of these initiatives have generated policy support for practitioner innovation, generally without imposing significant constraints on practice.

Data gaps and the complexity of the domain diluted the power and credibility of the preparation performance indicator. Although one can make a case that the Measuring Up preparation indicator is roughly accurate at the broad level of the state, the complexity of its construction and the variable definitions and availability of data among the states are disadvantages. Preparation for postsecondary success may eventually be measured more directly and compellingly if the assessments of college readiness based on the Common Core State Standards gain traction. Some of the subindicators Measuring Up used for preparation, such as high school course-taking patterns, might also become more robust if Common Education Data Standards and state longitudinal databases are fully implemented and operational.

Measuring Up's affordability indicator was not fully successful in making transparent the complexity and diversity of tuition and financial aid policies within and among states. The affordability indicator was difficult for many to fully comprehend, and when Measuring Up changed its procedure for calculating affordability grades, the communication problems were compounded. The development of student-level data systems may create opportunities for improving policy analysis in this domain.

Although Measuring Up did not master every technical challenge it confronted, the conceptual framework it developed is a major contribution to educational policy. *The Attainment Agenda: State Policy Leadership in Higher Education* by Laura W. Perna and Joni E. Finney is an impressive application of this framework to case-study analyses of state policy achievements and shortcomings in five states. Both the framework and the measurements developed by Measuring Up will be quite useful in any serious efforts to increase postsecondary attainment.[33]

Expansive Student-Level Data Systems and Common Education Data Standards

State longitudinal data systems and common education data standards could become enormously helpful for both policy and practice. But more and more consistently defined information will not automatically become a powerful tool for improvement. The potential benefits of better information cannot be fully realized without developing and implementing thoughtful strategies to use data for improvement.

Data systems professionals and vendors argue that consistent standards and data systems will enhance administrative efficiency and facilitate the development of more automated reporting with real returns on investment. From this perspective the goal would be for the systems to include every conceivable data element now used by schools and colleges. This is a fair description of what has been occurring, but imagining practical uses for all the parts of such a massive system boggles the mind.

Other voices, emanating in part from the "big data" community, are arguing that data systems can become a means of personalizing instruction for each student in order to become the "killer app" for educational improvement.[34] Like the educational data movement itself, the enthusiasm seems based in the exciting potential of an abstract idea, without extensive thought given to the workability of it in practice. Research on how students interact with computer-based instructional materials, as is being done by the Open Learning Initiative at Carnegie Mellon University and others,[35] may prove to be quite significant, but the case remains to be made.

Enterprising scholars should consider these voids as opportunities to make a contribution.

Of course, the ambiguity thus far about use and users of centralized data systems is a significant problem limiting the contributions of these initiatives. The very existence of such systems naturally raise fears that privacy will be breached and that top-down, intrusive policy initiatives will be harmfully imposed. These fears will not subside until and unless these initiatives accumulate years of productive use, without significant violations of privacy or overreaching misuses of data by policy makers.

In any event, the development of large-scale data systems and data standards has potential to significantly improve the accuracy, reliability, and validity of data and information on education. Both policy and practice can become better informed through the skillful use of administrative data systems, even if the more grandiose ambitions of data expansion advocates prove to be unrealistic.

Common Core State Standards for College and Career Readiness

The Common Core State Standards initiative lies squarely at the intersection of policy and practice, a location that gives it great potential for both benefit and harm. The problem addressed by the initiative is the multiplicity of different, not comparable, and frequently changing educational standards or learning objectives among the American states.

One might legitimately question whether educational standards at the state level should be established, but virtually every American state has settled that question in the affirmative. The extent of state-sanctioned learning objectives is another legitimate issue about which there is more debate: Should they include all domains of learning, including science and social studies, or should they be limited to language arts and mathematics?

At this writing, the first assessments of college and career readiness based on the Common Core are nearing implementation. A number of states are reengaging political debates over the Common Core and a handful have withdrawn or seem close to withdrawing support. Despite the defections, it seems unlikely that the movement will be completely sidetracked. How might this initiative serve policy makers and practitioners, and what risks need to be managed?

In this case, the question of fitness for purpose depends significantly on whether functional standards actually exist in society for the domains in question, or whether uncertainty and legitimate debate make functional standards impossible or undesirable. Universal agreement about instructional strategies or priorities within these domains may be infeasible and even undesirable, but I am persuaded that society has implicit, meaningful, and fairly rigorous standards for the use of language and mathematics. People not meeting those standards have limited opportunities for higher education, employment, and satisfying lives. Given these facts and the proliferation of state efforts to make such standards explicit, the absence of consistency in the definition of fundamental learning objectives and the measurement of attainment is a problem for both practitioners and policy makers.

With that said, common learning objectives and assessments present pitfalls as well as opportunities for both policy makers and practitioners. Rather than test-driven instruction, teachers must have and employ the freedom to develop creative, engaging approaches to help students master these skills. Policy makers need to suppress their tendency to establish high stakes around such assessments while ignoring the unavoidability of measurement error and the perverse side effects of high-stakes assessment. But it is difficult for this observer, at any rate, not to believe that clear learning objectives, assessments, and a logical progression of attainment through the elementary and secondary grades could be anything but useful for practitioners. Public policy will also benefit from such assessments, so long as policy makers find ways to help practitioners in general become more successful, rather than intervening clumsily with blunt, ineffective policy tools.

Let me take two short diversions into relevant side topics, the imposition of high stakes for assessments and the question of local control of schools.

An assessment of college and career readiness does not require high-stakes cut scores with direct consequences for either high school graduation or college admission. Test scores naturally have consequences, but an appropriate consequence for a subpar score on college or career readiness should be simply to indicate that some amount of additional learning is needed. This learning, depending on circumstances, could occur in a high school or in a postsecondary setting. The imposition of unnecessarily high stakes for students or teachers has typically resulted, not in increased motivation to learn, but in lowering standards or cheating, both of which are entirely counterproductive.

In their book *The Ordeal of Equality: Did Federal Regulation Fix Schools?*,[36] David Cohen and Susan Moffitt provide a telling analysis of four decades of largely unsuccessful efforts to reduce educational inequalities through Title I funding to local school districts. Their analysis suggests that the nation's deep commitment to local control of schools made it virtually impossible for a national effort to make progress on the systemic problem of educational inequality. Their analysis is not an argument for top-down centralization as the solution to national problems. But it suggests that a working consensus on fundamental goals and strategies is necessary to make progress on them. Both flexibility and focus have essential roles to play in dealing with complex issues. The Common Core State Standards for language arts and mathematics have the potential to give the U.S. education system greater focus on fundamental learning objectives without impairing in any way the flexibility of local teachers and school leaders in pursuing them.

So, much like expanded educational data systems, the Common Core State Standards have great potential for assisting both policy makers and practitioners. But to realize this potential, policy makers and practitioners will have to develop a division of labor for using the data that is tailored to their respective responsibilities and capabilities. This is a challenging, but not an impossible task. Scholars should play a useful role in assisting both policy makers and practitioners in this effort.

Let me conclude by addressing the final two questions of this analysis. The Common Core State Standards pose no more of a threat to privacy than all other assessments of individual learning. These should be easily managed, so long as artificially high stakes are not permitted to make private scores a public issue.

Finally, the assessments of the Common Core State Standards face all the familiar challenges for criterion-based learning assessments discussed in Chapter 3: sampling content in the construction of instruments and achieving valid, reliable results from the questions. These tasks, and the need to develop questions that assess the ability to use knowledge rather than simply choose the right option among multiple choices will continue to require expertise in psychometrics and test design. Compared to other assessments, however, the use of a well-defined common domain of knowledge and skill for Common Core assessments has the potential for materially improving the usability and benefits of the measurements.

Assessment of Higher Education Learning Outcomes (AHELO)

The Organization for Economic Cooperation and Development (OECD) has made significant contributions by addressing the many challenges of reliable and valid measurement and analysis on an international scale. Although OECD's educational and economic indicators have attracted criticism, policy makers and policy analysts across the globe have found OECD's work informative and useful. Because the OECD Programme for International Student Assessment (PISA) that focuses on the learning of 15-year-old students has been especially influential, OECD naturally was led to launch a feasibility study for assessing higher education learning outcomes.

International interest in postsecondary learning assessments emerged partially in response to the development and popularity of international university rankings (the Shanghai Rankings, QS World University Rankings, and Times Higher Education World University Rankings)[37] based largely on research accomplishments. These rankings are particularly popular in countries that have not enjoyed international prestige because they provide a means of gaining recognition for their achievements and improvements in quality. The interest in assessing student learning internationally reflects both this motivation and a sense that research rankings involve only a narrow, and fairly exclusive segment of postsecondary education worldwide.

The participation of many countries in AHELO detailed in Chapter 3 indicates that international interest in assessing student learning is more likely to grow than subside. But the AHELO feasibility study demonstrates by omission the importance of fitting the design of measurements and their administration to the capabilities and needs of potential users, both policy makers and practitioners.

The AHELO feasibility study created assessments in two disciplines and for general intellectual skills at the institutional level with the intent of helping institutions establish benchmarks and gain comparative perspective on teaching and learning achievements. Although the assessments themselves were, with some qualifications, robust and valid, the test administration design greatly reduced the potential for the assessment to be useful to institutions and their faculty: The assessments were administered only to a sample of students; the participation rate varied significantly among institutions; and students had, at best, weak incentives for doing their best work. Only

40% to 60% of students reported that they gave the assessment their best effort or close to their best effort.

To serve practitioners well, an assessment would need to have a high and consistent participation rate among students; to be administered universally or to a sizable random sample; and to have high enough stakes (perhaps an effect on a grade or supplemental individual recognition) so that students would be motivated to do their very best.

AHELO was not designed principally for the use of policy makers because no attempt was made to construct a representative national sample of students in the feasibility study. (In the design envisioned after the feasibility study, however, a random sample of students in various sectors of postsecondary education was planned.) But because OECD is essentially an association of governments, institutional representatives in countries with well-developed postsecondary education systems were and remain quite nervous about potential governmental misuses of AHELO-type instruments.

The wariness of institutions about the potential uses of AHELO compounded OECD's difficulties in constructing and administering a multinational assessment that might be useful in meeting the ongoing needs of faculty and institutions. Despite these difficulties, the attempt enabled participating nations to deepen their understanding of the potential and the limitations of inter-institutional, international assessments. Some participants also reported that the work of designing and implementing these assessments usefully illuminated areas of curriculum and instruction that need improvement.

OECD has recently administered a new assessment of adult competencies, PIAAC, which is modeled on the PISA test administration protocol and uses a national random sample.[38] The PIAAC and PISA assessments, because they focus on the nation as the unit of analysis, naturally yield themselves to policy relevance and usefulness. In many respects, the PIAAC assessment is relevant to education at all levels. These OECD assessments fully meet the criteria of useful, valid, fit for purpose, and proper protections of privacy outlined previously.

Concluding Thoughts on the Assessment of Learning

The Common Core State Standards initiative, AHELO, and other recent assessment efforts have generated sharper and deeper thinking about the challenges assessing student learning and the use of such assessments. Multiple choice, standardized tests to assess learning have increasingly lost credibility due to their shortcomings in informing instruction and assessing student achievement. Test preparation courses, which have demonstrated susceptibility to "score improvement" strategies not driven by authentic knowledge and skill have contributed to the loss of confidence. Educators are increasingly convinced that the most valid measurements of student learning require the demonstrated use of knowledge and skill, rather than the ability to respond correctly to scripted questions.

The inclusion of constructed-response questions in the AHELO and Common Core assessments is a response to these concerns. An increasing number of schools and colleges are employing a variety of assessment strategies, including portfolios of actual student work to assess student achievement. The assessment by expert judges of answers to constructed response questions and of portfolios may be a less reliable measure than responses to multiple choice questions, but increases in the depth, validity, and utility of assessments compensate for that loss.

In many respects, the ongoing evolution of the assessment field illustrates the importantly different perspectives and capabilities of practitioners and policy makers. Practitioners need and can use fine-grained information that reflects the complexity and sometimes ambiguity of practice. Policy makers need and can use coarse-grained information that is less valid and instructive for practice (e.g., PISA or PIAAC scores), but it is perilous for them to use such information to make interventions or policies that directly affect practice on the ground. An understanding of the difference between the domains, buttressed by trust and cooperation between policy and practice, is required to achieve better outcomes.

Notes

1. Piety, P. J. (2013). *Assessing the educational data movement.* New York, NY: Teachers College Press, pp. 3–21.

2. Data Quality Campaign. (2014, March 19). Success stories. Retrieved from http://dataqualitycampaign.org/success-stories/data-in-your-words/kipp-founda tion-finds-the-story-behind-the-numbers/

3. Piety, p. 19.

4. National Center for Education Statistics. (2014, March 20). *Graduate rate survey.* Retrieved from http://nces.ed.gov/ipeds/glossary/index.asp?id=812

5. Haley Will, K. (2006, July 23). Big Brother on campus. *Washington Post,* p. B07.

6. National Association of College and University Attorneys. (2014, March 20). *Higher Education Opportunity Act.* Retrieved from http://www.nacua.org/docu ments/heoa.pdf

7. National Center for Education Statistics. (2014, February 17). *Statewide longitudinal data systems grant program.* Retrieved from http://nces.ed.gov/programs/slds/stateinfo.asp

8. Mark R. Warner, U.S. Senator from the Commonwealth of Virginia [Web page]. (2013, May 9). *Sens. Warner, Rubio, Wyden introduce student Right to Know Before You Go Act.* Retrieved from http://www.warner.senate.gov/public/index.cfm/pressreleases?ID=b1ece1f5-a00a-4c25-8362-bfadfacd4785

9. McCann, C., & Laitinen, A. (2014, March). *College blackout: How the higher education lobby fought to keep students in the dark.* Retrieved from http://education.newamerica.net/sites/newamerica.net/files/policydocs/CollegeBlackoutFINAL.pdf

10. Loshin, D. (2003, March 1). Who owns data? *Information Management.* Retrieved from http://www.information-management.com/issues/20030301/6389-1.html?zkPrintable=1&nopagination=1

11. U.S. Department of Education. (2014, March 22). *FERPA general guidance for students.* Retrieved from https://www2.ed.gov/policy/gen/guid/fpco/ferpa/students.html

12. Shapiro, D., Dundar, A., Ziskin, M., Yuan, X., & Harrell, A. (2013, December 16). *Completing college: A national view of student attainment rates—Fall 2007 cohort.* Retrieved from http://nscresearchcenter.org/signaturereport6/ (Disclosure: The author serves on the board of the National Student Clearinghouse.)

13. Western Interstate Commission for Higher Education. (2014, March 25). *Facilitating development of a multistate longitudinal data exchange.* Retrieved from http://www.wiche.edu/longitudinalDataExchange

14. Dahl, R. A., & Lindblom, C. E. (1953). *Politics, economics, and welfare: Planning and politico-economic systems resolved into basic social processes.* New York, NY: Harper & Row.

15. Scott, J. C. (1998). *Seeing like a state: How certain schemes to improve the human condition have failed.* New Haven, CT: Yale University Press.

16. Ibid., p. 3.

17. Ibid., p. 4.

18. Ibid., pp. 3–6.

19. Ibid., pp. 132–146. In these pages, Scott develops his critique of high-modernist city planning relying significantly on the work of Jane Jacobs, *The Death and Life of Great American Cities* (New York, NY: Vintage Books, 1961).

20. Ibid., pp. 310–311.

21. Ibid., pp. 342–357.

22. Shulman, L. S. (2004). *The wisdom of practice: Essays on teaching, learning, and learning to teach.* San Francisco, CA: Jossey-Bass, p. 443.

23. Ibid., p. 194.

24. In 2010 the Spencer Foundation sponsored a series of papers and conversations among researchers, practitioners, and policy analysts on the uses of data for educational improvement. This collection of papers is a useful resource for exploring these issues in depth: Spencer Foundation Strategic Initiatives. (2015, April 14).

Data use and educational improvement. Retrieved from http://www.spencer.org/con tent.cfm/data-use-and-educational-improvement-activities

25. Jones, D. P. (1982). *Data and information for executive decisions in higher education.* Boulder, CO: NCHEMS, pp. 23–24.

26. Nussbaum, M. C. (2004). *Hiding from humanity: Disgust, shame, and the law.* Princeton, NJ: Princeton University Press, pp. 223–250.

27. Pawson, R. (2002). Evidence and policy and naming and shaming. *Policy Studies, 23*(3/4), 211–230; quoting Pulitzer, 1978, as quoted in Fisse, J., & Braithwaite, J. (1983). *The impact of publicity on corporate offenders.* Albany, NY: SUNY Press, p. 1.

28. Chui, M., Farrell, D., & Jackson, K. (2014, April 7). *How government can promote open data and help unleash over $3 trillion in economic value.* Retrieved from http://www.mckinsey.com/Insights/public_sector/how_government_can_promote_ open_data?cid=other-eml-alt-mip-mck-oth-1404

29. de Tocqueville, A. (1997). *Democracy in America* (Vol. 1). New York, NY: Alfred A. Knopf, p. 223.

30. Ewell, P. T. (1999). Linking performance measures to resource allocation: Exploring unmapped terrain. *Quality in Higher Education, 5*(3), 191–209.

31. Complete College America. (2014, April 7). *Complete College America.* Retrieved from http://completecollege.org

32. American Council on Education. (2014, April 7). *American College Application Campaign.* Retrieved from https://www.acenet.edu/about-ace/special-initia- tives/Pages/ACAC.aspx

33. Perna, L. W., & Finney, J. E. (2014). *The attainment agenda: State policy leadership in higher education.* Baltimore, MD: Johns Hopkins University Press.

34. King, M. (2014, April 1). Why data is education's "killer app." *Education Week, 33*(27), 28–29. Retrieved from http://www.edweek.org/ew/articles/ 2014/04/02/27king.h33.html?tkn=MXRFBsdCGluvqL5nPvU7iMuIaxIgqOgBy1p 7&cmp=ENL-II-NEWS2&print=1

35. Open Learning Initiative. (2014, April 9). *Open Learning Initiative.* Retrieved from https://oli.cmu.edu

36. Cohen, D. K., & Moffitt, S. L. (2009). *The ordeal of equality: Did federal regulation fix the schools?.* Cambridge, MA: Harvard University Press.

37. Ranking of world universities. (2014, April 10). In *Wikipedia.* Retrieved from http://en.wikipedia.org/wiki/Academic_Ranking_of_World_Universities

38. Organization for Economic Cooperation and Development. (2014, April 10). *OECD skills surveys.* Retrieved from http://www.oecd.org/site/piaac

5

GETTING BETTER: THE USE OF EVIDENCE IN PRACTICE

"The point is not just to know what makes things better or worse,
it is to make things actually better."[1]

—Donald M. Berwick, foreword to *The Improvement Guide*

Henry Kissinger contrasted the work of scholars and statesmen as follows:

Intellectuals analyze the operations of international systems, statesmen build them. And there is a vast difference between the perspective of an analyst and that of a statesman. The analyst can choose which problem he wishes to study, whereas the statesman's problems are imposed on him. The analyst can allot whatever time is necessary to come to a clear conclusion; the overwhelming challenge of the statesman is the pressure of time. The analyst runs no risk. If his conclusions prove wrong, he can write another treatise. The statesman is permitted only one guess; his mistakes are irretrievable. The analyst has available to him all the facts; he will be judged on his intellectual power. The statesman must act on assessments that cannot be proved at the time that he is making them; he will be judged by history on the basis of how he managed the inevitable change and, above all, how well he preserves the peace. That is why understanding how statesmen have dealt with the problems of world order—what worked or failed and why—is not the end of understanding contemporary diplomacy, though it may be its beginning.[2]

Kissinger's statesmen (and stateswomen, I might add) dealing with the great crises of human history may face higher stakes and even more urgent time pressures than practitioners and policy makers working on more commonplace problems. Nevertheless, the fundamental characteristics of making decisions on the ground are similar for all complex problems. Life rarely grants practitioners the luxuries of time and control over circumstances employed by scholars in their work.

With limited resources and very little time for reflection, practitioners must make decisions involving uncertainties, complex interactions between countervailing forces, and trade-offs between competing values. Scholars, especially those seeking fundamental insights by reducing the complex to the simple, can strike practitioners as "ivory tower intellectuals," either blissfully unaware of or greatly underestimating the forces constraining practice and the difficulty of decision making and action in the "real world." Practitioners, however, may miss opportunities to get better results because they become creatures of habit; hang on to preconceptions; fail to explore innovative approaches; or fail to learn from evidence, reflection, and analysis.

The natural tendency toward mutual disrespect between practitioners and scholars must be overcome in order to unlock the potential of evidence and research to improve outcomes. Bridges must be built to help scholars develop a more sophisticated understanding of the challenges and techniques of skillful practice and policy making. Bridges must be built to help practitioners see the value of systematically collecting evidence about practice as a tool for improving performance rather than a weapon for placing blame on them. And scholars and practitioners must learn how to work together to achieve better performance. Such bridges can only be built by organizing data and inquiry in ways that reflect the situational complexity and variable circumstances faced by practitioners.

Technical Rationality and Reflective Practice

Donald Schön's classic analysis, *The Reflective Practitioner: How Professionals Think in Action*, is a useful resource for scholars seeking to inform practice. With examples from various fields, he demonstrates the limits of *technical rationality*, which generally has dominated thinking about professional practice and education. From the technical rationality perspective, professional practice consists of "instrumental problem solving made rigorous by the application of scientific theory and technique."[3] Further, "the knowledge base of a profession is thought to have four essential properties. It is specialized, firmly bounded, scientific, and standardized." Professional practice consists of three components: (a) standardized, basic scientific knowledge as the foundation of professional practice; (b) applied science or engineering to diagnose problems and derive solutions; and (c) skills and attitudes involved in the actual provision of services to the client.[4]

The literature concerning professional practice outlined by Schön contrasts what he calls "major professions" (e.g., medicine, law, and engineering, which have a foundation in generally standardized knowledge) and "minor professions" (e.g., architecture, social work, city planning, education, etc.). The so-called minor professions do not enjoy the benefits of relatively unambiguous, one-dimensional professional aims such as curing a disease, designing a bridge, or winning a case in court, which can often be informed by standardized scientific knowledge. Professional education in the so-called major professions typically begins by grounding the student in the science or abstract fundamental principles (in the case of law) of the profession. Training in the application of these principles and the skills of clinical practice follows in the educational program, often with somewhat lower status. In the minor professions, training often follows a similar pattern, but the scientific base of the profession typically is less thoroughly developed and more a matter of discussion and debate.

Although science and fundamental principles have important roles in professional practice, Schön argues that the perspective of technical rationality is an incomplete, inadequate depiction of effective practice in *all* professions because many problems are not "in the book." As illustrated by Schön's examples, all professionals, including the major professions and basic scientists, must employ the skills of reflective practice in order to cope with complexity and uncertainty in at least some of the situations in which they work. Any aging person who has discussed health matters with a wise physician understands this.

As discussed earlier, practitioners or policy makers face a threefold challenge in applying general knowledge to improve outcomes in particular situations:

1. Does the available general knowledge apply to the contexts and circumstances?
2. Can I apply the knowledge effectively in this situation?
3. Can I achieve the necessary responses and cooperation from other people, who have the freedom to see things differently and to actively or passively resist my efforts?[5]

The answers to these questions vary across circumstances and situations. Sometimes general knowledge is sufficient, but when practitioners and policy makers are faced with complex situations involving human variables and interactive dynamics, general knowledge is of limited use. General knowledge must be supplemented with reflective practice—particular knowledge of the situation at hand and skillful professional judgments involving experimentation, observation, and adaptation.

Increasingly, more sophisticated views of practice have led to partnerships between practitioners and scholars that use evidence and theory developed in context to improve results. Such research must be just as disciplined and evidence based as normal scientific inquiry, but it involves methods and procedures that consider and are grounded in particular circumstances and situations.

Qualitative Research

Thus far, much of this volume has described the challenges complexity presents to quantitative and experimental research methods. Qualitative methods, which were briefly considered in a review of the development of program evaluation in Chapter 2, are useful—in fact, essential—to understand the dimensions of complexity. They are limited, however, in generating useful knowledge across settings and measuring improvement. The contributions and limitations of these methods to practice and policy will be explored somewhat more fully here.

The *SAGE Encyclopedia of Qualitative Research Methods* explains the difference between quantitative and qualitative research as follows:

> Where quantitative approaches are appropriate for examining *who* has engaged in a behavior or *what* has happened and while experiments can test particular interventions, these techniques are not designed to explain *why* certain behaviors occur.[6] Qualitative approaches are typically used to explore new phenomena and to capture individuals' thoughts, feelings, or interpretations of meaning and process.[7]

The *SAGE Encyclopedia* includes two volumes with roughly 500 entries describing various aspects of qualitative research. Its entry on the history of qualitative research indicates that a range of disciplines are responsible for the rise and continued development of qualitative approaches, including history, medicine, nursing, social work, and communications. The encyclopedia further notes:

> Subdisciplines of social sciences, health sciences, and humanities, including cultural anthropology, symbolic interactionism, Marxism, ethnomethodology, phenomenology, feminism, cultural studies, and postmodernism, each with its own conception of reality, and its own methodological preferences, have played significant roles in the continued development of qualitative

research. Despite the differing theoretical assumptions and methodological preferences, these disciplines and subdisciplines are united in their reasons for employing qualitative research—to identify, analyze, and understand patterned behaviors and social processes.[8]

Qualitative inquiry, or disciplined observation, is the first step in all human understanding, including formal scientific inquiry. The science of astronomy, for example, is entirely based on regularities observed in the physical world, even though its observations have been greatly enhanced by sophisticated analytical and measurement tools. Although the other physical and biological sciences have achieved great advances by supplementing observation with controlled experimentation, qualitative observation plays a critical and foundational role in every scientific area in the formation of theory and hypotheses, the design of research projects, and the exploration of new frontiers.

Disciplined observation may be even more critical in the social sciences where complexity and the difficulties of designing and implementing social experiments pose formidable challenges to understanding. A powerful example of productive qualitative inquiry is Alexis de Tocqueville's classic *Democracy in America*.[9] This nineteenth-century tour de force of disciplined observation and analytical thinking continues to engage and influence students of government. Much like an anthropologist or community sociologist, de Tocqueville immersed himself in an interesting and unfamiliar society; sought to "make sense" of how democracy in the United States worked; and assessed its advantages and weaknesses for meeting human needs, protecting freedoms, and serving what he considered the legitimate purposes of government. Although de Tocqueville's genius was an essential ingredient in his study, no other method for studying democracy in American could possibly have been more productive and influential.

At times, a shortcoming of what Lindblom and Cohen called *professional social inquiry* (discussed in Chapter 1) is inadequate regard, or even disrespect for the insights of practitioners. *Qualitative research,* almost by definition, avoids this pitfall by placing the perspectives, insights, and judgments of participants at the very center of inquiry. Rigor in qualitative research derives from the breadth and sophistication of the topics explored by an experienced and skillful interrogator and from the practice of obtaining and examining critically the perspectives and observations of multiple participants and observers. In many respects, psychotherapy, business consulting, executive coaching, teaching—virtually all of the helping professions—employ qualitative research. In the hands of skillful practitioners, these disciplines continue to be quite effective and helpful.

From my perspective, unfortunately, qualitative research and its practitioners have often placed themselves or have been placed by others in intractable opposition to quantitative methods. Part of this is undoubtedly driven by excessive faith in the capabilities of quantitative methods to yield conclusive information, by the uncritical acceptance and use of inconclusive quantitative data, and by disrespect for nonquantitative approaches. These legitimate reservations about quantitative methods have been the focus of much of this book.

But on the other side of the coin, qualitative research has significant inherent limitations. A central goal of science is parsimony—discovering principles or laws that can efficiently explain some of nature's complexity. Qualitative research, by its very nature, can never achieve parsimony. The best qualitative research is coherent and compelling, but in working to achieve rigor qualitative researchers sometimes accumulate and present so much information that they fail to achieve coherence and clarity.

Qualitative research's appropriate bias in favor of openness may also detract from its coherence. Without a strong theoretical orientation, it is very difficult to set appropriate, disciplined boundaries for the collection of data and the interpretation of what is observed. Unfortunately, when a strong theoretical orientation is present (e.g., in psychoanalytic theory), a commitment to theory may excessively dominate the analysis and reduce openness to divergent information.

The absence of a grounded epistemology and consilience among qualitative researchers are even more serious limitations for its use in policy and practice. The previous quotation from the *SAGE Encyclopedia* refers to many disciplines and subdisciplines "each with its own conception of reality, and its own methodological preferences."[10] From one perspective, this can be viewed as an honest and appropriately modest acceptance of human limitations and the importance of open-mindedness. On the other hand, a proliferation of conceptions of reality and methodological preferences is likely to produce more confusion and argument than progress in solving real problems. It is not surprising that decision makers in policy and practice find unhelpful scholarship that, due to many competing perspectives, offers very little potential for closure or clear guidance.

The absence of consilience among qualitative research approaches is less of a problem than the lack of agreement on a "conception of reality." Given the inability of any single research methodology to cope with complex problems of policy and practice, a strong argument can be made for what Tom Cook called *postpositivist critical multiplism*.[11] No single methodology, quantitative nor qualitative, deserves unchallenged authority; the wise researcher will employ or, at the very least, give regard and attention to the contributions of multiple methods. As Cook suggests, one should cultivate one's critics.

Postmodern epistemology, on the other hand, seems to reject the idea that inquiry can be useful in building consensus about knowledge for the purpose of improving policy and practice. After suggesting that "all movements tend to extremes," E. O. Wilson starkly summarized the conflict between postmodernism and the Enlightenment as follows:

> Postmodernism is the ultimate polar antithesis to the Enlightenment. This difference between the two extremes can be expressed roughly as follows: Enlightenment thinkers believe we can know everything, and radical postmodernists believe we can know nothing.
> The philosophical postmodernists . . . challenge the very foundation of science and traditional philosophy. Reality, they propose, is a state constructed by the mind, not perceived by it. In the most extravagant version of this constructivism, there is no "real" reality, no objective truths external to mental activity, only prevailing versions dominated by ruling social groups. Nor can ethics be firmly grounded, given that each society creates its own codes for the benefit of the same oppressive forces.[12]

Extremists on both sides of the quantitative/qualitative divide are visible and numerous, but the middle ground may well be better populated. In its inaugural year of 2007 the *Journal of Mixed Methods Research* includes two articles worth citing in this context. Johnson, Onwuegbuzie, and Turner,[13] provide an extensive discussion of mixed methods research and outline its evolution from the dialogue among ancient Greek philosophers to the debates among and the practices of twentieth-century researchers. And David L. Morgan[14] argues for research driven, not by metaphysics, but by methodology focused on pragmatism and problem solving.

Improvement Science in Medicine

Ironically, or perhaps inevitably, the profession of medicine, which has made effective use of the experimental method for evaluating pharmaceuticals and treatment regimens, has learned that successful practice requires much more than the straightforward application of "proven" treatments. The medical profession has led the way in developing instructive models for using evidence from practice to improve outcomes.

The quality improvement movement in medicine gained considerable momentum during the past two decades following the 1994 report of the Institute of Medicine (IOM) of the National Academy of Sciences, *America's Health in Transition: Protecting and Improving Quality.*[15] After the release of this study, the Institute of Medicine launched the Crossing the Quality Chasm initiative, which continues to issue reports addressing topics as diverse as reducing the incidence of human error in health care, improving the provision of health care in rural areas, providing financial incentives for improved performance in Medicare, developing and using electronic record systems, and improving the quality of care for mental illness and substance abuse.[16] This movement explicitly responds to the complex interactions among contexts, systems, and individuals, which limit the utility of technical rationality.

Atul Gawande, the author of *Better: A Surgeon's Notes on Performance*,[17] (which inspired this chapter's title) and many other articles and books on medical practice, has been quite influential in raising public awareness of this movement in medicine.[18] Although a little less well known to the general public, Donald Berwick, former president of the Institute for Health Care Improvement,[19] has been a seminal leader both of theory and practice in the health care improvement movement. In his 2008 *JAMA* article "The Science of Improvement," Berwick writes:

> The two endeavors [improving clinical evidence and improving the process of care] are often in unhappy tension.
>
> Neither disputes that progress toward health care's main goal, the relief of illness and pain, requires research of many kinds: basic, clinical, systems, epidemiologic. The disagreement centers on epistemology—ways to get at "truth" and how those ways should vary depending on the knowledge sought. Individuals most involved in day-to-day improvement work fear that if "evidence" is too narrowly defined and the approach to gathering evidence too severely constrained, progress may be the victim. For example, the RCT [randomized clinical trial] is a powerful, perhaps unequaled, research design to explore the efficacy of conceptually neat components of clinical practice—tests, drugs, and procedures. For other crucially important learning purposes, however, it serves less well.[20]

Berwick goes on to explain that the "other crucially important learning purposes" he has in mind are, in fact, the challenges of learning how to improve outcomes in the context of complex individuals and environments. Referring to the work of Pawson and Tilley in *Realistic Evaluation* (cited in Chapter 2), Berwick argues that improving outcomes in complex environments requires examining the effects of specific interventions or mechanisms in context; RCTs are not able to deal with the complicated contextual realities associated with either the individual subjects of an intervention, the organizational systems in which they live, or those of multifaceted interventions themselves.

Many assessment techniques developed in engineering and used in quality improvement—statistical process control, time series analysis, simulations, and factorial experiments—have more power to inform about mechanisms and contexts than do RCTs, as do ethnography, anthropology, and other qualitative methods. For these specific applications, these methods are not compromises in learning how to improve; they are superior.[21]

Improvement science in medicine, although still a young and growing field, has led to significant reductions in complications from infection associated with surgery and hospitalization, and improvements in the regimens used to treat complex diseases, such as cystic fibrosis.[22] The fundamental approach of improvement science is to monitor outcomes systematically and then seek to understand the ways that different systems and practices contribute to adverse or better outcomes. Dramatic results from improvement science in medicine have come from interventions such as frequent, perhaps even obsessive handwashing and implementing rigidly systematic approaches for common medical procedures.

Such dramatic results are possible when a fundamentally simple problem (e.g., complications from infection) can be avoided or ameliorated by systematic (even if difficult and complicated to implement) improvements in practice. Of course, many problems are not fundamentally simple, and achieving systematic improvements in practice is often quite challenging. But the achievements of improvement science in medicine demonstrate that the systematic analysis of practice, in context, and in collaboration with reflective practitioners, can be rewarding. The payoff comes both from the research and from engaging the insights, wisdom, and commitment of practitioners in research for improvement.

In summarizing the evolution of his field, John Steiner, senior director of the Institute for Health Research in Denver, told me:

> For decades we tried to improve medical care by improving the knowledge and skill of physicians. But there are limits. Doctors are incredibly busy and have to deal with a never-ending stream of immediate health concerns. To make real progress we have learned that it is also necessary to improve the *systems* in which they work.[23]

Networked Improvement Communities: Improvement Science in Education

In recent efforts to apply improvement science to education through *networked improvement communities*, Anthony Bryk and his colleagues at the

Carnegie Foundation for the Advancement of Teaching have synthesized and articulated the fundamental ideas of collaborative improvement initiatives as they have evolved in industry and health care.[24] This brief introduction to the Carnegie work is intended to motivate further reading and exploration of these ideas. It draws on a series of Carnegie publications and my participation in several Carnegie workshops.[25]

The word *community* in the name of the Carnegie initiative signifies a robust partnership between practitioners, researchers, and improvement scientists at local sites. The communities are networked in order to share learning among practice settings to deepen knowledge and generate improvement at scale. Sharing knowledge across settings is similarly the goal of the Cochrane Collaborative and the Campbell Collaborative, two initiatives that chronicle and organize experimental research findings in order to make them available to individual practitioners and organizations. But the focus of the Cochrane and Campbell Collaboratives is on the evaluation of standardized treatments or interventions based on experimental research, not research situated in the practice setting. And in these collaboratives, *knowers* and *users* are separate communities, not members of a single community engaged in dialogue and discovery. In improvement science, the users are critical agents in developing knowledge about how to improve their work.[26]

Bryk and colleagues acknowledge employing aspects of translational research and action research in their work, but they distinguish improvement research in important ways from these other approaches to improve practice. Translational research attempts to "push" research findings on an intervention or protocol into practice.[27] The intervention generally is well specified based on previous research, and the researcher seeks to implement the finding in multiple settings, disseminating innovation at scale. A priority is to maintain the fidelity of the intervention to the established protocol and to measure results using standard measurements across settings. In many respects, the development and dissemination of Success for All discussed in Chapter 2 has been presented as translational research. An extensive review of its practices by Donald Peurach suggests, however, that the actual dynamic of the program is more interactive between research and practice.[28]

In translational research, the basic scientist is clearly in the lead, but feedback from practitioners may add value to the process. In the words of Smith and colleagues:

> [Translational research] require[s] productive interactions of basic scientists (from several disciplines) and clinicians. The basic scientists keep the clinicians informed of recent scientific developments while the clinicians bring back to the laboratory intelligence and resulting reactions of patients dur-

ing experimental protocols. The information sharing and subsequent discussions synergize new ideas and concepts that help guide future research directions and efforts.[29]

Although such collaborations have often been productive, in translational research the traffic on the bridge between research and practice may be asymmetrical, with practitioners playing a minor role. Unsurprisingly, relationships between researchers and practitioners sometimes become frayed, as the incentives and problems faced by researcher and practitioners are often different. These differences are well explicated in an account of a research practitioner partnership involving Johns Hopkins researchers and Experience Corps in Baltimore and in the research of Coburn and colleagues in education.[30]

Action research focuses on issues of practice in a particular setting, with practitioners in the driver's seat. The work of action researchers may involve extensive measurement and analysis, but the purpose is local improvement, without reference to broader concerns or the field as a whole. Although disciplined, rigorous "action research" may facilitate great improvements, it is unlikely to advance a field without expanding the focus beyond a single location.[31] As in action research, the Carnegie initiative engages practitioners deeply, but it adds an explicit partnership with scholars and a networked community in order to advance the field.

Improvement research is situated in practice and draws on the insights, initiative, and motives of practitioners. But it also employs the disciplined measurement and field-wide perspectives of traditional experimental or rigorous observational research. As expressed by Bryk and colleagues, improvement research employs common protocols in order to "allow participants to share, test, and generalize local learning across a professional community of practice."[32] By making the measurement of outcomes and the protocols of interventions comparable across sites, it becomes more feasible to generate improvement at scale.

Based on the established practices of the field, the straightforward components of improvement science in Carnegie's networked improvement communities are

- understanding the problem to be improved, including the systemic factors (personal, organizational, environmental, etc.) that contribute to the problem;
- establishing clear, measurable goal(s) for improvement;
- developing and testing theories of action to generate improvement; and
- analyzing results in order to guide subsequent action.

Bryk contrasts the research of the networked improvement communities to traditional models for program improvement and evaluation on two dimensions, scale and time. When research is not situated in and directly informed by practice, the tradition has been to make large interventions and study them with complex, time-consuming studies—to change big and learn slow. In the networked improvement communities, the approach to learning is to make small changes, quickly examine their effects, make changes based on what has been observed, and repeat the cycle of experimentation/adaptation—to change small and learn fast. The objective is to learn quickly how to implement improvements that ultimately can achieve quality outcomes at scale. It is no surprise that practitioners are more receptive to research that informs practice, provides quick feedback, and generally avoids large-scale disruption while attempting to learn.

The avoidance of large-scale disruption does not imply the avoidance of large-scale change. According to Corey Donahue from Carnegie:

> Tests are initially done on a very small scale (one classroom, one teacher, in one school) but over time, the scale of these tests increases when successful. We often refer to the scale as 1-5-25, but the basic idea is that after testing with one teacher, you might next test with a handful of teachers across different settings. This "ramp" allows for validation of the intervention through replication under diverse circumstances, an understanding of its effectiveness across different settings, better will building through involving practitioners, and potentially eventual full-scale implementation.[33]

The key to learning in a networked improvement community is through the cumulative contributions of a large number of small experiments. Those that fail (typically most) contribute to the learning at a modest cost; those that succeed contribute to learning, generate ideas for refinement, and are replicated, eventually at scale.

The Carnegie Foundation is developing several networked improvement communities in education. In this brief summary, I will share specific examples from its Community College Pathways initiative which has two components: Statway, focused on statistics; and Quantway, focused on quantitative reasoning. This initiative seeks to address the problem that a large number of community college students fail to graduate due to their inability to get past remedial mathematics.

Understanding the Problem in Systemic Terms

Getting better results from practice begins with achieving a sufficiently accurate and *shared* systemic understanding of the problem among practitioners and researchers. Multiple factors tend to be important in the development and resolution of serious problems, and the understanding of the problem cannot be superficial or one dimensional. At the same time, a handful of factors typically play a disproportionate role. Existing research findings and the judgments and observations of practitioners should be used to construct a shared, working (not static or definitive) understanding of systemic issues and the factors most likely to be significant.

Factors with causal impact exist within individuals, within their immediate social environments (families and peers), within the immediate organizational settings, and within the broader environments. Inevitably, disputes or differences of opinion arise concerning the role of different problem factors and the potential for them to be ameliorated by feasible interventions. Especially when under intense pressure to improve outcomes, practitioners tend to focus on factors arguably beyond their ability to influence. Urban teachers may focus on the challenges posed by poverty and perhaps the relative absence of parental support (associated with poverty and limited parental education) for their work. Community college faculty may mention the difficulty of overcoming inadequate academic preparation. Medical professionals may express frustration with the persistent failure of patients to follow instructions for taking medications or modifying dysfunctional behaviors.

Such factors are clearly significant, but if any single presenting factor is judged to be an insuperable obstacle to improvement, practitioners obviously will find it difficult to be enthusiastically engaged in working for improved outcomes. But when practitioners are engaged in analyzing problems from a systemic perspective, the analysis normally results in an appreciation of the problem's multiple dimensions, several of which may provide openings and fresh insights that lead directly toward ideas to improve the outcomes of practice.

The medical profession, for example, has come to realize and accept that many of the "complications" that arise after surgery or during hospitalization are not inevitable random events, but consequences of errors, or failure to scrupulously observe all the requirements of good practice. Atul Gawande's *Checklist Manifesto: How to Get Things Right*[34] and his related work to improve medical practice have made a compelling case for rigorously specifying and observing proper procedural guidelines in medical care. Highly specific procedural checklists are clearly good approaches for improving performance for systems problems where good practice can be systematically described, perhaps even scripted, where the direct consequences of a failure to observe good practice are likely to be obvious and measurable, and where a community of practitioners can adopt and hold itself accountable for appropriate standards.

Problems of practice in aviation, medicine, manufacturing, and other areas where relatively straightforward biological or physical mechanisms are in play are particularly appropriate for scripted routines. Even when more complex situations (e.g., surgery) require responsiveness to variable or unpredictable circumstances, routines or protocols of good practice—standard checklists that may stop a little short of a script—are the foundation of good practice.[35]

In fields seeking to build human capability such as education, social work, and mental health, routines of good practice are likely to be more difficult to "script" because the individual variation is great and human interaction compounds the complexity. The relevant individual factors include genetics, prior experience, attitudes, and the social context of the individual. The environmental context; the systemic resources available; and the capabilities of the teachers, therapists, and organizations seeking to help the individual are also relevant.

Despite the complexity, the objective of improvement science is to discover actions and interventions, protocols, if you will, that will enable practitioners to improve results. The first step in developing a testable improvement strategy is to describe the system and to develop a *sufficient understanding* (that typically draws on both practitioner knowledge and available research) of the relative importance of factors contributing to the circumstances.

Sufficient understanding of the system does not require absolute certainty, comprehensive knowledge, or unanimity of understanding. It does require a working consensus on the factors within the system that are likely to be important in contributing to the problem and subject to change within the resources available. This working consensus is necessary to develop improvement strategies, which can then be tested. And the understanding of the system itself, the working consensus, should be tested and enhanced through the process of reflective practice.

The Carnegie Foundation's Community College Pathways initiative developed a *system improvement map* to illustrate the different dimensions of the system related to high failure rates for students taking remedial mathematics in community colleges. As shown in Figure 5.1, the various dimensions of the system involved the personal characteristics and preparation of the students; instructional practices and expectations before, during, and after community college enrollment; institutional policies and practices; the human and financial resources available to the institution; student supports; the available information infrastructure; and the governance of the system. Some of these dimensions can be addressed at the instructional or classroom level, others may require institutional change, and others may require broader change in the field or system, such as changes in the supply of resources.[36]

Figure 5.1 System Improvement Map for Community College Pathways

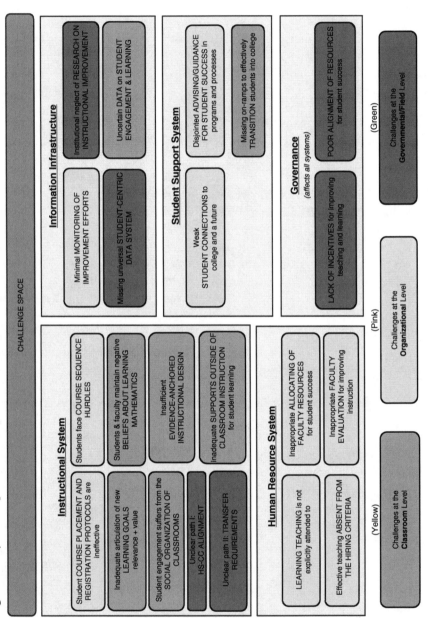

CHALLENGE SPACE

Information Infrastructure

Minimal MONITORING OF IMPROVEMENT EFFORTS

Missing universal STUDENT-CENTRIC DATA SYSTEM

Institutional neglect of RESEARCH ON INSTRUCTIONAL IMPROVEMENT

Uncertain DATA on STUDENT ENGAGEMENT & LEARNING

Student Support System

Weak STUDENT CONNECTIONS to college and a future

Disjointed ADVISING/GUIDANCE FOR STUDENT SUCCESS in programs and processes

Missing on-ramps to effectively TRANSITION students into college

Governance
(affects all systems)

LACK OF INCENTIVES for improving teaching and learning

POOR ALIGNMENT OF RESOURCES for student success

Instructional System

Student COURSE PLACEMENT AND REGISTRATION PROTOCOLS are ineffective

Inadequate articulation of new LEARNING GOALS relevance + value

Student engagement suffers from the SOCIAL ORGANIZATION OF CLASSROOMS

Unclear path I: HS-CC ALIGNMENT

Unclear path II: TRANSFER REQUIREMENTS

Students face COURSE SEQUENCE HURDLES

Students & faculty maintain negative BELIEFS ABOUT LEARNING MATHEMATICS

Insufficient EVIDENCE-ANCHORED INSTRUCTIONAL DESIGN

Inadequate SUPPORTS OUTSIDE OF CLASSROOM INSTRUCTION for student learning

Human Resource System

LEARNING TEACHING is not explicitly attended to

Effective teaching ABSENT FROM THE HIRING CRITERIA

Inappropriate ALLOCATING OF FACULTY RESOURCES for student success

Inappropriate FACULTY EVALUATION for improving instruction

(Yellow)

Challenges at the **Classroom** Level

(Pink)

Challenges at the **Organizational** Level

(Green)

Challenges at the **Governmental/Field** Level

Of course, it is not possible to change the entire system simultaneously, but total system change is rarely necessary to generate positive results. The objective in analyzing the system is to construct hypotheses about significant causal factors whose impact, negative or positive, might be mitigated or enhanced through an intervention. If progress can be achieved by harvesting "low-hanging fruit," it may increase the ability to generate the will and resources to tackle more challenging aspects of a system.

Establishing Clear, Measurable Goals for Improvement

The next component of improvement science is to establish clear, measurable goals for improvement. Without measurement it is impossible to meaningfully pursue improvement, it is impossible to know the extent to which the effort has been effective, and it is impossible to learn how to improve.

The ultimate goal of the Community College Pathways initiative is for students to complete a postsecondary certificate or degree. The initiative's specific goal initially was to double the proportion of students who earn a college credit in math after one year of continuous study. Because the baseline rate of success was only 5%, this goal was quickly achieved. The goal was then increased to 50% of developmental math students enrolled earning college math credits after a year of study. The latter goal has been achieved for three successive years. The broad goals of the initiative include both greater success in learning mathematics and student persistence; these measurable, operational goals reflect both dimensions.

Both practitioners and external observers must consider the measurable goal to be meaningful and significant. Attaining the goal or making progress toward it must be worth the effort involved. In addition to being ambitious and measurable, the goal must also be judged feasible, not entirely impossible from the perspective of practitioners responsible for performance. Otherwise, it is unlikely that they will engage seriously in the improvement initiative.

Although some of the same measurements can be used for both accountability and improvement, in a successful improvement initiative it must be quite evident that the primary purpose of measurement is improving performance, not the evaluation of practitioners for purposes of reward or sanction. When improvement is the focus, measurements are more frequent, the immediate stakes or consequences of the measurement are low, and process measurements, or leading indicators of subsequent outcomes, may be more frequently employed. The purposes are to identify interventions that yield better performance; to test the extent to which interventions, once attempted, have been effective; and to guide a continuous learning and improvement process.

When accountability is the principal focus, the purpose is to evaluate and identify exemplary or substandard performers—process is less relevant than outcomes, measurements are less frequent, and stakes are higher.[37] As illustrated by the extensive discussions in Chapters 3 and 4, when accountability is the focus, more energy is often expended in debating the validity of the measure or evading measurement than in improving performance.

A Carnegie paper, *Practical Measurement*, distinguishes measurement for improvement in practice from measurement for accountability and measurement for theory development, both of which seek to address general questions relevant to, but somewhat distant from day-to-day practice. At its core, practical measurement is systematically and deeply embedded in the day-to-day work of practitioners. It is employed to assess change as it occurs, predict risk of failure, guide interventions to mitigate risk, and establish priorities for achieving improvement. Unlike measurement for accountability or theory development, practical measurement often focuses with greater specificity on intermediate processes and actions, the effects of which are likely to vary for different students. And practical measurement must be efficient, not employing tools that require hours of assessment separate from instruction, but measurement tools that can be easily and frequently embedded in the course of normal practice.[38]

In the Community College Pathways initiative a great deal of sophisticated effort was invested in the development of measures to inform and improve practice. Both practitioner experience and an extensive research literature were tapped to identify student characteristics and instructional practices likely to be important causes of failure to persist and succeed in developmental mathematics. Then additional time and effort were invested to design efficient tools for measuring the extent to which risk factors are present and whether they are being mitigated by specific actions or interventions in the program. Eventually 26 survey questions, briefly and frequently administered, provided continuing feedback to instructors on key factors such as: students' confidence they belong in the course, their engagement in the course, the level of anxiety related to the course, their connection with peers, and their feelings of faculty support.[39]

In addition to the usual psychometric concerns of reliability and validity, other dimensions are also critically important. Can the measures be used to infer what actions might lead to improvement? Are the summative measures inherently consequential, both to practitioners and to others with a stake in improvement?[40]

Perfect comparability on universally accepted scales (one of E. O. Wilson's criteria for science in Chapter 1) is unrealistic in education, but reasonable and practical outcome and process measures can be devised relatively easily. Such measures also can be used to provide comparability among sites. In improvement science the most important purpose of measurement is to support learning in and across sites of practice.

Developing and Testing Theories of Action to Generate Improvement

Before developing and testing theories of action to generate improvement, the Carnegie initiative performs a *causal systems analysis* to explore why the system consistently generates the results that constitute the problem. This involves developing hypotheses about important factors contributing to the problem and hypotheses about actions at the system level or by practitioners that might ameliorate those factors.

The design of actions to generate improvement requires combining a systems perspective with what is known or suggested by research on interventions in the field and the *ordinary knowledge* (see Lindblom and Cohen in Chapter 1 for a definition) accumulated by practitioners working on the ground. When both kinds of knowledge contribute to the causal model used in an improvement initiative, intervention strategies will benefit from both broader knowledge of the problem and the insights of practitioners in the particular situation. In addition, the engagement of practitioners in the implementation of interventions will be enhanced through the collaborative process of designing an intervention strategy.

A systems perspective typically yields a constellation of potentially important factors contributing to the problem and potential solution strategies for each of them. As Bryk and his colleagues note:

> Intellectually powerful forces anchored in personal belief and role-specific experiences tend to direct garden-path interveners away from systems thinking and toward silver-bullet solutions. A tool kit that includes system improvement maps and driver diagrams can discipline a community of interveners to see problems with larger, common eyes even as they may intervene in very specific ways.[41]

Bryk and his colleagues employ a "driver diagram" to present potential solutions to ameliorate factors contributing to the problem. Figure 5.2 illustrates five conditions identified in the Community College Pathways project as significant requirements for student success in remedial mathematics.[42] The absence of these conditions is judged to be a significant cause of student failure. The secondary drivers identify particular components of the primary drivers that might be enhanced through specific actions or interventions. The testing of hypotheses concerning particular actions is the next step in the improvement process.

Figure 5.2 A Framework for "Productive Persistence" (Tenacity + Effective Strategies) in Developmental Math

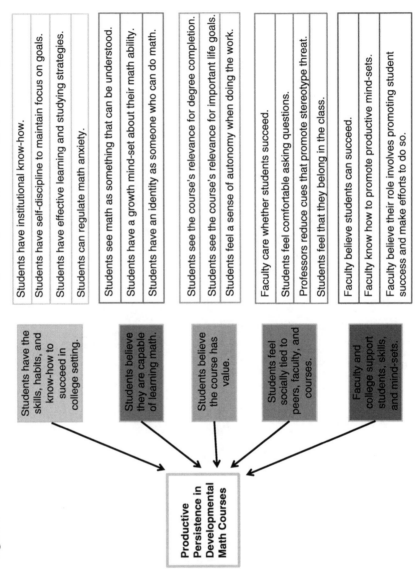

Analyzing Results to Guide Subsequent Action

In view of the frequently-observed finding that results for specific interventions tend to vary across sites, Bryk and colleagues suggest that the key analytical question in improvement science is not "What works?" but "What works, when, for whom, and under what sets of circumstances?"[43] In addition to understanding the reasons for variation in student performance, understanding the reasons for variation across sites is important. What site-specific factors undergird exemplary performance or retard improvement? How can interventions become effective in the hands of different practitioners? Practitioners need not a single silver bullet, but a portfolio of interventions and strategies for the array of circumstances they confront.

The speed of measurement, and the ability to intervene quickly are also key to improvement. Measurement needs to be part of day-to-day work. If an intervention fails to get the intended result, or if a student veers off track, a quick adaptation based on observation in practice may be very helpful. For example, the Community College Pathways initiative draws on research indicating that student disengagement frequently occurs early in the community college experience. Accordingly, it monitors student behavior intensively during the early weeks of enrollment. Real-time data on student disengagement is necessary for quick interventions to address an adverse event.

A Continuous Cycle of Learning and Improved Performance

Theories of action to generate improvement are created and tested through a widely used cycle of activities: plan, do, study, act (PDSA).[44] Illustrated by Figure 5.3 as employed by Carnegie, the steps in the cycle are summarized here.

Plan consists of an analysis of the problem, of the system encompassing the problem, and possible interventions to address the problem. What factors, and causal relationships among which factors, contribute to the problem? What interventions, targeted on which factors, might successfully improve performance? A key to planning is developing a specific hypothesis concerning the effects of an intervention. If it fails to work as planned, investigators seek to understand why the theory didn't work out.

Do consists of implementing a single intervention designed to improve outcomes toward a measurable goal.

Study consists of learning quickly from what has happened during and following the intervention. What can be learned from the process of intervening, both from the experience of those implementing the intervention and the results observed? What are the implications for the validity of the plan (the understanding of the system) and the theory undergirding the planned intervention? Should the intervention or its implementation be

Figure 5.3 PDSA Cycle for Learning and Improving

modified based on what has been learned? Should a different intervention be attempted in order to yield the desired result? Are the results promising, suggesting that the intervention should be continued, intensified, and tested through replication by others in diverse settings? Or are they discouraging, suggesting a return to the drawing board?

Empirical data are central to the study phase of the improvement cycle. As Bryk and colleagues observe:

> It is human nature to believe in the efficacy of one's work, and the field of education is replete with individual testimonials about effective programs. Improvement research, however, requires adherence to rudiments of experimental design in order to create an empirical warrant for such assertions. This is captured succinctly in the phrase (often attributed to Deming): "In God we trust; all [others] bring data." Each PDSA cycle must establish a plausible counterfactual and test local outcomes against it. In practice, improvement researchers often employ an interrupted time series design. An outcomes baseline is established, and subsequent performance is tracked against this baseline. Observed gains over and above the baseline provide evidence of an intervention's effect. In this design, the baseline functions as the counterfactual—the outcomes we would have expected to occur absent the intervention.[45]

Although observed gains above a baseline may not satisfy the most rigorous standards for causal inference, from the perspective of the practitioner, improvement, not incontrovertible causal inference, is the primary objective. A deeper understanding of the effects of an intervention is a means toward further improvement. In addition to hard, quantitative data, qualitative observations about the process of intervention and the results are used to create hypotheses to test in subsequent PDSA cycles.

Act consists of the adaptive responses based on the questions addressed in the study of the intervention. These actions will shape the next iteration of the PDSA cycle, refining the understanding of the system, modifying hypotheses concerning causal factors and interventions, guiding the continuing design of interventions, and determining whether an intervention should be tested in additional settings.

The strategy of the Carnegie initiative is based on the theory that learning to improve practice requires multiple PDSA cycles in a particular setting. Moreover, learning to improve practice at scale requires multiple intervention settings across a networked improvement community. Figure 5.4 illustrates the organization of such a community, and how it is intended to work.[46] Hunches, theories, and ideas will be tested through multiple PDSA cycles in multiple contexts, yielding comparable data, more effective practices, and deeper understanding.

The Carnegie initiative has drawn extensively on the work of improvement science in health care, which has benefited from relatively clear outcome measures and relatively consistent treatment protocols in the field of medicine, at least in comparison to the field of education. In addition, the field of medicine has benefited from the presence of large health maintenance

Figure 5.4 Multiple PDSA Cycles to Generate Learning and Improvement at Scale

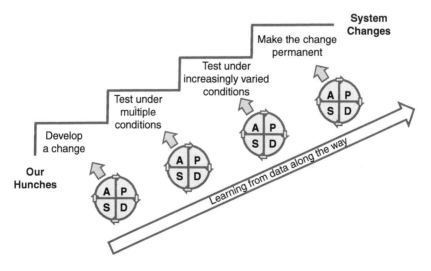

organizations and hospitals, with mechanisms to facilitate organization-wide improvement initiatives. In education there is less consensus on the measurement of important outcomes, perhaps more variety in instructional and student support strategies and protocols, and perhaps greater difficulty in establishing and coordinating improvement efforts among practitioners. These differences between medicine and education are likely to create challenges for the Carnegie initiative.

Bryk and his colleagues have thought deeply about these challenges and are seeking to learn how to address them in the networked communities of the Carnegie initiative.[47] Their ultimate success will depend both on more widespread implementation of the practices of improvement science in education and the development of effective mechanisms for learning across local sites.

What Is Evidence-Based Practice? How Can It Improve Outcomes?

Fundamentally, *evidence-based practice* is simply using empirical evidence to inform and improve practice. The evidence used can be generated from local data and applied locally, or it can be obtained from research and studies elsewhere and applied in a local practice situation. The term as it is used most often in medicine and other helping professions refers to the application of external research findings in practice.

Parenthetically, in medicine as well as in other fields, *practice-based research*, systematically collecting data from practice, has also been employed as a means of advancing knowledge and speeding improvements in clinical practice. In 1999 Nutting, Beasley, and Werner described the contributions of practice-based research networks in reducing costs and improving health outcomes by using actual clinical experience to challenge the effectiveness of research-based clinical practice recommendations.[48] Westfall, Mold, and Fagnan in 2007 further articulated the case for and contributions of practice-based research as an essential supplement to traditional research.[49]

The nature and the potential effectiveness of evidence-based practice in yielding better results depends on (a) the complexity of the situation in which it is applied; (b) the relevance of the evidence to the particular situation confronted; (c) the quality of the evidence and measures employed to analyze practice; and (d) the ability of the practitioners to find, analyze, and make use of the evidence. All of these factors play a role in determining its effectiveness, whether evidence-based practice is focused on a single situation or case, or whether, as in the Carnegie networked improvement communities or improvement science in medicine, the objective is to improve practice in an entire field.

The Complexity of the Situation

The relative complexity of a situation and the characteristics of its complexity create challenges which define and limit the potential contributions of evidence to practice. To illustrate, the discipline of evidence-based practice pioneered by the field of medicine has been spreading into the profession of social work during the past decade. The differences between social work and medicine are reflected in how the social work profession is attempting to implement the basic concept and in the debates occurring within the field.

Medicine focuses primarily on a single individual, it most often addresses a particular disease or illness, and it usually is reasonably easy to measure success. If the problem and the intervention are "conceptually neat" (to use Berwick's phrase), it is more possible to develop robust evidence on the effectiveness of the intervention. Of course, even medical problems often are not conceptually neat because people vary in genetics, medical histories, and other characteristics, such as multiple diseases, that can complicate clinical judgment and decision making. Particular people tend to get results that vary considerably from the "average" finding of an intervention found in a clinical trial.

Social workers focus on the individual in context—in the context of a family, a work situation, and a life history. Treatment is almost always complex, and "success" is likely to be more difficult to measure. The individual may have a problem with stress management, substance abuse, homelessness, mental illness; or be a victim or perpetrator of child abuse or neglect; or have conflict with an employer, spouse, children, or parents, or difficulty in dealing with the problems of significant others in one's life. Quite frequently, social workers deal with multiple problems simultaneously (*comorbidity* is the technical term), such as stress, substance abuse, mental illness, and dysfunctional family dynamics. (Sandra Mitchell's analysis of mental illness, referenced in Chapter 1, explains the difficulty of dealing with problems with multiple, interacting causal factors.)

The situation of teachers is likewise quite complex. Teachers work with students who bring different life experiences, cognitive frames and abilities, and personal issues into the classroom. These differences, along with the complexity of the instructional content itself and the complexity of the organizational factors and constraints that shape the school, must be addressed in a successful instructional process. Efforts to bring evidence to bear in improving education have often addressed only one or two variables, typically outcome measures associated with a single intervention. They have rarely been successful in addressing complex issues in ways that actually improve outcomes.

More comprehensive efforts, such as the research of the Consortium on Chicago School Research, have been more successful in positively affecting policy and practice. Its work will be discussed in Chapter 6.[50]

The Relevance of Evidence to the Situation

Summative evidence on performance (did the student learn, did the patient recover) has its uses, but by itself contributes little to the improvement of results. Practitioners need to understand not only "what works," but also what works in a particular situation, and why it worked or why not. In writing about the need to train teachers to learn from practice, Deborah Ball and David Cohen assert:

> Practice cannot be wholly equipped by some well-considered body of knowledge. Teaching occurs in particulars—particular students interacting with particular teachers over particular ideas in particular circumstances.[51]

Evidence useful for practice needs to be connected to an understanding of each particular situation and theories about actions and interactions that might improve outcomes. Available general knowledge is frequently relevant to elements of each particular situation (e.g., a trusting relationship between worker and client is important to good results in social work, and self-confidence affects a student's ability to learn), but such knowledge is only part of what a practitioner must know. A practitioner also needs a clear objective and a conceptual (theoretical) model of the factors in the situation that are relevant to that objective. And a practitioner also must know how and when to apply what is known to good effect.

Effective practitioners possess (and stay current with) general knowledge in the field, but they must supplement general knowledge with evidence developed from the experience of their own practice. Successful outcomes in the aggregate consist of individual events for individual people, each of which emerges from a complex set of causal factors and interactions. The "art" of successful practice comes not from knowing all there is to know in advance, but from knowing how to explore and work with the relevant factors in a situation.

Deborah Ball and Francesca Forzani have argued, for example, that educational research must get to the core of instruction—the interaction of individual teachers, individual students, and specific content—in order to help teachers become more effective.[52] Individual students vary substantially in how they respond to and understand content presented to them. Teachers need to observe and understand how particular students are thinking about content in real time in order to reinforce their learning or correct misunderstanding. This is not to suggest that every student thinks in a unique way, but that teachers must connect with how individual students are thinking in a given situation in order to be effective.

Research on actual learning must be situated in practice, and the accumulation of evidence from such research is unlikely to ever reach the level of generality sought through scientific reductionism. With that said, practitioners can learn from the direct evidence of practice and from sharing their learning process with other practitioners. Useful learning about practice is unlikely to come from any other approach.

The Quality of Evidence and Measurement

Educators and parents are showing signs of becoming weary of the educational data movement and assessments of student learning. Such feelings are understandable in view of the huge investments of money and time that have been made without obvious benefit. But there is no substitute for data and measurement. It may be possible to improve practice without measurable evidence, but without defined objectives and measurement of outcomes in a particular situation, it is not possible to know whether improvement has occurred or to learn from what may have been accomplished.

A program's objectives and measures of progress may not need to be elaborate or technically sophisticated in order to be useful. In the Carnegie Community College Pathways initiative, a key measurable outcome is the progression of a student to a credit-bearing college mathematics course. This admittedly coarse-grained indicator is "good enough" as an aspirational goal and measure of progress because it signifies meaningful attainment (even if imprecisely), and historically, few students in remedial mathematic courses persist and succeed to that point. The indicator also has the advantages of being simple to calculate while being meaningful and roughly consistent across all the community colleges participating in the program. More sophisticated measures are required for some purposes, but meaningful, easily accessible information is often sufficient for measuring improvement in practice.

Understanding what is actually going on in a practice situation is difficult to capture with quantitative performance measures, even though direct quantitative measures or systematic ratings based on observation are necessary to measure results. Constructing a theoretical model of the situation and deciding what interventions to attempt requires the thoughtful appraisal of the many factors operating in the situation. Ball and Cohen suggest that simple nonquantitative artifacts (videos, examples of student work, curricular materials, and teachers' notes) can be usefully employed in the analysis and evaluation of practice.[53] And the Community College Pathways project has quite usefully employed frequent brief surveys of student attitudes and perceptions.

Using evidence from other settings to guide practice requires assessing its relevance to the presenting problems and its quality. Following fairly closely the medical model, social work scholar Bruce Thyer has suggested that evidence-based practice consists of five steps:

1. Convert one's need for information into an answerable question.
2. Track down the best clinical evidence to answer that question.
3. Critically appraise the evidence in terms of its validity, clinical significance, and usefulness.
4. Integrate this critical appraisal of research evidence with one's clinical expertise and the patient's values and circumstances.
5. Evaluate one's effectiveness and efficiency in undertaking the four previous steps, and strive for self-improvement.[54]

Posing an "answerable question" typically involves asking about the usefulness of a particular approach for addressing the problem at hand. For example, Thyer suggests several examples involving the utility of specific interventions for the treatment or diagnosis of post-traumatic stress disorder or childhood sexual abuse.

Thyer suggests that practitioners should track down the "best clinical evidence" from books and journals (aided perhaps by the Campbell and Cochrane Collaborations), the Internet, and evidence-based practice guidelines developed by practitioners that are available for many mental health problems.

Appropriately, given the complexity of social work practice, Thyer suggests that practitioners may benefit from examining evidence from a broad spectrum of analytical studies, including anecdotal case reports, correlational studies, single-subject research designs, uncontrolled clinical trials, randomized clinical trials, and multisite RCTs. In addition to appraising the validity and significance of research findings, the practitioner must consider their utility in addressing the immediate problem.

The practitioner is then advised to consider the patient's values and circumstances and the practitioner's clinical expertise before taking action. Some interventions are likely to be beyond the expertise of the practitioner or inappropriate for or unacceptable to the client.[55]

The Ability of the Practitioner to Use Evidence

A simple Internet search on the words "evidence-based books" will demonstrate the intuitive appeal of evidence-based practice. The sheer number of books and articles in health care fields and in social work is impressive. Reading any of them, however, demonstrates the complexity of using research evidence drawn from other settings in practice.

In "Limitations of Evidence-Based Practice for Social Work Education: Unpacking the Complexity," Kathryn Betts Adams, Holly C. Matto, and Craig Winston LeCroy[56] offer a thorough analysis of the challenges and limitations facing social workers seeking to apply research evidence from other settings in their practice. The tone and content of their article reflects the dilemma facing practitioners who, as an ethical matter, want to provide the best possible service to their clients, but find it challenging to employ the procedures described by Thyer.

The first challenge is that the best available evidence is rarely conclusive and rarely provides direct assistance in knowing what to do in a particular situation. For example, the controls employed in randomized clinical trials frequently screen out clients with complex, multifaceted problems in order to achieve a more robust finding, but in real life many clients have complex, multifaceted problems. The results of research studies typically offer evidence of effectiveness to some extent, for some fraction of those served. The practitioner is left to determine to what extent these results might apply in the case at hand.

The second challenge is that few practicing social workers have the time to conduct a thorough search of the literature for evidence on a question of practice. Even if that were possible, few social work practitioners (and I would suggest perhaps only a fraction of physicians) have the expertise to assess the research literature skillfully enough to avoid errors of misinterpretation or misapplication. Judging the validity of a large body of scientific work requires the skill of a specialist, and settled knowledge frequently becomes unsettled when new findings emerge. Some have sought to address these problems by developing treatment manuals and practice guidelines. Adams et al. suggest that such manuals are limited in the range of clinical problems addressed; they typically require special training and extra cost; and they must be supplemented with flexible, adaptive clinical practice. The problem of evidence-based practice is not solved by such efforts.[57]

Many people, including social scientists and policy makers, who advocate the use of RCTs for shaping policy and practice in nonmedical fields seem unaware that this tool works well only for "conceptually neat components of clinical practice" in medicine.[58] The scope and complexity of the research enterprise and variation in the medical condition of individuals often make the utilization of research findings quite difficult. A recent initiative, the Patient Centered Outcomes Research Institute (PCORI), has been launched by the National Institutes of Health to address these difficulties.

The following summary and quotations drawn from an editorial in the *Journal of the American Medical Informatics Association* (*JAMIA*) illustrate the challenges.

> An analysis of the science underlying 2,700 practice recommendations of cardiology professional societies found that only 11 percent were based on multiple, well-done randomized trials. Nearly half were based solely on expert opinion. The vast majority of ongoing clinical trials are too small to provide evidence relevant to patients and clinicians . . . .
>
> Too often, clinicians cannot tell patients which therapies are likely to work best for individuals like them. Too often risks, benefits, and impact on quality of life are uncertain. Providing accurate answers based on the highest levels of scientific evidence for the majority of unresolved clinical questions is a revolutionary dream shared by patients, providers, payers, health plans, researchers, and policy makers alike.
>
> PCORnet aims to build a national research network, linked by a common data platform and embedded in clinical care delivery systems. This network will enable studies, and in particular randomized trials, that have been impractical to conduct to date—and to do so with economies of scale. Examples of questions this network will be able to address are: "What are the best management strategies for localized prostate cancer? Which of the available treatment strategies for children with attention deficit hyperactivity disorder are most effective? What are the best treatment strategies for lower back pain? What interventions are most effective for reducing disparities in hypertension outcomes?" . . .
>
> PCORnet holds the promise to transform clinical research—but many challenges lie ahead. For ultimate success, all those involved in shaping this revolutionary dream must maintain the bold and visionary attitude that enabled its creation. This is not your father's clinical trial network.[59]

The PCORnet initiative is an attempt to employ the tools of big data to clinical research in medicine. Unlike big data initiatives that utilize naturally occurring, unstructured information, PCORnet will require a common data platform with standardized definitions and data models, much like those described for the Common Education Data Standards discussed in Chapter 3. PCORnet is a logical next step in the effort to use evidence to improve policy and practice, and it may make important contributions that go well beyond those of the Cochrane Collaboration, "your father's clinical trial network." It remains to be seen, however, how successful such initiatives can be in overcoming the fundamental challenges of developing and applying knowledge in complex human situations.

Concluding Thoughts on Using Evidence to Improve Practice

In *Fixing Urban Schools*, Paul Hill and Mary Beth Celio suggest that every reform contains a "zone of wishful thinking."[60] This is their label for the presumption that the necessary conditions for better results will follow if an intervention is implemented, including conditions not directly influenced by the intervention. The idea that measurement alone ("You get what you measure!") can automatically generate improvements in practice is a case in point. The idea that evidence based on research studies can reshape practice and yield better results is another. Both measurement and research are essential for improving outcomes in practice, but much more is required.

The first necessary step, of course, is to measure what outcomes are important. Practitioners cannot get better results without measuring what they and their stakeholders value. With that said, if measures are employed principally to place (or deflect) blame rather than to guide improvement, progress will surely be slowed by practitioner resistance and debates over technical issues.

The next step is to acknowledge the enormous variation in the relative simplicity and complexity of problems relevant to practice, and the (almost always) complex human and organizational situations that must be managed to deal with problems, whether simple or complex. Some relatively simple problems (e.g., disease spread from unsanitary water or the hands of health care professionals) can be very effectively addressed, but solving them often requires considerable human effort and cooperation. Improvement science in medicine is addressing the health care problems that can be solved in this way, following the leaders of continuous quality improvement in manufacturing. Much, perhaps most, human progress has come from using inquiry to identify available opportunities and building a willing consensus to make the changes needed to exploit them.

The final steps, and the most significant challenges, are in bringing research to bear on the more complex problems facing practitioners. Skillful individual practitioners have used evidence to improve for a very long time, and they continue to do it every day. But all the professions have struggled to find effective ways of training skillful practitioners and to bring practical skill to scale. This is most especially true in the so-called minor professions where the goals and the problems are complex and multifaceted.

Deep, mutually respectful collaborations between scholars and practitioners may be the only effective pathways for employing evidence to improve practice. One pathway to progress may be more intensive attention to practice at the molecular level: What is really happening when an individual teacher works to help an individual student learn particular content or a sophisticated skill? How can understanding the student's thinking, predispositions, and other characteristics help the teacher become a more successful instructor?

Deborah Ball and her colleagues are doing interesting work on understanding the instructional process and helping teachers acquire such skill.

Another promising pathway is the PDSA cycles of the improvement science community and the Carnegie Foundation Networked Improvement Communities. This model combines reflective practice with systemic thinking, experimentation, and adaptation. It avoids the silver bullet predisposition that seems to infect the evidence-based practice field, and it emphasizes rapid learning and adaptation rather than quixotic search for natural laws and robust causal inference across variable particular situations. There are other communities of practice (e.g., Success for All and the National Wraparound initiative in child mental health[61]), but assuring the fidelity of a pre-designed intervention may often take priority over learning and adaptation in the local situation.

In the end, the effective use of evidence to improve practice will require respect for the complexity of practice and the wisdom of practitioners combined with respect for scholarship—systemic analysis, the development and pursuit of theory (or hunches) about causal relationships, measurement, experimentation, and adaptation. Advances in data systems in measurement, in basic science, and in creative ways of marrying the wisdom of practice with systemic inquiry are increasing the potential for significant progress. But easy victories remain elusive.

Notes

1. Langley, G. J., Moen, R. D., Nolan, K. M., Nolan, T. W., Norman, C. L., & Provost, L. P. (2000). *The improvement guide: A practical approach to enhancing organizational performance*. San Francisco, CA: Jossey-Bass, p. xii.

2. Kissinger, H. (1994). *Diplomacy*. New York, NY: Simon & Schuster, p. 27–28.

3. Schön, D. A. (1983). *The reflective practitioner: How professionals think in action*. New York, NY: Basic Books, p. 21.

4. Ibid., p. 23–24, citing Moore, W. (1970). *The professions*. New York, NY: Russell Sage Foundation, p. 56; and Schein, E. (1973). *Professional education*. New York, NY: McGraw-Hill. 39–43.

5. Donald Schön's elaboration on these points was presented in Chapter 1.

6. This statement, asserting that quantitative research and experiments cannot explain *why* behaviors occur, seems to refer to the reliance of experiments on *succession*, defined as the results observed after the treatment, as the basis for causal inference. Without delving further into the philosophical and scientific issues involved in the argument concerning whether causation can be observed (Chapter 2, pp. 34–39 contains a brief discussion of the matter), it is fair to observe that the same obstacles to certainty on *why* behaviors occur confront both quantitative and qualitative methods. Qualitative methods, however, can probe how people interpret causation and other aspects of their experience.

7. Given, L. M. (Ed.). (2008). *The SAGE encyclopedia of qualitative research methods.* Los Angeles, CA: SAGE, p. xxix.

8. Ibid., p. 706.

9. de Tocqueville, A. (1835/2003). *Democracy in America.* New York, NY: Penguin.

10. Given, L. M. (Ed.). (2008). *The SAGE encyclopedia of qualitative research methods.* Los Angeles, CA: SAGE, p. xxix.

11. Cook, T. D. (1985). Post-positivist critical multiplism. In R. L. Shotland & M. M. Mark (Eds.), *Social science and social policy.* Beverly Hills, CA: SAGE Publications, pp. 21–62.

12. Wilson, E. O. (1999). *Consilience: The unity of knowledge.* New York, NY: Random House Digital, p. 40.

13. Johnson, R., Onwuegbuzie, A. J., & Turner, L. A. (2007). Toward a definition of mixed methods research. *Journal of Mixed Methods Research,* 1, 112–133. doi:10.1177/1558689806298224.

14. Morgan, D. L. (2007). Paradigms lost and pragmatism regained: Methodological implications of combining qualitative and quantitative methods. *Journal of Mixed Methods Research, 1,* 48–76. doi: 10.1177/2345678906292462

15. National Academies Press. (1994). *America's health in transition: Protecting and improving quality.* Retrieved from http://www.nap.edu/openbook.php?record_id=9147&page=R1

16. Institute of Medicine of the National Academies. (2015, July 15). *Crossing the quality chasm: The institute of medicine's health care quality initiative.* Retrieved from http://iom.nationalacademies.org/Reports/2001/Crossing-the-Quality-Chasm-A-New-Health-System-for-the-21st-Century.aspx

17. Gawande, A. (2007). *Better: A surgeon's notes on performance.* New York, NY: Henry Holt & Company.

18. Gawande, A. (2014, May 5). Atul Gawande [website]. Retrieved from http://atulgawande.com

19. Institute for Health Care Improvement [website]. (2015) Retrieved from http://www.ihi.org/Pages/default.aspx

20. Berwick, D. M. (2008). The science of improvement. *Journal of the American Medical Association, 299*(10), 1182–1184.

21. Ibid.

22. Gawande, A. (2004, December 6). The bell curve. *The New Yorker.* Retrieved from http://www.newyorker.com/magazine/2004/12/06/the-bell-curve

23. John Steiner (personal interview with author, February 8, 2011).

24. Carnegie's work has drawn heavily on Langley, G. J., Moen, R. D., Nolan, K. M., Nolan, T. W., Norman, C. L., & Provost, L. P. (2009). *The improvement guide: A practical approach to enhancing organizational performance.* San Francisco, CA: Jossey-Bass.

25. See: Bryk, A. S., Gomez, L. M., & Grunow, A. (2010). Getting ideas into action: Building networked improvement communities in education. *Carnegie Perspective.* Retrieved from http://www.carnegiefoundation.org/spotlight/webinar-bryk-gomez-building-networked-improvement-communities-in-education

Bryk, A. S., Gomez, L.M., Grunow, A., & LeMahieu, P. (2015). *Learning to Improve: How America's schools can get better at getting better.* Cambridge: Harvard Education Press.

Carnegie Foundation for the Advancement of Teaching. (2014, November 18). *The six core principles of improvement.* Retrieved from http://www.carnegiefoundation .org/our-ideas/six-core-principles-improvement/

26. Anthony Bryk (personal correspondence with author, November 16, 2014).

27. Havelock, R. G. (1971). *Planning for innovation through dissemination and utilization of knowledge.* Center for Research on the Utilization of Scientific Knowledge, University of Michigan: Ann Arbor. This volume by Havelock and his collaborators at the Institute for Social Research at Michigan provides a thorough history and analysis of efforts to push research knowlege into agriculture, medicine, education, and other human endeavors.

28. Peurach, D. (2011). *Seeing complexity in public education: Problems, possibilities, and success for all.* Oxford Scholarship Online: Oxford University Press, doi:10.1093/acprof:oso/9780199736539.001.0001.

29. Smith, R. V., Densmore, L. D., & Lener, E. F. (in press, 2015). *Graduate Research: A guide for students in the sciences (4th ed.).* Academic Press/Elsevier, Boston.

30. Tan, E. J., McGill, S., Tanner, E. K., Carlson, M. C., Rebok, G. W., Seeman, T. E., & Fried, L. P. (2014). The evolution of an academic-community partnership in the design, implementation, and evaluation of Experience Corps. Baltimore City: A courtship model. *The Gerontologist, 54*(2), 314–321. Also: Coburn, C. E., & Stein, M. K. (Eds.). (2013). *Research and practice in education: Building alliances, bridging the divide.* Lanham, MD: Rowman & Littlefield.

31. For comments on action research, see Bryk, Gomez, & Grunow (2010, pp. 20–22). For an extensive discussion of action research see: Reason, P., & Bradbury, H. (2008). *The SAGE handbook of action research: Participative inquiry and practice.* (2nd ed.). London, England: SAGE Publications.

32. Ibid., p. 20. The Carnegie networked improvement initiative draws heavily on the continuous improvement work of Deming and Juran in industry and the use of these principles in health care.

33. Corey Donahue (personal correspondence with author, November 16, 2014).

34. Gawande, A. (2009). *Checklist manifesto: How to get things right.* New York, NY: Metropolitan Books.

35. Bennett, B. (2014, October 23). The standardization paradox. *Carnegie Commons* [website]. Retrieved from http://commons.carnegiefoundation.org/what-we-are-learning/2014/the-standardization-paradox/

36. Bryk et. al. (2010), pp. 16–17.

37. Solberg, L., Mosser, G., & McDonald, S. (1997, March). The three faces of performance measurement: Improvement, accountability, and research. *Journal on Quality Improvement, 23*(3), 135–147.

38. Yeager, D., Bryk, A., Muhich, J., Hausman, H., & Morales, L. (2014). Practical measurement. Retrieved from http://cdn.carnegiefoundation.org/wp-content/ uploads/2014/09/Practical_Measurement_Yeager-Bryk1.pdf

39. Ibid.

40. Bryk et al. (2010), pp. 23–26.

41. Ibid., p. 20.

42. Yeager et al., p. 55. Used with permission.

43. Ibid., p. 25.

44. Langley et al., pp. 23–25.

45. Bryk et al. (2010), p. 30.

46. Carnegie Foundation for the Advancement of Teaching. Used with permission.

47. Bryk et al. (2010), pp. 31–38.

48. Nutting, P. A., Beasley, J. W., & Werner, J. J. (1999). Practice-based research networks answer primary care questions. *JAMA, 281*(8), 686–688. doi:10.1001/jama.281.8.686

49. Westfall, J. M., Mold, J., & Fagnan, L. (2007). Practice-based research—"blue highways" on the NIH roadmap. *JAMA, 297*(4), 403-406. doi:10.1001/jama.297.4.403

50. A broad description of the categories of Consortium research and links to specific studies can be found online (https://ccsr.uchicago.edu/research).

51. Ball, D. L., & Cohen, D. K. (1999). Developing practice, developing practitioners: Toward a practice-based theory of professional education. In L. Darling-Hammond & G. Sykes (Eds.), *Teaching as the learning profession: Handbook of policy and practice* (pp. 3–32). San Francisco, CA: Jossey-Bass, p. 10.

52. Ball, D. L., & Forzani, F. M. (2007). 2007 Wallace foundation distinguished lecture—what makes education research "educational"? *Educational Researcher, 36*(9), 529–540. Retrieved from http://edr.sagepub.com/content/36/9/529

53. Ball & Cohen, p. 14.

54. Thyer, B. A. (2004). What is evidence-based practice? *Brief Treatment and Crisis Intervention, 4*(2), 167–176, esp. p. 168.

55. Ibid., pp. 168–174.

56. Adams, K. B., Matto, H. C., & LeCroy, C. W. (2009). Limitations of evidence-based practice for social work education: Unpacking the complexity. *Journal of Social Work Education, 45*(2), 165–186.

57. Ibid., pp. 176–177.

58. Berwick, p. 1182–1184.

59. Collins, F. S., Hudson, K. L., Briggs, J. P., & Lauer, M. S. (2014). PCORnet: Turning a dream into reality. *Journal of the American Medical Informatics Association: JAMIA, 21*(4), 576–577. doi:10.1136/amiajnl-2014-002864

60. Hill, P. T., & Celio, M. B. (1998). *Fixing urban schools.* Washington, DC: Brookings Institution Press, p. 16–23.

61. Walker, J. S., Bruns, E. J., Conlan, L., & LaForce, C. (2011). The national wraparound initiative: A community of practice approach to building knowledge in the field of children's mental health. *Best Practices in Mental Health, 7*(1), 26–46.

6

RESEARCH AND EVIDENCE IN GOVERNMENT AND ORGANIZATIONS

The study of politics is the study of influence and the influential. . . .
The influential are those who get the most of what there is to get. Available values may be
classified as deference, income, safety. Those who get the most are elite; the rest are mass.[1]
—Harold Lasswell, 1950

T he objective of this chapter, to consider how research and evidence might inform and improve the making of policy in government and organizations, is inherently complex. It will begin with a relatively abstract discussion of the process of influence and the roles of interests, views, information, negotiations, and settled "knowledge" in decision making. It will continue with a brief discussion of the political interests and views at play in the highly politicized education policy environment, which, not coincidentally, also are often at play in other domestic political issues. Finally, it will turn to the challenges and opportunities for useful research under these circumstances and identify a few examples of such work.

Influence, Interests, Views, Information, Negotiation, Knowledge

To understand the role of research and evidence in government and organizations, one must understand how decisions are made within them. It is not the entire story, but Lasswell's terse definition of the study of politics at the beginning of this chapter is a good place to start.

Influence

Politics and policy are about important decisions that shape opportunities, establish incentives, govern behaviors, allocate resources, distribute rewards,

144

and in government, determine who pays what taxes. Elites have the most influence over such decisions.

Although elites tend to get more of what there is to get—desirable things such as deference, income, and safety—they don't get it all. The distribution of deference, income, and safety varies; some societies are more equitable than others, and the distribution of these values changes constantly. Also, exceptional cases occur. Some elites (e.g., certain powerful political or religious leaders) may not be personally wealthy. At the highest level, elite status can be dangerous: Lasswell cites a study finding that over time, 31.9% of 423 monarchs in different countries suffered a violent death.[2]

According to Lasswell, elites work to protect their influence using the following methods: (a) invoking powerful symbols, often religious or patriotic; (b) violence; (c) distribution of goods and privileges; and (d) other practices to preserve influence and manage and reduce discontent, which vary according to circumstance. Further, he suggests that the tools used by elites to gain and secure influence include: (a) skill in problem solving, organization, oratory, or management; (b) sensitivity to and exploitation of class divisions in a society; (c) personal traits that are powerful in certain circumstances (e.g., fighting ability in war or even Lincoln's sadness and gentleness, which helped him gain support for his leadership in a time of crisis); and (d) sensitivity to and the ability to exploit ingrained attitudes in a society. Such ingrained attitudes might include prejudice against outsiders, a disposition to favor individualism, or conversely, an inclination to rely on tribal bonds and mutual support systems.

Non-elites compete continuously to be among the elite, and elites may lose their influence. Counter-elites have sometimes dramatically achieved a redistribution of influence and the values that come with it. (Witness the American, French, and Russian revolutions.) The success of a counter-elite inevitably results in the redistribution of resources, but it does not result in a fundamental change in the realities of the political process. A successful counter-elite initiative simply represents the replacement of one influential elite by another. Lasswell argues that elites are inevitable.[3]

This description of politics might suggest that influence and the values distributed through influence constitute a zero-sum game. Some win, some lose, and the sum of winnings and the sum of loses are offsetting. Such a view is too narrow; political processes can be positive-sum games that increase valuable outcomes for the masses, members of the elite, or both. Influence can be reciprocal—that is, elites bargain among themselves and with counter-elites—and such bargaining can result in mutual advantage.

Interests

People compete for influence over decisions based on their interests. A legislator once told me with unforgettable conviction, "Higher education doesn't cost, it pays." I happen to share his belief, but the fact that the University of Illinois was in his district undoubtedly strengthened his conviction. Public support for higher education "pays" very directly many of the people who elected him to office. The ends people seek unavoidably shape their beliefs and policy preferences, whether their interests are purely personal or extend to a concern for others.

Philosophers, religious leaders, psychologists, and economists have examined the extent to which people care, and debated the extent to which they should care about the interests of others as well as their own. It is evident that nearly all people do care about the welfare of those closest to them, family, friends, and perhaps neighbors, but distance—psychological, cultural, physical, and social—seems to diminish the intensity of caring instincts. At one polarity, Ayn Rand's objectivist philosophy[4] argues that the rational pursuit of one's self-interest is the proper moral purpose of each life. At the other polarity lies the philosophy of Auguste Comte, who coined the word *altruism*. Comte wrote, "We are born under a load of obligations of every kind, to our predecessors, to our successors, to our contemporaries." The duty of human beings is to live for others, he argued.[5]

Most people seem to live their lives between the polarities of undiluted self-interest and undiluted altruism. The belief that individual rights, freedom, and a drive for advantage and self-realization are valid and morally right coexists with a sense of obligation to family, community, nation, and humanity. Both perspectives play a role in how people understand their interests and express them in the political process.

Views

People also have different views on what mechanisms work best for achieving outcomes, even when they may share a common interest. Dahl and Lindblom's classic, *Politics, Economics, and Welfare*,[6] analyzes the strengths and weaknesses of the following fundamental social processes for achieving desirable outcomes: (a) markets (a price system), (b) hierarchy (command and control with flexibility, without fixed rules), (c) bureaucracy (enforcement of fixed rules), and (d) polyarchy (negotiation and bargaining). Many people are predisposed to favor one of these approaches for addressing social or organizational issues. Often policy makers who share a common objective will differ on the best way to achieve it.

Interests and views about effective mechanisms often converge in mutually reinforcing ways. Those who have capital and skills in the marketplace may favor market-based strategies; those without capital or who feel disadvantaged or exploited in the marketplace may favor centralized hierarchal or bureaucratic regulatory solutions to perceived problems. Polyarchy (negotiation and bargaining) may be employed to resolve differences among competing interests and viewpoints for solving problems.

Information

Information plays a role in how interests are understood and the views of policy makers concerning the effectiveness of different means for achieving an objective. As discussed in Chapter 3, information is different from data. Data exist independently from context and use. Information involves the organization of data into meaning in order to serve the purposes of a user or a group of users.[7] So in decision making, whether for organizations or government, information is inextricably linked to and shaped by those who use it.

Data may be absolutely objective, but information cannot be entirely objective. Users shape and judge the relevance and acceptability of information, in part by the standards of accuracy, reliability, and validity applicable to data, and in part by employing screens based on their interests and views. Previously acquired information influences the interests and views of decision makers. It also influences what new information they embrace, what they use, and their openness to information that might challenge or expand the information they have previously embraced and used.

Figure 6.1 illustrates the reciprocal interrelationships between interests, views, and information. All three factors may have an independent influence on policy preferences and actions. They can be in conflict with each other in the mind of a decision maker. When facing such conflicts, decision makers tend to seek and find a way to make them congruent, either by modifying their assessment of interests, the nature of one's views, or the information that is accepted and used.

This is not to suggest that new information has little power in influencing decision makers; for some it may have considerable influence. But no decision maker receives information on a blank slate. All information is screened and interpreted by decision makers in the light of previous information, their interests, and their views. Decision makers tend to enjoy receiving "new"

Figure 6.1 Reciprocal Relationships in the Minds of Decision Makers

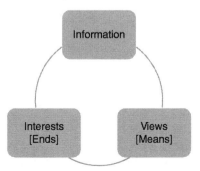

information that reinforces established beliefs and promotes their interests. They will seek such information, just as scholars seek to find evidence that reinforces their theories of how the world works or their beliefs and interests.

Decision makers naturally vary in their receptivity and openness to dissonant information. Some are quite open and curious, and others are quite settled in what they believe and why they believe it. Mature people, no matter how open they are generally to new ideas, tend to have fairly settled views on some topics. This means that dissonant information must be quite powerful in order to overcome strong predispositions. This is true across the political spectrum, but it seems to be more true as one approaches the extremes of left and right.

Negotiation

Because decision makers have different interests and views, negotiation is intrinsically a significant part of the decision-making process. Although political parties tend to be organized around generally shared views, negotiation occurs both within and among political parties. Individual members of all parties vary in their particular personal interests and in how closely they adhere to the dominant policy views of the party. In a two party system if one party drifts toward the center (in the direction of the opposition) or drifts too far from the center, factions in the party will take actions, perhaps to the point of organizing another party, to reverse the direction of the drift.[8]

The interplay of varied interests and viewpoints in decision-making frequently appears to be incoherent. The evident confusion of the process as a whole does not signify that the individual actors or the process itself are fundamentally irrational. Each actor typically employs a rational strategy in pursuing a relatively coherent, consistent set of interests and views buttressed by the information they have incorporated. The objectives, a combination of interests and views on how to achieve them, pursued by a political decision maker may not be well founded, may even be incoherent to some extent, but the means by which these objectives are pursued is almost always highly rational.[9] When decision makers set aside or defer the pursuit of one of their preferences in order to achieve another, seemingly irrational behavior is simply a matter of setting priorities.

Figure 6.2 illustrates the influence of interests; views; and two types of information, consonant and dissonant, on the formation of policy preferences and actions. *Consonant information* reinforces existing views and assessments of interests and *dissonant information* challenges them. Although individual policy makers tend to be sensitive to changing conditions and constantly reassess their interests (How do my constituents or board members feel about this? Am I at risk in the next primary or general election?),

Figure 6.2 The Formation of Policy Actions and Preferences

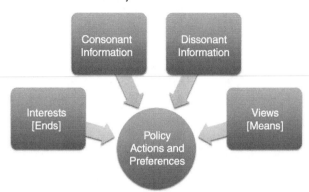

their views (favoring market-based strategies or, conversely, willingness to pass new laws and regulations that give power to government, etc.) tend to be more stable.

Dissonant information is less likely to influence settled views and more likely to influence the assessment of interests. This difference will be considered later in the discussion of the variable influence of research topics and findings. Dissonant information tends to be screened out by decision makers when it challenges settled views. It may be more readily embraced if it provides early warning of a threat or a new way to advance one's interests.

Information, both consonant and dissonant, can come from many different sources—supporters and opponents in political negotiations, constituents, lobbyists, the media, and from researchers and policy analysts. Information is shaped and used by political actors in negotiations, and it can play an especially important role in influencing swing votes, those individuals whose interests and views are susceptible to influence from information.

The political process leads to decisions that determine who gets what in the competition among interests and viewpoints. Action is a decision to change the status quo. Inaction, whether deliberate or due to a stalemate, is a decision not to change the status quo. Decisions may be hotly contested and closely divided with clear winners and losers; or they may be relatively uncontested with large majorities of support; or they may involve compromise between strongly held positions in order to achieve an action acceptable to both sides, or at least to a central majority drawn from both sides.

Compromise can be a beneficial means of balancing different views capable of coexistence, or it can be employed in order to achieve an immediate objective without reconciling irreconcilable positions. The development and ratification of the U.S. Constitution illustrates both cases. Some of the compromises at the Constitutional Convention, such as the use of checks and balances, have survived more than 200 years even though they are still debated by politicians and political scientists. The compromise concerning the practice of slavery was likely necessary to achieve ratification at the moment, but it eventually proved corrosive and almost fatal to the Union.

In theory, scholarship and evidence may provide authoritative information to resolve disputes and build bridges to reconcile different interests and viewpoints. But as Lindblom and Cohen astutely observed (see Chapter 1), scholarship and evidence in themselves are rarely, if ever, controlling factors in decision making. Scholars may seek to marshal facts and generate proof, but they generally can only assemble evidence and generate arguments.

> Problem complexity denies the possibility of proof and reduces the pursuit of fact to the pursuit of those selective facts, which, if appropriately developed, constitute evidence in support of a relevant argument. We do not mean here that evidence is manufactured without respect to data, or that contrary evidence is suppressed, or that argument is indifferent to such facts as can be established. We mean only to call attention to the inevitably incomplete character of attempts at proof, the consequent reduction of such attempts to informed argument, and the highly selective search for just those facts that bear on argument as evidence for or against the argued position. There is, consequently, a need for new rules of verification or proof suitable to what [professional social inquiry] can actually accomplish.[10]

Knowledge

The discipline of *knowledge management*[11] emerged in the 1990s as a tool to help organizations and businesses capture, share, and use knowledge in order to better meet organizational goals. *Wikipedia* makes a distinction between knowledge management and *information management*,[12] describing information management essentially as the process of collecting, protecting, and managing data. Knowledge management, according to those who exercise this discipline, is a higher-order process, the systematic use of data and information to develop organizational strategies and improve performance. When invited in 2003 to work on a knowledge management system for higher education public policy, I encountered a serious conceptual problem. How does one develop a "knowledge" management system for a decision-making environment in which facts and information are widely contested and there is very little settled knowledge? I expect that even in the knowledge management systems of hierarchical organizations one will find less settled "knowledge" and more "information" as Dennis Jones has described it previously and as I use it here.

But as an operational matter, settled knowledge can exist in organizations and even in political decision-making systems. Every item of information is not contested; some bits of information are widely, perhaps even universally accepted, even when the underlying data may require complex calculations and analysis. The Dow Jones Index and other indices of investment markets are universally accepted as valid indicators of economic health. Measures of inflation, employment, population data, and other demographic indicators are rarely questioned. Although educational data are more frequently challenged, some information is widely accepted. For example, improved data collection systems have yielded more confidence in information concerning high school completion reported to the Department of Education, and the data of the National Student Clearinghouse have enabled institutions and policy makers to learn the postsecondary completion rates of students who move among institutions.

Scholars and policy analysts should never underestimate the potential benefits of improving the quality of information available to policy makers so that indicators of matters that require attention or indicators of progress or performance can be more widely accepted. Even though decision makers will always select facts and information to advocate particular positions, the quality of political debate and negotiations and, ultimately, the quality of decisions can only be improved if better data and information are available.

The Essential Role of Measurement

Although some very important things are not easily or precisely measurable in quantitative terms, the concept of *improvement* requires measurement, whether quantitative, qualitative, or both in combination. Similarly, purposeful action, and especially purposeful collective action in society, requires an objective, which implicitly or explicitly must be measurable.

The virtually universal urge to measure is evident. We have created ratings of child well-being, ratings of consumer products and service providers, "league tables" of college and university quality, and so on—a constantly expanding array of measurement information, frequently of quite variable quality in terms of reliability and validity.

If people generally (or universally, to use E. O. Wilson's standard) accept the measures or scales used to describe a social condition, scholarship and evidence can help to bridge differences of viewpoint and interest. If there is no common framework of measurement, it is quite difficult or even impossible to agree on whether improvement has occurred or to organize action to achieve it.

The significance of these fundamental ideas is evident in the measures that are commonly accepted in society. With general agreement we measure life-span, income, wealth, rates of employment and unemployment, inflation, levels of education, and more. Some of these measures, such as life-span, are easy, but others are more complex and require sophisticated definitions, data collection, and calculations.

Over time, more complex measures (e.g., indicators of inflation or employment) have become widely accepted through rigorous scholarship and analysis. Scholarly work to create better, more reliable and valid, more widely accepted measures of important social conditions is a vitally important, inadequately honored, and underappreciated contribution to policy and practice. The intellectual effort unsuccessfully deployed to establish significant causal relationships in complex situations might be better used to improve the quality of measurement available to guide practitioners and policy makers.

Newly emerging human priorities, such as environmental quality or higher and more widespread educational attainment, frequently require new or better quality measurements. Examples of such work in education include the Measuring Up initiative and ongoing efforts to measure knowledge and skill described in Chapters 3 and 4. In environmental policy, the creation of new indicators of air quality and of global warming are obvious examples. Such indicators are bound to be controversial at the outset, but scholarly efforts to develop and refine measures and build a consensus on questions of measurement can be especially useful.

The Politicization of Educational Policy

A dispassionate, abstract analysis of the role of research and evidence in policy making (which is being attempted here) cannot ignore the fact that educational policy debates in the United States have been passionately contentious and not the least bit abstract for decades. It would take a substantial library to do justice to the various viewpoints in the public debate, but a brief summary of major themes may be sufficient for the present purposes.

The Culture Wars

The transmission of cultural norms and religious beliefs to children has always been an important educational objective. Parents are deeply and instinctively invested in transmitting cultural practices, beliefs, and values to their children, whether their practices and beliefs are conservative or liberal, highly prescriptive and normative, or nonprescriptive and tolerant. Like-thinking individuals organize themselves into social, religious, and political groups to preserve their cultural commitments and, wherever possible, to advance them in the broader society.

Although the U.S. Constitution sought to separate religion and the state, defining the boundary between them has always been in dispute. In the field of education, religious and cultural commitments affect decisions about textbook selection, policies concerning tax support for church-related schools, disputes over the teaching of evolution, sex education, and more. These views unavoidably shape policy debates, and they are especially difficult to address with data and analysis.

Cultural conflict also extends beyond religious and moral issues to encompass attitudes concerning the interpretation of history; implicit or explicit criticism of a country or group; and different cultural traditions and beliefs related to gender, ethnicity, race, and other types of identities. Many authors have written on these issues. Among the books on my shelf that treat them, often with widely divergent perspectives, are: *Schooling America: How the Public Schools Meet the Nation's Changing Needs*[13] by Patricia Albjerg Graham; *Left Back: A Century of Battles Over School Reform*[14] by Diane Ravitch; *Cultural Politics and Education*[15] by Michael W. Apple; and *No Excuses: Closing the Racial Gap in Learning*[16] by Abigail Thernstrom and Stephan Thernstrom.

Markets, Hierarchy, Bureaucracy, and Pluralism

As explained in Dahl and Lindblom's analysis[17] mentioned previously, the options for making decisions and allocating resources in society are present in all governments and organizations. These mechanisms all have strengths and weaknesses, and people naturally vary in their assessment of which mechanism is most effective for achieving specific purposes. Among them, however, the market is favored by some as the best, most efficient means of organizing all, or less extremely, nearly all aspects of life. The fall of communism in the former Soviet Union and the economic liberalization of China have strengthened the convictions and assertiveness of those holding such a view.

In education, as well as in other publicly supported endeavors, including corrections and even national defense, promoting competition among providers and contractors has been increasingly advocated as an effective means of achieving efficiency and increasing quality. The market is proposed as the preferred solution whether government is the buyer, whether the exchange is purely between suppliers and consumers, or whether government provides resources to consumers (in the form of a voucher or a direct cash transfer) to enable them to choose among suppliers. Market-based allocations are urged whether the supplier is a for-profit or nonprofit organization. Sometimes using for-profit providers for public services is urged based on the argument that investment capital and the profit incentive are necessary to achieve sufficient resources to finance innovation.

The reinventing government movement in the early 1990s, well articulated by a best-selling book by David Osborne and Ted Gabler,[18] sought to incorporate many of the principles of market competition into governmental operations. Vice President Gore during the Clinton administration led a highly visible effort to improve the functioning of the federal government based in part on these principles.

The arguments for market-based policy are powerful and persuasive, but they do not go unchallenged. Among other factors, those questioning reliance on the market for important functions cite the inadequacy or unavailability of information to guide consumer decisions and restrictions on choice due to location, poverty, and inequitable access to information. In education, unlike many goods and services, the high stakes and the difficulty of recovery when time and money are sunk costs make the consequences of market failure particularly costly in human and economic terms.

Critics of the market mechanism also argue that the incentives of for-profit providers do not line up squarely with the public interest. Market incentives in higher education naturally lead suppliers to focus on the most profitable opportunities, perhaps neglecting socially important but less profitable fields such as philosophy, art, literature, languages, and graduate work and research in the sciences. And some argue that the incentive to maximize profits may also lead to cutting corners on the quality of service, especially to less advantaged, unsophisticated consumers.

Unsurprisingly, those advocating or opposing market-based educational policy frequently turn to research and analysis for supporting evidence. Although in this situation analytical research conceivably could help bridge differences of opinion, it is far easier to find dueling than converging research studies. A recent exchange between researchers affiliated with the Center for Reinventing Public Education (CRPE) and the National Educational Policy Center (NEPC) on the performance of charter schools provides a good example among many.[19]

The CRPE study found modest positive effects from charter schools on math achievement. (In my judgment the research was free of apparent bias, and the findings were appropriately qualified, statistically significant, but modest in size; interesting, but hardly a compelling case.) The NEPC review strongly asserted the findings were "overstated" and made a number of specific criticisms. In rebuttal, the CRPE researchers strongly defended the integrity of their presentation of the data and interpretations of the findings. On one side of this exchange the emotional energy clearly comes from strong opposition to charter schools. On the other side of the exchange, the emotional energy seemed driven largely by a perceived insult to scholarly integrity. Neither side claimed or could show evidence for a compelling, substantial effect in favor of or in opposition to charter schools. As is often the situation, research gauging the effectiveness of broad policy options on which people disagree philosophically rarely yields results strong enough to end or even to shape the argument.[20]

Conflict Among Special Interests

Although the term *special interests* usually has a pejorative ring, individuals naturally, unavoidably, and legitimately have particular interests and views based on their vocation, their views and political affiliations, and their personal history and social relationships. These interests often become conflated in ways that shape policy debates and limit the potential influence of information and analysis in shaping policy.

Over the past half century, educational policy in the United States has become increasingly polarized along the labor/management divide. Teachers unions and sometimes principals unions, generally supported by and active in the Democratic Party, have become especially active politically. Unsurprisingly, teachers unions have become a rhetorical and policy target of members of the Republican Party.

For example, one conservative thinker, Thomas Sowell, viewing substandard educational attainment among disadvantaged urban minorities, has long suggested that support for school vouchers can be an effective strategy for Republicans to increase political support from African American voters.[21] In his view, teachers unions are a principal cause of poor student performance in urban schools. Accordingly, he advocates breaking up the public school "monopoly" as a strategy for improving educational opportunity and attainment, as well as enhancing the electoral success of the Republican Party and conservative politics among minorities.

Teachers unions quite naturally find the causes of substandard educational attainment in other factors such as poverty, the difficulty poorly educated parents have in supporting their efforts, and inadequate support for their challenging work. And they vigorously oppose policy initiatives that might tend to siphon away support from public schools. Both teachers unions and their critics claim to have the interests of students and the public at heart, and both frequently use the label "special interests" to describe their policy opponents.

So somewhat apart from the substance of particular issues, differences in the way people frame and understand problems, political competition, political alliances, and appeals to swing constituencies and conflict between "special interests" play significant roles in educational policy debates. These interests and perspectives have stimulated a large body of research on issues such as vouchers, charter schools, class size, the need for flexibility (or consistency) in school practices, the utility of and effective approaches for evaluating and improving performance, and the role of incentives and rewards for excellence in educator performance. The polarization in the field, however, is not conducive to research that builds consensus or advances knowledge.

Social Justice: Income, Class, Opportunity, and Privilege

Dueling perspectives on issues of social justice—income, class, opportunity, and privilege—play a significant role in the politicization of education, as well as the politicization of many other public policy issues. In order to provide context for the challenges facing research and evidence, the following paragraphs attempt a brief description of the ends of the political continuum, right and left, on issues of social justice.

On the political right, people tend to believe the natural gift of intelligence combined with discipline, creativity, and hard work generally explain why some people have more income and advantages in life. Equality of opportunity is an acknowledged value, and bad luck and cases of historical domination and oppression are admitted. Nevertheless, greater emphasis is placed on merit, through both natural endowment and effort, in explaining differences in the human condition: People can rise above circumstances, and it is their responsibility to do so. Birth into a prosperous family may be acknowledged as an advantage, but these advantages are part of the natural order; parents are naturally motivated to help their children, and they have a right and an obligation do so. Government cannot do much to address inequalities in the human condition. Its efforts to do so are typically inefficient as well as ineffective, and therefore unfair to the deserving taxpayer. Progressive taxation, it is argued, reduces the incentive for productive investment by the wealthy, and therefore reduces the efficiency of the economy and dampens job creation and opportunity for all. Competition in the free market is the best, most efficient, and most just mechanism for pursuing and achieving human happiness and prosperity. Government efforts to address inequality reduce the motivation to work, create dependence, and degrade character. They are inherently less efficient than the market.

The political left acknowledges the role of talent and effort, but argues that people who are privileged through inherited wealth and advantaged social backgrounds have unfair advantages. Equality of opportunity is a fundamental human right, and the playing field is tilted against the poor and disadvantaged. Opportunity cannot be truly equal when income and assets, both financial and social, are grossly inequitable, and when historical oppression and domination are perpetuated over generations through inherited privilege, racial and ethnic discrimination, exclusion, and economic disadvantage. The marketplace is not free to all: The market strongly favors those with capital assets, privileged connections, and sophisticated information. Public policies that fail to address inequality of opportunity perpetuate injustice and oppression under a deceptive cloak of economic freedom. Prosperity and human happiness require social and governmental policies that address inequality of opportunity; that ensure the fundamental needs for food, shelter, and health care are met; and that provide education so all people can realize their potential. It is both unjust and unwise not to address gross inequality of opportunity and wealth. To neglect these issues deepens poverty, social conflict, and crime; it does not advance prosperity.

These brief descriptions inadequately capture the sophistication of the intellectual arguments in the literature on these thorny issues and the range and nuances of view and opinion between these poles that exist in the thinking of individuals. But they may serve the purpose of illustrating how different views of the human condition and of the causes and "cures" of human problems come into play in the policy and political arena.

Although the thinking of some people may be well-described by the "left" or "right" viewpoints presented previously, many people, perhaps most, acknowledge that each perspective contains some valid points. Governmental policy in democracies typically reflects compromises forged through the resolution of conflicts among particular interests; a blend of views concerning inequality and social justice, cultural issues; and the effectiveness of markets, bureaucracy, and hierarchy in solving social problems.

What Education Studies Are Influential in Political Environments?

In "Education Research That Matters," the concluding chapter of *Education Research on Trial,* Pamela Barnhouse Walters and Annette Lareau[22] assess the influence of different contributions to education research by employing a number of perspectives and indicators. Unsurprisingly, the values and purposes of different users of research matter greatly.

In their own research and writing, educational researchers most frequently cite scholars who have made important theoretical or methodological contributions. The top three scholars cited in a review of 129 education journals over 20 years were Jean Piaget (3,816 citations of work emphasizing stages of cognitive development in young children), Albert Bandura (3,338 citations of work on social cognitive theory and self-efficacy), and John Dewey (2,847 citations on theory, democracy, and education). Others in the top 13 most frequently cited scholars (1,500 citations or more) made contributions illuminating issues such as learning styles, impact of social class, theories and measurements of intelligence, self-concept, motivation, and other factors.[23]

Another indicator of influence, the Distinguished Contributions to Research in Education Award of the American Educational Research Association (AERA), similarly reflects the inclination of professional education researchers to value broad theoretical and methodological contributions. Of some 44 awardees from 1964 to 2007, Donald Campbell and Julian Stanley in 1980 and 1981 were honored for their contributions to the theory and methodology of experimental and quasi-experimental research. But Walters and Lareau suggest than none of the awardees were "primarily known for *conducting* random-assignment evaluation studies in education or other kinds of assessments of the efficacy of particular educational programs or interventions." Instead, they suggest that the AERA awardees were honored for focusing on core issues of broad significance that "modified, challenged, or advanced the literature" of the field.[24] Walters and Lareau argue that, even though its direct relevance to policy may not be immediately evident, such scholarly research has been and remains consequential for policy and practice.[25]

Policy professionals, however, may not readily recognize the influence of the scholarly contributions highly valued by the research community. A 2006 study by the Editorial Projects in Education (EPE) sought to identify studies, organizations, people, and information sources that were most influential in educational policy during the prior decade.[26] The studies were rated using three sources of information, a survey of expert ratings, news coverage, and scholarly citations. The EPE study (also analyzed by Walters and Lareau) found that the nature of influential studies varied substantially.

By a wide margin, the two most influential studies (according to all three indicators, expert survey, news citations, and scholarly citations) were not discrete research projects but assessment reports, the *National Assessment of Educational Progress (NAEP)*[27] and *Trends in International Mathematics and Science Study (TIMSS)*.[28] Another category of influential studies included highly publicized commission reports or collaborative national panel studies: *Report of the National Reading Panel; Preventing Reading Difficulties in Young Children; How People Learn: Brain, Mind, Experience, and School; What Matters Most: Teaching for America's Future;* and *Ready or Not: Creating a High School Diploma That Counts.*[29] One experimental study, Tennessee's *Student/ Teacher Achievement Ratio (STAR)*,[30] made the list of 13 influential studies. The remaining influential studies on the list consisted of a body of work of individual scholars (and one organization) on particular topics: William L. Sanders on value-added methodology; the Education Trust on teacher quality; Jay P. Greene on high school graduation rates; Paul E. Peterson on school choice and vouchers; and Richard F. Elmore on school reform.

All of these studies have attracted the interest of policy makers and educators, and in different ways have shaped policy and practice. From the vantage point of a single observer, however, the impact of these studies on the behavior of policy makers has been quite different among the categories.

Over an extended period of time the assessment projects, NAEP and TIMSS, have attracted the attention of policy makers and practitioners and prompted them to take action to improve outcomes. No assessment is technically perfect, of course, so they have not been accepted uncritically. But these assessments are technically robust enough to be taken seriously as a continuing benchmark of progress or a reason for concern. Because they do not in themselves provide much guidance for what policy makers or practitioners should do to improve outcomes, the responses to these assessments have varied greatly. But they have provoked action.

As one might expect, the commission reports and collaborative panel studies generally were quite impressive, thoughtful, wide ranging, and balanced. These efforts typically draw on the best thinking and research in the field, and they have likely shaped the choices policy makers and practitioners make in their efforts to improve outcomes. The contributions of such efforts should not be underestimated, but breadth and balance in a report is not conducive to crisp, causal impact. It is common for both practitioners and policy makers to use the phrase "another commission report to gather dust on the shelf," not because the reports themselves are poor quality, but because it is not easy to implement broad, multifaceted recommendations.

The impacts of the remaining "influential studies" vary in interesting ways. Although its findings were not universally accepted (perhaps largely due to the cost implications), the Tennessee STAR experiment prompted policy interventions to reduce class sizes, particularly in California. The unanticipated effects of creating a teacher shortage and reducing the average quality of the teaching force apparently diminished the positive effects of the intervention.[31] Class size remains a controversial policy issue.

The nature and extent of influence of the individual scholars (plus the Education Trust) on particular issues seems to vary according to the topic and the nature of the research. Sanders's work on the educational gains associated with particular teachers (value-added) attracted and still attracts great attention. The use of student learning outcomes as a factor in teacher evaluation and performance continues to be on the policy agenda, but the implementation of this approach has been slowed by persistent questions about the validity and reliability of "value-added" assessments for particular teachers. The Education Trust's work documenting the tendency for teacher placement policies to compound the disadvantage of underprivileged students continues to generate policy attention, even though the obstacles to change remain substantial.

Greene's work on high school graduation rates focused on particularly egregious inconsistencies in data collection and reporting. This, in comparison to other issues, was a relatively simple problem, and it has largely been solved. Greene was not alone in focusing on the problem, but he deserves a good share of the credit for stimulating a solution. Peterson's work on school vouchers has played a role in the debate concerning the role of the market-place in public education, but the debate continues without a clear resolution in sight. Elmore's sophisticated work on school reform (especially, but not limited to, the role of instructional leadership) has certainly caught the attention of policy makers and practitioners but evidently not in entirely satisfying ways. His most recent writing reflects deep skepticism about the potential for the reform of established schools and institutions to improve student learning.[32]

Walters and Lareau conclude their essay by describing educational research in two categories—research that has had an impact on future research and research that has had an impact on policy. The Coleman Report on the effects of socioeconomic status on school outcomes and Bandura's work on social cognition are offered as examples to illustrate the research-influential category. To illustrate the policy-influential category, they suggest the STAR class size study and Peterson's work on vouchers. The policy-influential cat-egory is, in their words, "often very focused and narrow, often a theoretical, timed to mesh with a new policy interest, consistent with the political agenda of existing interest groups, [and] sometimes seen as high quality and some-times not."[33] In contrast, they characterize the research-influential category of research as broader, informed by theory, timed to respond to develop-ments in the scholarly field, rarely connected with a political agenda, and widely viewed as high quality.

I do not quarrel with the general description of Walters and Lareau's two categories; they are useful in the same ways my previous description of the political left and right may be useful, but they risk being too categorical. In a field such as education, where the primary purpose is not to gain abstract knowledge but to transmit knowledge and skill, it is a problem if the research community is, or even appears to be, excessively self-referential on the one hand or driven by political agendas on the other hand. The remainder of this chapter explores how research and evidence have and might further engage directly and improve the outcomes of policy and practice.

Consequential and Less-Consequential Research

Walters and Lareau's chapter assessing the influence of various research efforts on policy makers and other researchers is a good point of departure for con-sidering how research and evidence can be *more* than influential. How can research and evidence help policy and practice actually improve? This section of the chapter will explore the difficult task of using research and evidence to help policy makers become more successful in reaching their goals. It will consider three challenges: (a) resistance to dissonant information; (b) the difficulty of sorting through cause and effect connections due to complexity and change over time; (c) the difficulty of tailoring inquiry to the structure, dynamics, and power distributions of the decision-making system.

Resistance to Dissonant Information

The resistance of policy makers (and humans generally) to dissonant information is a significant obstacle to the improvement of policy through inquiry and evidence. People commonly have relatively settled and divergent views on the major issues involved in making policy. While "research" is frequently employed as a tool of argument and advocacy, in politically competitive environments the goal of a "researcher duelist" often is to design and implement a "killer" study.

In organizations with an overriding, straightforward purpose such as generating profits, a "killer" study may be feasible under some circumstances. In government and nonprofit organizations with complex purposes and competing worldviews, debates over purposes and strategies for achieving purposes have rarely been settled by a research study. Typically, a sizable fraction of decision makers on both sides of an issue will be quite settled in their views and resistant to all but overwhelmingly conclusive research. For such decision makers, the most persuasive studies supporting the opposing side of an issue are more likely to generate energetic rebuttals rather than the modification of their views. The issues of school vouchers and class size reduction offer many examples of this dynamic.

More fertile ground for research contributions lies in the middle of the political spectrum where decision makers are more open to dissonant information. Studies that are visibly "advocacy research," tilting toward either end of the political spectrum or one side of an issue, have no chance of persuading those who are firmly opposed to the arguments of the studies, and they even have difficulty influencing those in the middle ground. In my view rigorous studies that carefully avoid the appearance of predisposition and bias have more power to shape opinions in the middle of the political spectrum.

Part of the solution to this problem lies in the framing of a study. Studies that focus narrowly on a politically contentious intervention or policy issue will inevitably be viewed as advocacy research, welcomed and applauded by the already converted, and attacked by established opponents. Broader studies that are visibly exploratory are more likely to have an educational impact across the political spectrum, or at least the central part of it. Such studies may not have a dramatic immediate impact, but they are more likely to move policy over time than research focused on polarizing issues.

A good example of such research is *Crossing the Finish Line: Completing College at America's Public Universities* by Bowen, Chingos, and McPherson.[34] This study examined previously untapped institutional data to explore the factors associated with successful completion (or noncompletion) of degrees by students in public universities. Its database was large enough to be persuasively representative of the entire sector, and it rigorously explored the role of academic preparation, financial assistance, and other factors in predicting successful college completion. Perhaps unsurprisingly, but convincingly, it found that financial assistance has the greatest impact on the success rates of lower-income students. More surprisingly to some, it found that the completion rate of low-income students is lower when they attend institutions that are less selective than other institutions to which they could have been admitted. "Undermatched" students do worse than similar students attending a more selective, perhaps more demanding, institution.

This study contributed to policy and practice by confirming existing evidence that financial assistance is most powerful in advancing completion when it address genuine financial need and that academic preparation is a necessary complement to financial assistance. Its finding regarding undermatched students suggests both that the educational culture of less-selective institutions might usefully become more demanding and that it is harmful, not helpful to funnel able low-income students into less demanding, less-selective institutions. Finally, it demonstrated the utility of mining administrative, student-level databases to learn ways of improving policy and practice.

Resistance to dissonant information is also less of a problem when information is presented that adds fresh, policy-relevant perspective on issues that are not politically fraught. For example, challenging, time-consuming paperwork is unpopular all across the political spectrum. An experiment using H&R Block tax preparers to help low-income families complete the federal financial assistance application (previously cited in Chapter 2)[35] confirmed that the form itself is a barrier to participation in higher education. This research surely has contributed momentum to efforts to simplify the application process for financial assistance.

Advocacy research, of course, will always exist, and it has its place. But researchers who want to move policy are likely to be more successful if they find ways of working around resistance to dissonant information.

Sorting Through Elusive Connections Between Cause and Effect

The complexity of social problems and social interventions typically makes it quite difficult for social research to be conclusive. Ray Pawson's discussion of mentoring programs summarized in Chapter 2 is a good example of a situation in which a constellation of requirements must be addressed in order to achieve the desired objective of an intervention. Different programs might be quite successful in meeting one, two, or three such needs while failing to meet a fourth or a fifth. When programs are evaluated on "bottom line" results, significant achievements could be masked by partial failure.

The STAR research focused on class size discussed previously is an example of a slightly different sort. In this case, evidence suggests that smaller class sizes help improve teaching and learning, but the experimental condition of "other things being equal" cannot be assured in the real world. More teachers to staff smaller classes might not be as skillful as a smaller number of teachers with larger classes, or the financial costs of smaller classes might result in trade-offs that reduce the quality of other important factors, including academic supports or even adequate compensation to attract and retain strong teachers.

Certainly "bottom line" results are what ultimately matter, but for most complex problems, simple interventions rarely yield impressive results. This is why the simple intervention of charter schools or other silver bullet "solutions" fail to yield the results that would gratify their advocates or silence their critics. Charter schools alone cannot solve all of the problems that impede the success of disadvantaged students, even though they might solve some of them. Many other factors that vary among charter schools (as well as among non-charter public schools) play a role in their success or failure.

A good example of the challenges complexity offers to public policy analysis can be found in a retrospective analysis of Lyndon Johnson's War on Poverty. Ronald Reagan famously quipped, "Lyndon Johnson declared war on poverty, and poverty won." Reagan was clearly right if the measure of victory is the total eradication of poverty. But a recent analysis of the full spectrum of issues tackled by the War on Poverty suggests it achieved some significant victories as well as suffered some failures. Also, changes in the underlying challenges facing poor people partially thwarted the strategies adopted by the Johnson administration.[36] The difficulty of assessing social policy is compounded both by complexity and by changes over time in the surrounding environment.

The War on Poverty included multiple campaigns. One campaign, reducing poverty among the elderly, was clearly a success. Comparing the poverty rate in 1962 to the rate in 2012, Bailey and Danziger found the changes displayed on Table 6.1 for different groups within the national population.[37] (Because this analysis excludes food stamps, housing allowances, and the earned-income tax credit, it actually understates poverty reduction during this 50-year period.) Although the general direction of change is

TABLE 6.1

Results of the War on Poverty (Based on Income Below the Poverty Line)

Population Component	Percentage in Poverty, 1962	Percentage in Poverty, 2012
All groups	20%	14%
Elderly	30%	9%
Blacks	40%	22%
Children under the age of 18	22%	20%

positive, a number of contextual changes over this period worked to increase poverty despite the governmental interventions:

- Wage inequality increased from 1963 to 2009.
- Male incarceration rates, nonmarital childbearing, divorce rates, and female-headed households all grew.
- The non-elderly poor are increasingly Latino; the percentage of non-elderly poor who are Black or White has dropped significantly.[38]

These environmental changes would seem to be the major factors explaining why childhood poverty has decreased so little, if at all.

When individual programs are examined, it is typically difficult to pin down their effectiveness due to the number of external variables with an impact on their intended outcomes. The initial academic gains associated with Head Start seem to fade over time. Is this due to weakness in the program, or due to the quality of schools serving poor children as they progress through the elementary grades?[39]

Significant need-based aid for higher education has contributed to higher participation, but college costs have risen faster than Pell Grants and large disparities by race and income remain.[40] Title I support for the K–12 education of disadvantaged children has reduced the gaps between inputs and outputs in rich and poor states and schools, but the gaps are still quite large.[41] (In *The Ordeal of Equality*, David Cohen and Susan Moffitt suggest that the failure to increase the capabilities of teachers and school leaders for educating disadvantaged children and the fragmentation of school policy due to local control largely explain the failures of Title I.)[42] Finally, workforce development programs had some positive effects, which varied for different populations, but rapid increases in skill requirements in the job market made it much more difficult to train and place in jobs the hard to employ.[43]

Since launching the War on Poverty, the nation has reduced elderly poverty and infant mortality while substantially increasing access to medical care, housing assistance, food assistance, and life expectancy.[44] It seems reasonable to attribute at least some of these gains to the interventions of the War on Poverty, but it is not possible to trace a causal chain that would convince all skeptics of the benefits of the effort and investment. And despite all these efforts, childhood poverty apparently has not improved at all.

What are the implications of complexity for researchers and policy makers? First, it is unrealistic to expect simple, one-dimensional interventions to yield dramatic solutions for complex problems. Second, all the elements of complex, multifaceted interventions can rarely be implemented consistently with necessary quality in single locations, and, perhaps, never with fidelity across locations. Third, both time and the capability of adapting in response to learning or change are required to make progress on social problems. The expectation or requirement that all social programs must be proven to "work" through experimental studies (as recently suggested by policy analysts Peter Orszag and John Bridgeland, each of whom, respectively, had major roles in the Obama and George W. Bush administrations)[45] inevitably leads toward the conclusion that nothing "works."

This is not to suggest, of course, that "everything works" or that policy should not be tested by analysis. It would be more accurate to say that no policies "work" all by themselves. Policy makers frequently have control over part of the solution to social problems, typically the allocation of financial resources, but they rarely can control or even materially influence many of the other factors important to the outcomes they seek. Effective policy is likely to require a sensitive balance between necessary interventions into local conditions along with respect for practitioners and the challenges of practice. Policy should avoid regulations that substantially constrain the ability of practitioners to respond to local context and complexity. Research and analysis can and should play a role informing both the macro levels of policy and the micro levels of practice, but it takes recognition of complexity and deliberate, wise decisions to well synchronize policy and practice.

College student financial assistance is a good example of the failure to meet this challenge. The U.S. government has made a significant investment in Pell Grants and in guaranteed student loans to enable and encourage widespread participation in postsecondary education. The policy objective has been to enable all qualified and motivated low- and moderate-income students to obtain a postsecondary education. The actual work of enrolling and educating them occurs in states and institutions.

The federal programs (supplemented by state and institutional programs) have clearly made a significant impact on postsecondary participation and completion; however, in too many cases the policies have been inefficient and ineffective on two related dimensions: adequately meeting financial need and avoiding the wasteful expenditure of funds. In many cases financial aid is insufficient to meet the need, and in other cases aid is provided where government support is not needed or where students and institutions are not prepared to achieve the program's objectives. Let me elaborate.

Despite a large federal investment, it is evident that the lowest-income students rarely have adequate aid to attend college full time. A full Pell Grant, added to the earnings from substantial part-time work during the academic year and full-time work over the summer, is just adequate to cover living and other nontuition expenses, which range from $12,000 to $18,000. Unless the states or institutions themselves provide enough assistance to cover tuition costs (a few do, but most do not), very low-income students have two unattractive choices: work full time while attending school part time, or borrow all the funding required for tuition expenses. A common choice has been to work full time and attend school part time; failure to complete is frequently the result.

Part of the reason financial assistance is inadequate for so many low-income students is that a substantial portion of the public investment in student assistance is unproductive in terms of the main program objective. Some states emphasize merit aid, allocated without regard to financial need, and even much of the federal aid is allocated to tax credits and loans available to higher-income families. These investments are defended because they reduce the cost of college to middle-income families and, in some cases, induce strong students to go to college in their home state. But on the margin, merit aid to middle- and upper-income families influences where students go to college, not whether they will go. Virtually all of these students would enroll without the aid.

Another reason funds are inadequate (and a political weakness of the program) is that too many grant recipients, poorly prepared to succeed in postsecondary education, fail to succeed after enrolling. Some institutions (both nonprofit and for-profit) are complicit in this failure by taking money allocated for the education of low-income, "high-risk" students without the ability and commitment necessary to help them succeed. During the George W. Bush administration, Congress tried to address the academic preparation problem by providing federal financial incentives for taking a rigorous college preparatory curriculum in high school. In principle this was a good idea, but it proved cumbersome and unworkable at the federal level. The Obama administration considered dealing with the complicit institution problem through a federal system to rate institutional performance, but eventually decided simply to expand the information available to the public without formally ranking institutions.

In this case, as for many social problems, policy and practice are interdependent. A policy focusing resources on a problem cannot succeed without effective "on the ground" practices to address the problem. At the level of practice, schools and colleges (and their self-regulating accreditors and professional associations) need to improve student preparation and institutional effectiveness. Both resources to support practice and resources and policies designed to improve practitioner capability are required.

The American student financial assistance system has, by and large, been successful, but it has not fully met its objectives. At the policy level, it is quite clear that substantial state and federal sums have been allocated to make college more affordable (often for middle-income students) without adequately enabling and increasing postsecondary educational attainment for large numbers of lower-income students. At the level of practice, educators have failed to assure that a large number of students who might benefit from the program have the right level of preparation and support to succeed. The analysis of data and evidence can best increase the success of policy and practice when the complexity of problems and the mutual interdependence of policy and practice are recognized.

Tailoring Inquiry to the Decision-Making System

It has often been frustrating to be a policy professional committed to using evidence and analysis to inform and improve policy. My greatest disappointment is not the resistance of policy makers to dissonant or challenging information; that is natural and inevitable, simply a problem to solve. My greatest disappointment is the number of missed opportunities to make important contributions by talented, caring scholars. These missed opportunities most often come from a failure to recognize and acknowledge the limitations of research, especially traditional research seeking to establish general knowledge, and a failure to understand how policy decisions are made.

Research or evidence has the greatest power to influence decisions in government or organizations when it is tailored to the structure, dynamics, and power distributions of the decision-making system. Let me suggest five characteristics of research efforts that are successfully "tailored" to be consequential. Consequential research and evidence is more likely to be

1. focused on realistic, potentially consequential operational options in decision making;
2. focused on salient, significant issues, where the demand for improvement is high, and the consequences of inaction are serious;
3. reasonably accessible to intelligent, educated decision makers who may lack sophisticated knowledge of statistical analytical techniques;
4. based on credible *local* data about the places to be affected by the decision or directly and clearly relevant to these places; and

5. studies where the likely effect sizes are neither trivial in size nor a close call in terms of differences among alternatives if causal effects are inferred.

Let me elaborate on each of these in turn.

Realistic, operational decision options. Scholars, too often graduate students looking for a dissertation topic, frequently seek to discover whether some broad, general characteristic of a state (the form of governance employed, the use or nonuse of formulas in the budgeting process, the allocation of funds to student assistance, the existing level of educational attainment, etc.) can explain an important part of the variance in a valued outcome, such as the generosity of state support, student enrollment, or student attainment. I have read many such studies (including one chapter in my own dissertation), and I have never observed, nor can I imagine one of these studies influencing a policy decision.

The first problem is that studies of the impact of general characteristics, no matter how Herculean the effort, cannot control for enough of the relevant variables to produce a sizable effect. Even if a statistically significant result is obtained, it rarely (if ever) explains enough of the variance to persuade most scholars of its importance or enough variance to be a decision-influencing factor, even for those policy makers who can understand the statistics.

The second problem is that the broad general characteristics examined in such studies are either not realistically under the control of policy makers, or that decisions are highly unlikely to be made based on the logical relationships examined (especially with weak results) in such studies. Take the case of governance. I have observed a number of cases where states have changed in some ways their system for governing or coordinating higher education. These decisions happen infrequently, they are always controversial (requiring the expenditure of considerable political capital), and they typically are made because of frustration or annoyance with the way the people involved in the current system are working with policy makers. While to some extent they change the dynamics of the decision-making process, such governance changes rarely result in fundamental change in the results generated by the higher education system. Many other factors are more influential in determining outcomes.

More consequential research is focused on realistic operational options and on decisions actually under the control of decision makers. Studies to evaluate whether a *particular* policy decision has yielded the intended effects such as Susan Dynarski's study of the Georgia HOPE scholarship program[46] and Joseph Burke's work on performance funding[47] are good examples of useful and consequential research. Such studies may not cause policy makers to pursue or avoid a particular course of action, but they add directly relevant evidence to the policy debate.

Focus on salient, significant issues.   A study is most likely to get the attention of policy makers and make a contribution to policy when it addresses a question of immediate policy concern. This observation may be too obvious to deserve mention, but scholars and policy analysts who focus on issues that are already on the minds of policy makers will capture their attention more readily than scholars whose first priority is to shape what policy makers think about.

The budget director of a large state (serving a Democratic governor with a Democratic legislature) was once heard to say, "We have three big problems in this state: K–12 education, health care, and pensions. Higher education isn't doing much to solve any of them." No doubt his opinion was unfair and inaccurate (at least to some extent), but if and where it exists, the perception of disengagement from important public issues is a problem for scholars. It can be a challenge for researchers and policy analysts to be relevant to policy debates without becoming a tool for one side or another in a philosophical disagreement, but the rewards of relevance will grow over time.

The Consortium on Chicago School Research, founded in 1990, is an outstanding example of a successful research effort focused on a salient public policy issue. The Consortium was created when improving the quality of public education in Chicago was an urgent priority. Reflecting the public mood and visible problems, not any sort of empirical review, then U.S. Secretary of Education William Bennett suggested in 1987 that the Chicago public schools were the "worst in the nation."[48] The state passed legislation that dramatically decentralized Chicago public schools in 1988, creating individual local school councils and reducing the power of the school board. Then in 1995, legislation was passed to give the mayor of Chicago power to appoint both the school board and the CEO of the Chicago schools. (These somewhat contradictory changes in governance still exist in uneasy tension, suggesting that governance changes of any kind are incomplete solutions to problems.)

The Consortium, then led by University of Chicago sociology professor Tony Bryk, drew on the resources of many of the universities in Chicago as well as the data resources of the Chicago public schools to employ research and data analysis to help "school reform" succeed. The complexity of the system and the depth of the interrelated problems—urban poverty, bureaucratic dysfunction, multigenerational educational disadvantage, difficult labor relations, and many more—defied silver bullet solutions.

Over many years Consortium-affiliated researchers sought to understand how the schools succeeded and failed to succeed by employing multiple research methods. (One dimension of the complexity of the problems was illustrated to me in an early meeting in which data concerning student mobility were presented—a shockingly high percentage of students attended different schools both during and between school years.) Consortium research projects ranged widely, including, for example: classroom observation to identify variance in the amount of time actually spent in instruction, interaction with students, and administrative activities; surveys of teachers, students, and parents in an effort to understand school culture and the community environment; and finding a way to estimate and compare the average contribution of individual schools to student progress, which required a painstaking analysis of the differences between versions of the Iowa Basic Skills test and controlling for student mobility among schools.

The breadth, depth, and persistence over time of this research program has yielded important general insights about elementary education, such as the relationship between higher levels of trust among the adult staff of a school and student learning, and particular insights about policies and practices in Chicago. A particularly dramatic contribution came from studies demonstrating that failure to graduate from high school frequently can be predicted by getting off track in eighth or ninth grade. Chicago's high school graduation rate has steadily increased to reach 69% in the 2013–2014 academic year,[49] apparently due in part to aggressive efforts to take corrective action in eighth or ninth grade when teachers and counselors observe a "getting off-track" incident such as failing a course or a suspension.[50] A thorough discussion of the Consortium's contributions can be found at its website and in *Organizing Schools for Improvement: Lessons from Chicago*, published in 2009.[51] Chapter 7 describes in more detail its initial work focused on elementary education.

Reasonable accessibility. Rigorous scholarship typically involves exhaustive reviews of the literature; scrupulous attention to detail; complete documentation of research methods; and often elaborate, fully documented statistical analysis of data. The skills and requirements of doing and presenting rigorous scholarship to an audience of scholars are often counterproductive in a policy environment. Outstanding PhDs who find themselves working in policy often have to learn new skills in order to design and present their work effectively.[52]

Scholars, and especially recent graduate students, frequently feel compelled to demonstrate a comprehensive grasp of a topic—a compulsion that is normally counterproductive, possibly fatal in a policy environment. *Not* presenting everything known about a topic is not "dumbing down." To the contrary, it takes considerable skill and intelligence to know what is essential to make a case and to understand how to capture and hold the attention of an audience managing information overload and many demands on its attention.

Similarly, elaborate statistics may be necessary for some analytical tasks, but a non-technical audience will be more persuaded by the face validity of a study than the statistics. If complex statistics are essential, they must be done well and stand up to potentially competitive (if not hostile) scrutiny. But statistical display to a policy audience is more likely to arouse suspicion than trust—if the message is hard to understand, then the messenger is less likely to be trusted and more likely to be suspected of deception or subterfuge.

When framing, conducting, and presenting research to a policy audience, simple, straightforward, and easy-to-grasp arguments add power and persuasiveness. Unnecessary words, potentially distracting information or side arguments, and difficult-to-understand mathematics subtract from the impact of the message. Achieving clarity and simplicity in research is challenging when the realities of the life and policy and practice themselves are inherently complex. But powerful policy research, just like a powerful scientific theory, is parsimonious.

Locally focused data and analysis.   Typically, the goal of science is generalizable knowledge. How can inferences from a sample of data, from experiments in a few places, be generalized to other settings or to the population as a whole? Social science knowledge that can be generalized across settings is quite valuable, of course, but it is also rare and very difficult to acquire.

Researchers and policy analysts can dramatically increase their contributions by obtaining and analyzing *local data* that by definition are directly relevant to the interests and concerns of local policy makers. When the data studied includes the entire population, the confusing issues of statistical significance are side stepped, and sampling error is not an issue. Policy makers can quickly decide for themselves whether substantive significance is present. For example, the local focus of the Consortium on Chicago School Research discussed previously guaranteed that local decision makers would pay attention.

Let me illustrate the difference that a local focus might make with an example of findings from the National Center for Education Statistics Longitudinal Study, 1988 to 2000. Figure 6.3, first published by the National Advisory Committee on Student Financial Assistance demonstrates a very strong relationship between socioeconomic status (SES) and college participation, despite academic ability.

This chart has been frequently shown to policy audiences with the powerful message that high achievement, low SES students enroll in college at a rate 20 percentage points lower than high achievement, high SES students, and at essentially the same rate as low achievement, high SES students. Figure 6.4, taken from the same longitudinal study, compares baccalaureate degree completion

Figure 6.3 The Effects of SES on College Participation for High- and Low-Ability Students

College Participation by Achievement Test and SES Quartile		SES Quartile	
		Lowest	Highest
Achievement Quartile	Highest	78%	97%
	Lowest	36%	77%

Source: U.S. Department of Education Advisory Committee for Student Financial Assistance, February 2001.

Figure 6.4 BA Completion by Age 28 by SES Quartile and Estimated SAT Scores

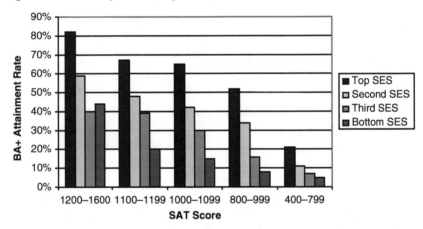

Source: Anthony Carnevale, *Liberal Education*, Fall 2008, p. 58.

by age 28 for students in each SES quartile when controlling for estimated SAT score. This analysis shows that roughly two thirds of top quartile SES students with average ability (SAT scores in the 1000–1099 range) complete BA degrees by the age of 28. Only about 15% of similarly academically qualified students in the lowest quartile of SES had completed a BA degree by the age of 28.

These analyses have been shared with numerous audiences, and they quite possibly have had an impact on state and national student assistance policies in the past decade. But I don't believe they have galvanized many policy makers into action. I've often wondered what the policy response might be if similar data were available at the state and local level. How many high ability (or average ability) low SES students are not receiving a postsecondary education in our city or state? How does our success rate compare to other states and cities?

It is fairly common to see data that rank states and cities along various single dimensions of wealth, business activity, unemployment, or educational attainment. But such descriptive, one-dimensional rankings can be dismissed as simply describing "fate," the hand that has been dealt to a city or state, not an assessment of performance or possible neglect. If the analysis of these figures were commonly available at a local level, they could be used to stimulate corrective interventions and to monitor progress over time. Local evidence and local research is much more powerful in the policy arena than "general" research.

Focus on nontrivial effects.   While thinking about writing this book, I asked a respected economist who has studied educational issues to share his thoughts on the many well-executed studies with disappointingly small or inconclusive findings. He sent me a copy of one of his studies, which found statistically significant, but relatively small positive effects of an after-school support program, accompanied by the plaintive question, "What size effect do people expect to get?"

Given the complex lives of poor urban youth, the relatively modest footprint of an after-school program in those lives, and the difficulty of designing and implementing a robust experimental study on such programs, I can understand why he believed that his study and the effect it found was an achievement. But elaborately conceived and executed experimental research with mixed, or even consistently positive results of small size do not move policy.

The experience of the past several decades suggests that very few if any single interventions or programs can consistently generate sizable effects. The What Works Clearinghouse in education has examined thousands of such studies, and the research community continues to generate dueling studies finding trivial differences on controversial interventions and policy strategies. These do not add up to positive change. It is difficult to argue for significantly increasing investments in similar research studies.

Sizable effects typically require multiple interventions in a multifaceted campaign, focused on clear goals and sustained (with intelligent adaptation) over time. Research and analysis can play important roles in such campaigns, as it has done in improvements in manufacturing, in health care, in education, and in social welfare through the still controversial War on Poverty and many other policy initiatives over time.

Concluding Thoughts on Research, Evidence, and the Politicization of Education

This chapter has ranged over a lot of territory. I have sought to make sense of political life as I have studied and experienced it, and then consider how research and evidence can help improve policy. It is evident that policy leaders and researchers of virtually every persuasion seek to employ data and evidence to support and advance their visions of what ought to be the social order. It is equally evident that research and evidence are unlikely ever to resolve once and for all the conflicts between dueling views of human nature and the world.

Political competition, however, is made more productive when research and evidence are employed in political debate. Evidence can be a mediator between conflicting worldviews, and in some cases it may even change worldviews. But evidence seems to be most powerful in the policy arena when it is modest in its aspirations—seeking to establish a shared view of the facts through commonly accepted measurements, focusing on local conditions and shared goals for improvement, and encouraging a frank and honest discussion of problems, limitations, and failures, as well as aspirations for improvement.

Notes

1. Lasswell, H. D. (1950). *Who gets what, when, and how*. New York, NY: Peter Smith, p. 3.

2. Ibid., p. 4.

3. Ibid.

4. Objectivism (Ayn Rand). (2014, September 24). In *Wikipedia*. Retrieved from http://en.wikipedia.org/wiki/Objectivism_(Ayn_Rand)

5. Altruism (ethics). (2014, September 24). In *Wikipedia*. Retrieved from http://en.wikipedia.org/wiki/Altruism_(ethics)

6. Dahl, R. A., & Lindblom, C. E. (1953). *Politics, economics, and welfare*. New York, NY: Harper & Row.

7. Jones, D. P. (1982). *Data and information for executive decisions in higher education*. Boulder, CO: NCHEMS, pp. 23–24.

8. Downs, A. (1957). *An economic theory of democracy*. New York, NY: Harper & Row, pp. 127–132.

9. Ibid., pp. 4–11.

10. Lindblom, C. E., & Cohen, D. K. (1979). *Usable knowledge: Social science and social problem solving*. New Haven, CT: Yale University Press, p. 81.

11. Knowledge Management. (2014, September 26). In *Wikipedia*. Retrieved from http://en.wikipedia.org/wiki/Knowledge_management

12. Information Management. (2014, September 26). In *Wikipedia*. Retrieved from http://en.wikipedia.org/wiki/Information_management

13. Graham, P. A. (2005). *Schooling America: How the public schools meet the nation's changing needs.* New York, NY: Oxford University Press.

14. Ravitch, D. (2000). *Left back: A century of battles over school reform.* New York, NY: Simon & Schuster.

15. Apple, M. W. (1996). *Cultural politics and education.* New York, NY: Teachers College Press.

16. Thernstrom, A., & Thernstrom, S. (2003). *No excuses: Closing the racial gap in learning.* New York, NY: Simon & Schuster.

17. Dahl, R. A., & Lindblom, C. E. (1953). *Politics, economics, and welfare.* New York, NY: Harper & Row.

18. Osborne, D., & Gabler, T. (1992). *Reinventing government: How the entrepreneurial spirit is transforming the public sector.* Reading, MA: Addison-Wesley.

19. Betts, J. R., & Tang, Y. E. (2014, August). *A meta-analysis of the literature on the effect of charter schools on student achievement.* CRPE Working Paper. Retrieved from http://www.crpe.org/sites/default/files/CRPE_meta-analysis_charter-schools-effect-student-achievement_workingpaper.pdf

Lopez, F. (2014, September 30). *Review of a meta-analysis of the literature of the effect of charter schools on student achievement.* Think Tank Reviews. Retrieved from http://nepc.colorado.edu/thinktank/review-meta-analysis-effect-charter

Betts, J. R., & Tang, Y. E. (2014, November 3). *Setting the record straight on charter schools and achievement: A reply to Francesca Lopez.* CRPE Working Paper. Retrieved from http://www.crpe.org/sites/default/files/crpe.response_to_lopez_review.11.3.2014.pdf

20. Inconclusive debates over the power of market competition to improve education are commonplace. For another example appearing while this was being written, see: The new school rules. (2014, October 11). *The Economist*, pp. 66–67; and a rebutting letter to the editor, Britain's schools. (2014, November 1). *The Economist*, p. 16.

21. Sowell, T. (2014, December 16). *Thomas Sowell Archives.* Retrieved from http://www.jewishworldreview.com/cols/sowell1.asp

See especially columns of: October 15, 2003; August 20, 2000; November 5, 1998; and April 10, 2008.

22. Walters, P. B., & Lareau, A. (2009). Education research that matters: Influence, scientific rigor, and policymaking. In P. B. Walters, A. Lareau, & S. Ranis (Eds.) *Education research on trial: Policy reform and the call for scientific rigor* (pp. 197–220). New York, NY: Routledge, p. 202.

23. Ibid.

24. Ibid., pp. 203–205.

25. Ibid., pp. 215–217.

26. Swanson, C. B., & Barlage, J. (2006, December). *Influence: A study of the factors shaping education policy.* Retrieved from http://www.edweek.org/media/influence_study.pdf

27. Institute of Education Sciences. (2015) *National Assessment of Educational Progress (NAEP)*. Retrieved from http://nces.ed.gov/nationsreportcard/

28. TIMSS & PIRLS. (2015, March 24). *TIMSS & PIRLS*. Retrieved from http:// timssandpirls.bc.edu/home/pdf/TP_About.pdf (from Bibliography)

29. National Institute of Child Health and Human Development (2000) *National Reading Panel: Teaching Children to Read*. Retrieved from https://www.nichd.nih.gov/publications/pubs/nrp/Pages/report.aspx

Bransford, J. D., Brown, A. L., Cocking, R. R. (1999) *How People Learn: Brain. mind, experience, and school*. Washington, DC: National Academy Press.

National Commission on Teaching and America's Future. (1996) *What Matters Most: Teaching for America's Future*. New York: National Commission on Teaching and America's Future:

American Diploma Project. (2004) *Ready or Not: Creating a High School Diploma that Counts*. Washington, DC: Achieve. Retrieved from http://www.achieve.org/files/ReadyorNot.pdf

30. Mosteller, F. (1995) The Tennessee study of class size in the early school grades. *Critical Issues for Children and Youths*, 5(2): 113–126. Retrieved from https://www.princeton.edu/futureofchildren/publications/docs/05_02_08.pdf

31. Walters & Lareau, p. 210.

32. Elmore, R. F. (2015, January 5). The future is learning, but what about schooling. *Inside Higher Ed*. Retrieved from https://www.insidehighered.com/blogs/higher-ed-beta/future-learning-what-about-schooling

33. Walters & Lareau, p. 211.

34. Bowen, W. G., Chingos, M. M., & McPherson, M. S. (2011). *Crossing the finish line: Completing college at America's public universities*. Princeton, NJ: Princeton University Press.

35. Bettinger, E. P., Long, B. T., Oreopoulos, P., & Sanbonmatsu, L. (2009). *The role of simplification and information in college decisions: Results from the H&R Block FAFSA experiment*. NBER Working Paper Series, 15361. Retrieved from http://www.nber.org/papers/w15361.pdf

36. Bailey, M. J. & Danziger, S. (Eds.). (2013). *Legacies of the war on poverty*. New York, NY: Russell Sage Foundation.

37. Ibid., p. 13.

38. Ibid., p. 17.

39. Gibbs, C., Ludwig, J., & Miller, D. L. (2013). Head Start origins and impacts. In M. J. Bailey, & S. Danziger (Eds.) *Legacies of the war on poverty* (pp. 39–65). New York, NY: Russell Sage Foundation.

40. Long, B. T. (2013). Supporting access to higher education. In M. J. Bailey, & S. Danziger (Eds.) *Legacies of the war on poverty* (pp. 93–120). New York, NY: Russell Sage Foundation.

41. Cacio, E., & Reber, S. (2013). The K–12 education battle. In M. J. Bailey, & S. Danziger (Eds.) *Legacies of the war on poverty* (pp. 66–92). New York, NY: Russell Sage Foundation.

42. Cohen, D. K., & Moffitt, S. L. (2009). *The ordeal of equality: Did federal regulation fix the schools?* Cambridge, MA: Harvard University Press.

43. Holzer, H. J. (2013). Workforce development programs. In M. J. Bailey, & S. Danziger (Eds.) *Legacies of the war on poverty* (pp. 121–150). New York, NY: Russell Sage Foundation.

44. Bailey & Danziger, pp. 21–25.

45. Orszag, P., & Bridgeland, J. (2013). Can government play moneyball? *The Atlantic, 312*(1), 63–66.

46. Dynarski, S. (2000). Hope for whom? Financial aid for the middle class and its impact on college attendance. *National Tax Journal, 53*(3), 2.

47. Burke, J. C. (2005). Reinventing accountability: From bureaucratic rules to performance results. In J. C. Burke and Associates (Eds.), *Achieving accountability in higher education: Balancing public, academic, and market demands* (pp. 216–245). San Francisco, CA: Jossey-Bass.

48. Schools in Chicago are called the worst by education chief. (1987, November 8). *New York Times.* Retrieved from http://www.nytimes.com/1987/11/08/us/schools-in-chicago-are-called-the-worst-by-education-chief.html

49. Ahmed-Ullah, N. S., & Byrne, J. (2014, August 27). Chicago public schools reports graduation rate up. *Chicago Tribune.* Retrieved from http://www.chicagotribune.com/news/ct-cps-graduation-rate-met-0827-20140827-story.html

50. Knowles, T. (2014, April 25). Pushing Chicago's graduation rates to new heights. *Chicago Tribune.* Retrieved from http://articles.chicagotribune.com/2014-04-25/opinion/ct-dropout-crisis-chicago-solution-perspec-0425-20140425_1_school-graduation-graduation-rate-new-heights

51. Bryk, A. S., Sebring, P. B., Allensworth, E., Luppescu, S., & Easton, J. Q. (2010). *Organizing schools for improvement: Lessons from Chicago.* Chicago, IL: University of Chicago Press.

52. Gill, J. I., & Saunders, L. (Eds.). (1992). *Developing effective policy analysis in higher education.* San Francisco, CA: Jossey-Bass. This publication offers a series of case studies that illustrate the mind-sets and skills involved in providing useful information for decision making. For a more pointed analysis, see: Layzell, D. T. (1990, October 24). Most research on higher education is stale, irrelevant, and of little use to policy makers. *Chronicle of Higher Education,* pp. B1–B3.

7

WHAT WORKS, WHEN, AND HOW: REFLECTIONS, OBSERVATIONS, AND OPINIONS

"When I look at the money spent, when I look at the programs created, when I look at the miserable outcomes and the high poverty rates, as a policy maker, (I say) 'We can do better than this and we need to figure out how.'"[1]

—Congressman Paul Ryan on LBJ's War on Poverty

"Medicare, Medicaid, Social Security, food stamps, housing programs, job training and more were all programs created and/or expanded through the War on Poverty and are some of the most powerful tools we have today to fight poverty. It's estimated that without government programs, the national poverty rate wouldn't be near today's 15 percent, or even 19 percent as it was in the 1960s, but a staggering 31 percent—almost a third of our population."[2]

—Dr. Sid Mohn, president of Heartland Alliance

This chapter (with a title obviously inspired by Harold Lasswell and the What Works Clearinghouse) will venture reflections, observations, and opinions on the two questions that have inspired this book: How can practitioners and policy makers become more successful? How can research and evidence contribute to their success?

Shaping Policy and Practice—Not Changing Worldviews

The quotes from congressman Paul Ryan and Dr. Sid Mohn illustrate starkly different perspectives and conclusions drawn from essentially the same data. Dr. Mohn, the theologically trained president of the Heartland Alliance and a member of the Ecumenical Order of Franciscans, has spent his life providing direct services to poor people—housing, job training, health care, refugee assistance. To Dr. Mohn, "ending poverty," the tagline of the Heartland Alliance, clearly requires direct assistance from government and nongovernment programs to help poor people overcome the challenges of their life situations.

As Congressman Ryan's quote indicates, he shares the objective of ending poverty. Yet, his quote and his political record make it clear that he believes that many of the government programs applauded by Dr. Mohn are ineffective and inefficient. He finds them too expensive, and he believes they interfere with personal incentives and with the market forces that, in his view, ultimately are the best means of ending poverty.

Congressman Ryan and Dr. Mohn have clear convictions about the question of poverty. It is unlikely any research or evidence will change either leader's fundamental worldview. This is not because either is intransigently resistant to dissonant evidence, but because each of their divergent views is founded on their life experience and their reading of history and current events. People who have thought about such issues tend to hold on to their opinions about how the world works. Rarely if ever can one assemble enough evidence to change a person's fundamental worldview. Even less persuasive to a person with firm ideas are arguments that his or her worldview lacks intelligence or moral standing.

Despite the persistence of conflicting worldview, policy is not established through the triumph of one worldview and the unconditional surrender of its opponents, especially in democracies and in organizations where power is shared. Policy emerges out of debate, argument, and sometimes even civil conversation among people with contrasting worldviews or blends of views. Evidence and research in some form has always played a role in shaping policy in a dialogue among diverse perspectives. Even though worldviews may resist fundamental change, policy changes continuously. Over time and generations worldviews also evolve, in response to both evidence and changing perspectives on justice and morality.

In a complex world where uncertainty is unavoidable and different views are inevitable, the task of analysts and scholars is to inform the debate among contending policy perspectives with the best available evidence. Analysts and scholars inevitably and legitimately also hold views about how the world works, but they are less likely to make a contribution when their work is focused on proving the validity or invalidity of a worldview. They are more likely to contribute by providing data and information to identify the issues warranting the attention of policy makers and to inform debates on how to address those issues.[3]

Even so, data and information do not and cannot stand entirely above the political struggle. Deborah Stone's book, *Policy Paradox and Political Reason,* is an elegant, comprehensive analysis of how different notions of policy goals, problems, and solutions depend largely, perhaps entirely, on the interests and views of different people. Differences among people (and among the circumstances of each particular political struggle) also influence how they see data and information. She writes,

> My central argument is that the categories of thought behind reasoned analysis are themselves constructed in political struggle, and nonviolent political conflict is conducted primarily through reasoned analysis. . . . Reasoned analysis is necessarily political. It always includes choices to include some things and exclude others and to view the world in a particular way when other visions are possible. Policy analysis is political argument, and vice versa.[4]

Stone's observation of pervasive, universal subjectivity does not, however, lead her to conclude that evidence has no useful role in political discourse. She astutely suggests that "while the interpretations divide people, the aspirations unite us. The process of trying to imagine the meaning of a common goal and fitting one's own interpretation to that image is a centripetal force."[5] Analysis and evidence may never be authoritative and definitive in the political process, but it can still be a powerful tool for shaping opinion, expanding mental horizons, and forging a wider, workable consensus on important issues.

Undesirable Variation: The Core Issue in Most Complex Social Problems

Our successes in solving many relatively simple, straightforward problems of policy and practice have misled some to imagine that science and evidence can just as easily solve more complex problems. Educating all children, improving health outcomes at scale, and achieving widespread economic prosperity and mobility are far more difficult than the nontrivial but simpler problems of providing clean water, proper sanitation, and effective transportation systems. In the real world, "what works" for complex problems is not going to be simple.

The confirmed skeptic or the frustrated, impatient practitioner and policy maker may conclude nothing works. More accurately, however, no *thing* works. No single program, no single policy, no simple pill-like interventions can solve complex problems of policy and practice. Successful parents, entrepreneurs, and teachers do not rely on one-dimensional strategies or formulaic guidebooks to raise children; build a business; or teach reading, mathematics, or piano. Instead, they learn what they can through observation and study; use what they have learned in a spirit of experimentation; and interact with children, colleagues, clients, or customers to discover what "works" in the particular situations confronting them.

Except in extreme situations, the problems facing policy makers and practitioners are not categorical; rarely are the results absolute failure or absolute success, life or death. The usual problems of policy and practice are unacceptable variation in results. Too many students fail to complete a course of study, too many people fail to find jobs, too many people fail to recover from illness, or too many people live in poverty. The work of reducing unacceptable variation in performance is intrinsically much more difficult than the work of achieving acceptable performance where it has already been achieved. Those in the population who are successfully educated, employed, or healthy are not a problem—the systems of policy and practice have worked for them. The challenge is to discover "what works" for the people left out.

Accordingly, to reduce or to eliminate (the putative goal of No Child Left Behind) undesirable variation in the outcomes of complex processes is a heavy lift by definition; one should not be surprised that it is hard to achieve dramatically significant results. In writing the history of Title I, David Cohen and Susan Moffitt suggest that raising national aspirations for educating poor children without increasing the capabilities of the educators working in the system redefined the educators as incompetent with no change in their abilities and effort.[6] This does not deny the importance of the goal; it simply recognizes that reaching a higher goal is likely to require different practices and capabilities from those required for less ambitious goals.

Chapter 1 argued that it is unrealistic to expect science to discover simple interventions that work for improving outcomes in complex human systems and social organizations. Chapter 2 reviewed the contributions of experimental science in improving practice and social policy, and concluded that the limitations of randomized clinical trials in identifying "proven" interventions are more evident than their contributions over the several decades they have been the "gold standard." It is unrealistic to expect dramatically significant results from controlled experiments testing solutions for complex problems, but nothing less than significant results can be wholly satisfying.

Following these downbeat discussions, Chapters 3 and 4 wrestled with the challenges of measurement in social policy. Chapter 5 considered the potential of qualitative research approaches and described initiatives to improve practice in medicine, remedial mathematics education, and social work. Chapter 6 stepped back to consider the challenges of using evidence in policy decision-making processes that are shaped largely by interests and previously established views. It also offered suggestions for influencing policy and connecting it to practice. The goal of this chapter is to draw on and pull together those observations in order to propose pathways for actual improvement. Although intended to be relevant to many areas of policy and practice, this chapter will focus primarily on the goal of increasing educational attainment at scale.

Measuring for Improvement, Despite the Land Mines

Measurement is difficult to get right; measurement is often misused; and measurement can be overrated as a solution to problems. Despite the land mines, it is not possible to improve policy or practice without measurement. The very concept of improvement requires a scale for measuring a condition and changes in that condition over time.

The power of measurement is demonstrated by the frequency and the variety of ways by which it is employed by people with a change agenda. The *equity scorecards* developed by Estella Bensimon and her colleagues focus attention on disparities in persistence and postsecondary academic achievement among students from different racial and social groups. Within institutions, these scorecards are used to identify and focus on practices that erect barriers and perpetuate inequities in outcomes for such students. From an internal perspective, the equity scorecards encourage faculty and administrators to recognize their responsibility to pursue more equitable outcomes.[7]

From a different angle, the practice of grading elementary and secondary schools *A* to *F*, notably in Florida but spreading to other states, is promoted as a means of externally forcing institutional change. Yet another example is the currently controversial practice of using measures of student achievement as a means of evaluating and rewarding teacher performance. Measurement in this case is intended to encourage and reward effective teaching and to focus corrective attention on ineffectiveness.

Although measurement is universally employed for such purposes, it is difficult to find universally accepted measures in social policy and practice. Disagreements on the acceptability of measures may be based on technical grounds such as reliability and validity. They may be also based on fears or evidence of misuse emanating from technical flaws or from disagreements about the implications of or the potential use of the data. One especially common misuse of data is focusing on a single measure, such as the average score of a school or the percentage of students above a single score. Typically, variation within an institution or classroom is much greater than variation among them. Proper use of measurement requires examining context and the distribution of scores, not simply the central tendency. George Kuh's article "Risky Business: Promises and Pitfalls of Institutional Transparency" provides a useful overview of these and other measurement land mines.[8]

Without question, some schools and teachers perform exceptionally poorly. It is rarely difficult to identify them because many measures—completion rates, test scores, teacher turnover, suspensions and expulsions, observations of classroom teaching, and the rest—usually point in the same direction. In these situations it is irresponsible not to take corrective action, even drastic corrective action if low performance persists. Experienced urban school superintendents have learned that knowing exactly what to do and how do to it are more challenging than knowing something must be done.

The misuse of measurement often occurs when a single measure or small group of measures is given undue weight in making decisions or judgments about people, schools, or educational strategies. For example, the large volume of research attempting to prove or disprove the superiority of charter schools over noncharter schools is essentially a waste of time, effort, and money. The amount of variation among charter schools and among noncharter schools far exceeds the variation different studies may find between the two organizational strategies. Much more useful is research learning what helps particular schools be successful within these two organizational approaches. The following research on Chicago Public Schools is an exemplary model.

Some argue that measurement is useful especially or even only when it is connected to high stakes. The theory of change for the new standards movement of the 1990s suggested that students and teachers would do what it takes to reach a higher standard if passing a well-designed, authentic assessment were required for high school graduation. This turned out to be a flawed theory. The behavioral responses to high-stakes standards have been multiple, noncomparable standards and assessments; cut scores placed low enough so nearly everybody could pass; cheating; and fraud.

A useful measure, one that can inspire and inform improvement, must be accepted as reliable and valid for the purposes for which it is intended by the policy makers, practitioners, and other stakeholders affected by its use. (The discussion of *consequential validity* in Chapter 3 elaborates on this point.) A measure can be useful for one purpose but not another. For example, learning assessments at the state or district level may be useful to identify issues that require attention but are too coarse-grained to evaluate the effectiveness of individual teachers or relatively small instructional units. Acceptability will be harder to win if the stakes are high and if it is complicated and difficult to measure the variable. Wide acceptance of a measure is also unlikely if it is employed, in fact or by implication, to force changes in behavior on unwilling people or institutions.

High stakes artificially amplify the significance of a single measure and emphasize categorical judgment; moderate stakes are more naturally proportionate to the situation. They keep measures in perspective and offer opportunities for improvement.[9] If the purpose of the measurement is improvement, not external accountability, and the stakes are moderate, stakeholders can often be convinced to "own" the data, to improve its quality as needed, and to use it constructively.

Uses of Measurement in Educational Policy

Policy is generally understood to involve the principles and guiding actions of a government or governing body (as well as the actions themselves collectively) that are intended to achieve specific purposes. The tools of policy include establishing laws and regulations requiring or prohibiting certain behaviors, allocating resources to achieve these goals, specifying the purposes for which resources may be used, and providing information to the public as a means of shaping choices in the marketplace.

The measurement of social outcomes is commonly and appropriately used to guide policy priorities and strategies. It is difficult to imagine a meaningful policy discussion without measurement of an outcome or situation that warrants policy attention. Especially recently, measurement has played a critical role in making education a high public priority in the United States. International measures of educational attainment have documented worldwide increases in educational attainment and the erosion of U.S. educational superiority in comparison to other developed countries.[10] A large, growing body of literature has debated the strengths and weaknesses of these measures, but given the consistency of their general direction, it is difficult to believe they are far off the mark.

In addition to the information provided by comparative international data, salaries and wages and employment rates in the United States have increasingly shown a high correlation among educational attainment, employability, and income. The implications of these data for economic prosperity and global competitiveness, combined with the importance of an educated population in democracies, have made educational attainment an urgent public policy priority across the political spectrum in the United States.

In response to this growing priority, new and improved measurement resources have been developed to make the components and drivers of educational attainment more visible. The Measuring Up initiative (described in detail in Chapter 3) provided a framework of benchmarks for state policy makers to identify barriers and establish priorities for improving educational attainment. Also as described in Chapter 3, U.S. educators have developed longitudinal student-record systems to improve understanding of educational pathways, significant new tools to assess student learning, and quite extensive common education data standards.

Improving the quality of data and measurement as a means of identifying policy issues and evaluating policy effectiveness is widely approved by policy makers across party lines. Benchmarking data from Measuring Up and its cousin Quality Counts stimulate action and appear as debating points in the policy making process. The U.S. Chamber of Commerce Foundation has developed its own publication, *Leaders and Laggards,*[11] for rating educational state policy effectiveness.

Although the use of data as a general source of information for guiding policy and setting priorities is rarely controversial, the use of data as an instrument for triggering specific policy actions has been a constant source of contention. The critical issues involve not only whether the validity and reliability of specific measurements are robust enough to justify direct policy responses but also who has the legitimate authority to take action based on the data.

As the precision, breadth, and depth of data and information have improved, both the federal government and state governments have increasingly employed or explored using performance measurement as a tool for allocating budgetary resources. The contributions and limitations of this tendency will be considered later in this chapter.

Uses of Measurement in Educational Practice

The measurement of learning has a long history in education. The purpose typically has been to determine which students are qualified to advance to the next level of instruction based on qualitative assessments and quantitative counts of the number of discrete problems solved correctly. Thomas Jefferson's recommendation for public education in Virginia is an instructive example of this purpose.

In his 1787 *Notes on the State of Virginia,* Thomas Jefferson advocated 3 years of free universal education. Believing democracy required voters who could read, Jefferson concluded 3 years of universal education were essential for democracy to survive. But Jefferson also believed in a natural meritocracy. He proposed that after 3 years the "boy of best genius" in each local school should be sent to one of 20 grammar schools for 1 or 2 more years of free education. Then the "best genius" in each grammar school would be given 6 more years of free education. Through this means, Jefferson wrote, "twenty of the best geniuses will be raked from the rubbish annually." Finally, the best 10 of these 20 students would be given a 3-year scholarship to William and Mary.[12]

Although I've seen no record that Jefferson's plan was ever implemented, it is a good example of high-stakes, nonstandardized assessment. In the twentieth century, the development of standardized college admissions tests was an effort to make such sorting/selecting functions for college admissions more objective and fair. Nicholas Lemann's *The Big Test: The Secret History of the American Meritocracy* is an engaging account of the initial but temporary effectiveness of standardized testing in broadening opportunity and fairness.[13] The generation that benefited from the development of standardized tests has now mitigated the objectivity and fairness of these instruments by purchasing test preparation services for its children. John Katzman, creator of the Princeton Review, is a particularly trenchant critic of standardized tests.[14]

In the twenty-first century, sorting and selecting with high stakes is still an important and perhaps still the dominant function of measurement in education. We are establishing cut scores for college readiness, grading schools from *A* to *F*, and assessing teachers in part based on the learning outcomes of their students. These purposes still reflect the sorting/selecting tradition, but within them are the seeds of a shift in the function of educational measurement. In fits and starts, measurement is becoming a tool for improvement and for pursuing more widespread attainment.

Although the theories of change have been questioned, the three examples in the previous paragraph are all associated with efforts to achieve broader and higher educational attainment. Clear assessments of college readiness are intended to help more students become adequately prepared; schools are being graded to expose high rates of failure and stimulate better performance; and assessing teacher performance based on student learning is intended promote better teaching. The critics of these efforts make the following charges:

- The pace of learning varies among children, and standard expectations by grade or age level are inappropriate because they are insufficiently sensitive to developmental variation.
- Standardized tests cannot accurately assess critical thinking and the ability to use knowledge and skill to solve problems, especially complex, "unscripted" problems.
- The benefits of grading schools *A* to *F* are outweighed by the negative effects of stigmatization in stimulating defensiveness and erecting greater barriers to improvement.
- It is unwise and potentially unfair to assess teacher capability on the basis of measured student learning. The measures are imprecise and unstable over time, too many factors not in the teacher's control are

in play, and no single measure can be sufficiently reliable and valid for assessing a teacher's impact on the complex process of student learning.

With some qualifications, I agree with all of these criticisms. Employing unavoidably imprecise measures to make decisions with high-stakes consequences tends to erect barriers to improvement rather than remove them. But the solution is not to resist measurement or to pursue impossibly perfect measurement. A better strategy is constantly to improve the quality and quantity of measurement about practice, while using measurement wisely for improvement, not primarily for categorical sorting and selecting.

Later in this chapter, I provide cases where measurement has been used as a tool to improve performance. Before getting to those concrete examples, the following list is suggested as a distillation of principles for the sound use of measurement:

- Improvement in policy and practice requires measurement. Within reasonable bounds of cost in relation to benefit, the more measurement, the better. Measurement adds discipline to analysis and broadens understanding. Measurement also can help practitioners and policy makers focus on priorities.

- The most powerful and useful measures are widely accepted as valid for the intended purpose by all relevant stakeholders. If the data and metrics based on the data are difficult to understand or their quality or appropriate use is in dispute, measurement has less value. It risks becoming a distraction and an impediment to improvement in policy and practice.

- Scholars and policy analysts can make significant contributions by developing and facilitating the use of relevant, high-quality measures of valued outcomes. Developing a robust, credible measure of an important outcome is likely to improve policy and practice significantly more than a portfolio of studies demonstrating modest causal impacts.

- "Good enough" measurement (rough indicators such as academic progression; feedback from quick, low-cost surveys as in Carnegie's "practical measurement"; etc.) can be quite valuable in guiding practice by signaling that an issue needs attention. When high stakes are avoided, modest, frequent investments in low-cost measurements or examining readily available administrative data can be very helpful.

- "Everything that counts can't be counted," Einstein is reported to have said, and qualitative inquiry is an important tool for developing theory and strategies for improving policy and practice. Improvement, however, depends on the discipline of benchmarks and relevant quantitative measures. Complex outcomes can be quantified through systematic, reasonably reliable ratings based on expert qualitative observations.

- The appropriate role of policy is to focus on broad issues and broad measures. When policy makers employ fine-grained data or take actions intending to directly influence or control practice, the potential for harmful error, cumbersome rigidity, and inefficiency increases significantly. Einstein also is reported to have said, "Everything should be made as simple as possible, but not simpler."

- The role of practice is to improve outcomes for individuals. Fine-grained measurement is vital, but the consequences of measurement error can be serious. Triangulation and multiple observations are critically important. And protecting the privacy of individual data is absolutely essential.

- The appropriate role of measurement is to inform the use of other tools in policy and practice. Measurement is not in itself an effective instrument for improvement. "Naming and shaming" is a misguided improvement strategy. Measurement isolated from context, used uncritically and mechanically, can make a problem worse, not better.

Measuring What Matters

The cliché "you get what you measure" is often heard in educational policy circles. But deciding what to measure is a nontrivial task in education, as it is for all organizations whose primary mission is creating nonmonetary goods.[15] The multiple-choice standardized test, which dominated educational measurement in the twentieth century, did a serviceable job when combined with high school grades of predicting who would succeed in college. As a tool for increasing actual educational attainment, or even measuring the educational outcomes that really matter, it is a weak reed.

The educational outcomes that really matter involve authentic understanding and the ability to use knowledge, not simply breadth of knowledge and the ability to answer the questions on an artificial test. In the 1980s, after extensive study, Arthur Chickering and Zelda Gamson concluded that seven factors undergird effective teaching and learning in undergraduate education: (a) contact between students and faculty; (b) reciprocity and cooperation among students; (c) active learning techniques; (d) prompt feedback; (e) time on task; (f) high expectations; and (g) respect for diverse talents and ways of learning.[16]

Other significant research on undergraduate education in this period, especially the work of Alexander Astin and Robert Pace, created a framework for understanding the factors that contribute to a quality postsecondary education.[17] This understanding, and a desire to create a substantive alternative to college "ratings" based on selectivity, class size, and other superficial factors associated with prestige, inspired the creation of the National Survey of Student Engagement (NSSE). NSSE has been used by more than 1,600 colleges and universities since 2000 to examine and improve the quality of undergraduate instruction.[18]

Contact between teacher and student may be presumed in K–12 education, but reports from the field suggest that teaching to multiple-choice tests has degraded active learning and student engagement. A high school version of the National Survey of Student Engagement is available, but it is not well known or widely used. More frequent assessments of student engagement in K–12 education would be a useful complement to direct assessments of student learning.[19]

Student engagement, of course, is an essential means to an end, not the ultimate objective. Gradually, both K–12 and postsecondary educators are developing both definitions and assessments of the learning that really matters. The Common Core Standards for Mathematics and English Language Arts sought to identify the learning objectives in those subjects whose attainment constitute essential preparation for college and careers after high school. The Essential Learning Outcomes, established by the Association of American Colleges and Universities as part of its Liberal Education and America's Promise (LEAP) initiative, describe and define the knowledge and skills associated with a baccalaureate degree. Building on and elaborating the LEAP objectives, the Degree Qualifications Profile describes the learning objectives for associate's, bachelor's, and master's degrees in postsecondary education.

The assessments of Common Core learning objectives developed by the Smarter Balanced Assessment Consortium and the Program for Assessing Readiness for College and Careers employ more questions that require constructed responses and writing in order to assess authentic understanding and the ability to use knowledge. In postsecondary education, the Collegiate Learning Assessment (CLA) has been an important advance in assessing critical thinking skills, writing, and problem-solving abilities.[20] Another important contribution is the

Critical Thinking Assessment Test (CAT) developed with National Science Foundation support at the Center for the Assessment and Improvement of Learning at Tennessee Tech University.[21] Moving beyond even these standardized tests, however, educators, especially in postsecondary education, are developing rubrics for comparable assessments of student achievement in complex assignments.[22] Taking this practice to its logical conclusion, some institutions are requiring students to create portfolios of their work as evidence of meeting the requirements of a degree.

The point of these efforts is not to improve assessments, but to develop assessment tools that can help generate more widespread, high-quality attainment. It may not be possible with great precision and reliability to measure problem-solving ability, knowledge utilization, and creativity, but it is possible to make useful comparative judgments of academic work products. A loss of precision in measuring authentic learning can be offset by gains in consequential validity and utility.

Over several decades, the leaders of the assessment movement in postsecondary education have achieved slow but steady progress in pursuit of this challenging goal. *Using Evidence of Student Learning to Improve Higher Education*, a recent publication by the National Institute for Learning Outcomes Assessment, is an impressive account of growing capabilities, more widespread impact, and the remaining challenges.[23]

Understanding the System: The Case of Research on Chicago Schools

Measurement is essential for identifying unacceptable variation in a social outcome and monitoring improvement. Understanding the systems that create and sustain unacceptable variation in outcomes is essential for improving those outcomes.

In 1990, stimulated by the Chicago School Reform Act that radically decentralized public schools, Anthony Bryk and his colleagues at the Consortium on Chicago School Research launched a sustained and still continuing effort to understand Chicago public schools in order to help them improve. The following paragraph from *Organizing Schools for Improvement* captures what may be the most important observation from their research:

> Schools are complex organizations consisting of multiple interacting subsystems. Each subsystem involves a mix of human and social factors that shape the actual activities that occur and the meaning that individuals attribute to these events. These social interactions are bounded by various

rules, roles, and prevailing practices that, in combination with technical resources, constitute schools as formal organizations. In a simple sense, almost everything interacts with everything else.[24]

The research of the Consortium sought to understand these schools and the factors and systems within and around them that contributed to their relative effectiveness or ineffectiveness. Without attempting to summarize this incredibly rich body of work, I will try to convey in the next few pages the research approaches employed, some of their major findings, and the principles that led and continue to lead to improvements in outcomes.

Comparable, Valid Measurement of Crucial Outcome Variables

Although many outcomes are important in Chicago Schools, none are more important than student attendance and progress in reading and mathematics. To be useful, the Consortium's research program had to be anchored in valid, reliable measures of these outcomes that were comparable among schools. Improvement on these indicators was the bottom line for improvement in school effectiveness.

Measuring attendance is quite straightforward, but it was necessary to adjust school attendance rates modestly to reflect changes in school demographics over time. Achieving comparability on learning and assessing actual learning gains was more complex.

Chicago Public Schools annually administered the Iowa Test of Basic Skills to most elementary students. Although these tests provided a source of data on student learning, considerable effort was required to turn the data into useful information for research. First, results from these tests typically were reported in a simple statistic—the percentage of students at or above grade level. This statistic is sensitive only to movement of students near the grade level point. Improved learning of those well below or well above grade level is not captured by gains or losses in this indicator, so deceptively strong gains might be reported by improving the performance of only 5% of the students—those just under grade level. The Consortium focused on the average scores of all students, rather than the percentage of those at or above grade level.

Second, the norm-referenced test scores for each grade were not comparable across grades, and different versions of the tests yielded different grade equivalents for the same students tested at the same time. The Consortium research team analyzed students' performance on individual items across different tests to create a content referenced test, rather than a norm referenced test so test scores at the end of fifth grade could be validly compared with test scores at the end of sixth grade for an individual student—actual learning gains.

Third, school performance was assessed only using pretest and posttest scores of students enrolled in a school for the full academic year. For a series of 7 years from 1990 to 1996 this analysis enabled the Consortium to identify by school whether students on average made normal progress during a year, lost ground, or gained more than average by grade level during each of the years.

Over 7 years, and without a system of high-stakes accountability, the average Chicago elementary school improved productivity (i.e., the size of annual learning gains) in reading by 5% and productivity in mathematics by 12%. More than 80% of schools improved at least somewhat in mathematics, and nearly 70% of schools showed some learning gains in reading.[25]

Probing to Discover the Drivers of Improvement

The Consortium's research was launched in part to examine the effects of Chicago's decentralization of public schools. Local school councils were elected with the power to hire and fire principals, and principals were given control over a meaningful amount of discretionary funds. Important research questions for the Consortium were: Did this reform lead to improvement? If so, where and why?

The data on attendance and student learning discussed previously provided information on school improvement in individual schools. Over 7 years, the Consortium found that roughly one third of Chicago's schools clearly moved forward with improvement, one third showed mixed results and signs of struggle, and one third showed little progress. Although the average performance of the system improved, it was important to educators and policy makers to understand the factors that helped some schools improve and those that seemed to hold others back.

From its research the Consortium developed a framework of five essential organizational supports for influencing student engagement and learning. They then examined the prevalence of these essential supports in improving and nonimproving schools. A variety of research techniques including direct observation and surveys were used to study schools using this framework over an extended period.

The five essential supports are:

1. *Leadership as the driver for change.* Principals scored high on this dimension if they encouraged inclusive faculty and community involvement, if they were actively and effectively engaged in instructional leadership, and if they actively implemented the school improvement plan (SIP) developed in collaboration with the local school council.

2. *Parent community ties.* This support was measured by assessing the extent to which teachers were familiar with the community, had personal ties to the community, and used community resources in their work. Teacher outreach to parents and parent involvement in the school were also assessed.

3. *Professional capacity.* Teachers' professional background, their knowledge and skill, and the frequency and quality of professional development were indicators of professional capacity. In addition, teachers' attitudes toward innovation and their commitment to the school, their "work orientation," was assessed. Finally, six measures of *professional community* were included in this category—public classroom practice, reflective dialogue, peer collaboration, new teacher socialization, collective responsibility for improvement, and a focus on student learning.

4. *Student-centered learning climate.* The climate for learning was assessed by examining two broad dimensions: safety and order, and academic support and press. The term *academic support and press* is shorthand for academic pressure, persistent demands for student effort, delivered in a supportive teaching and learning environment. These survey questions examined the norms for behavior in the school, the level of academic engagement, and peer support for academic work.

5. *Instructional guidance.* Two dimensions of instruction were examined: the extent to which the content and pacing of the curriculum in the school was coherent and aligned; and the relative balance among didactic, basic skills instruction, and instruction that promoted active student engagement and the application of knowledge.[26]

The Utility of Research Findings

The Consortium found persuasive evidence of strong relationships between these essential supports and gains both in student attendance and in reading and mathematics. Unsurprisingly, the relationships between supports and particular outcomes, and the interrelations between supports, are generally what one would expect. Leadership is highly correlated with the other essential supports. All the essential supports are correlated with improved student learning. A safe and orderly environment coupled with engaging, applied instruction is related to improved attendance. Problems with safety and order are more likely to occur in contexts with weak community support. Schools with problems in safety and order are also likely to overemphasize basic skills and didactic instruction.[27]

Two general findings from the Consortium research warrant special mention. First, the research found that relational trust among adults in the school community, facilitated by smaller school size and stability, is strongly associated with school improvement. High trust is strongly related to positive change in professional capacity (elaborated previously), parent involvement, and safety and order.[28]

Second, the Consortium examined the influence of the external community on schools in order to consider whether external factors make it especially difficult for some schools to develop the essential supports for improvement. In Chicago, many neighborhoods are poor and virtually all are predominantly non-White, but such neighborhoods are not all the same. Some have more social capital, as measured by participation in local religious organizations, a sense of collective efficacy, and connections to outside resources, than others.[29] Some have higher rates of crime and larger numbers of abused and neglected children enrolled in the schools. Schools in neighborhoods with low social capital, high crime, and many abused and neglected children rarely find the resources necessary for improvement.[30]

From an academic perspective, this research is a persuasive analysis demonstrating the importance of these essential supports in an effective school. From the perspective of policy and practice, it provides guidance for educators and policy makers who want to generate improvement. This kind of research can make visible and measurable the necessary system of essential supports for increasing educational attainment and addressing comparable social challenges. It also can provide the infrastructure for monitoring the presence and health of essential supports in order to achieve continuing improvement. Leaders who have the necessary vision and persistence can use such research to develop and guide the implementation of successful strategies for improvement.

Harnessing, Not Fighting, Human Agency in Accountability for Improvement

Accountability for improvement is and should be unavoidable. But productive accountability must take into account the role human agency plays in the complex, adaptive systems of policy and practice. The choices people make in supporting or resisting the implementation of a policy or practice are an enormously important factor determining its effectiveness.

Douglas McGregor's *The Human Side of Enterprise* described two sharply contrasting views of human motivation and behavior in organizations. Theory X presumes that workers are fundamentally uninterested in being effective and productive in their jobs. They must be closely supervised and held accountable in detail for the quantity and quality of their work. Theory Y presumes that people are motivated to be successful, take pride in their work, and, if so encouraged and permitted, will freely exercise creativity and self-discipline in order to be more productive.[31]

The distinctions Paul Hill and Mary Beth Celio make between intrinsic and extrinsic factors as drivers for improvement in *Fixing Urban Schools* are similarly relevant to human agency. Some theories of change argue that intrinsic factors such as teacher commitment; collaborative deliberation and learning, professional and community standards; voluntary professional development; and active parental participation are the primary drivers of improved school effectiveness. Others argue that the primary drivers of improvement are extrinsic factors such as performance incentives and the pressure of market choices and competition among schools, vendors, and educational products and systems.[32]

The presence and impact of all these contrasting perspectives on human motivation can be supported with empirical evidence. To an extent, all of them are always in play. With no extrinsic incentives (or sanctions), it is difficult to imagine that practitioners or policy makers will consistently do their very best. But it is equally hard to imagine that complex, challenging problems can be solved by people who lack intrinsic motivation, engagement, creativity, and capability. Most, perhaps all, significant human achievements seem to involve uncoerced motivation and personal investment.

Accurately or not, in the United States the accountability movement has been widely perceived by practitioners as externally driven, largely based on Theory X ideas about management. The accountability movement may have advanced educational progress, but I suspect that greater progress would have been obtained from approaches that struck a better balance among external pressure and support, external incentives, and intrinsic motivation.

Theory X and Theory Y were evidently in play in one chapter of my career. In 2005, the report of the State Higher Education Executive Officers' National Commission on Accountability in Higher Education sought to reframe the public dialogue on accountability, to encourage shared responsibility and a division of labor between policy makers and educators, and to promote accountability as an instrument of self-discipline and improvement.[33] For many reasons it did not achieve the public visibility and attention of the commission appointed a year later by Secretary of Education Margaret Spellings, which, while addressing comparable issues, struck a different, less collaborative tone.[34] Clearly, the Theory X approach, with the implicit threat of governmental sanctions, generated more conversation and attention than Theory Y. It is difficult to know whether the Spellings Commission's positive effects on actual practice (I believe there were some) outweighed the obvious resistance it generated.

Any effort to improve the effectiveness of policy or practice must consider the balance between extrinsic and intrinsic factors, between externally and internally motivated and driven change strategies. The Networked Improvement Communities initiative described in Chapter 5 is an example of a disciplined, accountable strategy for improvement that emphasizes internal motivation and expertise, and partnerships between practitioners and researchers, while keeping supervisory authority in the background. It begins with a collaborative effort in analyzing the problem and designing potential solutions. It also creates for participants a safe environment to examine data about comparative effectiveness as a catalyst for conversations about learning how to improve.

Deliverology, defined as "a systematic process for driving progress and delivering results in government and the public sector" by its leader Sir Michael Barber, is similar in analytic discipline, but it differs significantly in its top-down orientation with a management process led by a *delivery unit*.[35] The top-down approach of deliverology, an improvement strategy of the Labor Government of British prime minister Tony Blair, logically follows the structure of a parliamentary system with a unified executive/legislative government. In the United States, with its federal system including checks and balances embedded in every level of government, such a strategy would likely have a very steep uphill climb.

The deliverology approach is far too sophisticated to ignore the importance of human agency, but it leads with systems analysis and the design of problem-solving strategies. After more than 200 pages, the final section of the book, "Unleash the 'Alchemy of Relationships,'" acknowledges the importance of human agency. The inclusion of this section, even as an apparent afterthought, is yet another indication that a change strategy cannot fully succeed without achieving a synergistic balance between the intrinsic and extrinsic components of human motivation.

Balancing Measurement for Improvement and Accountability

Others have written extensively about the difficulty of resolving the tension between measurement for improvement and measurement for accountability.[36] This problem is similar to the tension between sorting through the many facets of complex, adaptive systems and the desire for simple proofs concerning what works in policy and practice. Identifying a single source of substandard performance is just as difficult as identifying a simple cure for it.

A valid, direct link between a measured outcome and accountability for performance is possible and appropriate only for discrete tasks—getting a base hit in baseball, completing an operation on an assembly line, showing up for work, responding to requests, properly inserting a needle into a vein, and the like. Such discrete tasks are part of every job.

The outcomes for more complicated processes, such as managing a factory or baseball team or teaching a student, however, are determined by not just by the performance of an individual worker but also by the situation and by the contributions of others. Summative judgments are necessary in complex situations, but such judgments are less likely to go astray when many factors, qualitative and quantitative, are taken into consideration and no single measurement is given undue weight.

Judging, confronting, and correcting inadequate performance is difficult, so supervisors and managers sometimes prefer automatic, measurable triggers that lessen their responsibility for making and defending difficult decisions based on complex judgments. Only weak or ambiguous evidence supports the notion that specific performance targets attached to rewards improve performance. Experimental studies by behavioral economist Dan Ariely suggest that high-stakes performance assessments based on specific metrics actually degrade rather than improve performance.[37] In my experience, performance assessment systems that employ multiple performance targets and metrics in an effort to reflect job complexity lead to fuzzy priorities and a false sense of precision in the validity of the assessment.

In collective bargaining situations, contractual rules are often designed to reduce or eliminate supervisor judgment in performance assessment. This reinforces the tendency of managers to devise and employ quantitative measures of performance, which generally are inadequate for assessing performance in complex jobs. Using explicit quantitative measures for accountability often has perverse side effects—gaming, cheating, setting easy targets, or the neglect of critical but less-measureable functions.

Accountability tools are needed to identify problems and to deal with the individuals and organizations that are incapable or are unwilling to improve. But the modest improvement in educational progress after decades of hard-edged accountability suggests that accountability by itself is not a very powerful instrument for achieving substantial improvement. Based on extensive analysis of successful businesses, Jeffrey Pfeffer observes: "The growing emphasis on individual accountability—something, by the way that is completely inconsistent with the lessons of the quality movement—hinders learning and even discovering mistakes." Cultivating a mind-set of shared responsibility to solve problems and achieve improvement is more productive.[38]

Actual improvement seems to require much deeper understanding of the organizations and situations involved and the willing engagement and cooperation of the people who work in them. The most useful approaches to accountability will acknowledge the complexity of policy and practice, the difficulty of isolating the independent contributions of any individual in complex tasks, and the difficulty of taking into account and measuring accurately all of the factors involved in producing an outcome. When an appreciation of complexity and a sense of shared responsibility are present, a leader is more likely to be able to engage the creativity and commitment of practitioners in finding pathways for improvement.

Such collaboration between management and labor seems uncommon, especially when collective bargaining contracts govern most of the relationships between managers and employees. I once heard the superintendent of Denver Public Schools, now senator, Michael Bennet say, "It is no wonder we have restrictive work rules in union contracts when you consider the command and control techniques we've traditionally used to manage education." It will not be easy to untangle the knots that make collaboration for improvement difficult in public education, but labor and management leaders should make it a priority.

Illuminating Fundamental Issues of Practice

Complexity makes it extremely difficult to discover neat solutions to most human problems, but it does not preclude the discovery of useful knowledge. Herbert Simon, in *The Sciences of the Artificial*,[39] suggests that *organized complexity* (as defined by Warren Weaver and considered in Chapter 1) takes the form of a hierarchy of interrelated subsystems. Physical and biological hierarchies are typically described in spatial terms, and social hierarchies are described in terms of interactions. Better understanding the fundamental subsystems at play within people and societies can enable us to solve problems, not with the mechanistic, reductionist knowledge feasible in the study of less-complex systems, but with approximate knowledge based on experience as well as research and analysis.

Lacking a generally accepted, precise definition of a *fundamental subsystem* or *issue of practice*, I mean here a characteristic of human beings or human relationships that exists independently from any particular context but operates in all or many situations. Such fundamental issues can be explored through research on, for example, the effects of stress on the body and on decision making, and the behavioral reactions of people in certain circumstances. Such fundamental social subsystems play a role in all situations of practice, even though the interplay among various factors produces variation in outcomes.

Simon summarizes the findings of research on human problem solving as follows:

> All that we have learned . . . points to the same conclusion: that human problem solving, from the most blundering to the most insightful, involves nothing more than varying mixtures of trial and error and selectivity. The selectivity derives from various rules of thumb, or heuristics, that suggest which paths should be tried first, and which leads are promising.[40]

Selective judgments are made based on feedback from the environment, the observation of stable patterns, and the lessons of past experience.[41] Policy makers and practitioners will not find easy, guaranteed solutions to complex problems, but they can improve their decision making by employing the findings of research, analysis, and experimentation on fundamental human dynamics.

Although we lack fully dependable solutions for the riddles of complexity, observing stable patterns can help. Management consultant Joseph M. Juran suggested from his experience that roughly 80% of the effects one finds come from 20% of the causes. He used the term *Pareto principle* to describe this rule because his experience paralleled Pareto's observation that 80% of the land in Europe was owned by 20% of the people, and 20% of pea pods in his garden contained 80% of the peas.[42] As a rule of thumb, this principle is employed by Anthony Bryk and his colleagues in Networked Improvement Communities to identify the most significant factors affecting student performance before designing interventions that might change a negative trajectory. Correlations found through data analytics (discussed next in this chapter) can also be employed to identify potential causal factors or promising points for an intervention.

Frequently, research that illuminates fundamental issues corroborates common sense, or ordinary knowledge, to use the language of Lindblom and Cohen. George Kuh's research on high-impact practices shows that students who participate in activities that include unusually high levels of effort over an extended period of time, substantive interactions with faculty and peers, and timely feedback are more likely to be academically successful.[43] Equally logical are the findings of the Consortium on Chicago School Research that improvement in student achievement is correlated with leadership in schools and trust within the school community.[44] So is the finding of Bowen, Chingos, and McPherson that able students do better when they attend institutions that challenge them and expect student success, rather than institutions that have lower expectations.[45]

When interrelated social systems are complex and without clear hierarchical relationships to simplify the understanding of interactions, it is harder to develop useful insights. For example, the many social and political subsystems that come into play in public education are not all organized in clear hierarchical relationships. In his analysis of Success for All, discussed more extensively in Chapter 2, Donald Peurach, citing Simon, suggests that the failure to recognize nonhierarchical complexity in a stubborn search for linear solutions is often a barrier to understanding and successful adaptation.[46]

Using Data Analytics to Improve Performance

Predictive analytics have long been used to help decision makers avoid risky decisions through sorting and selecting. Insurance companies have used predictive analysis to avoid insuring poor drivers or to charge them very high premiums to offset the risk. Selective colleges have used analysis to avoid admitting students likely to fail academically. They have also used analysis to predict admissions yield and to adjust pricing through tuition discounts in order to meet their enrollment and financial targets.

Now, however, exponential increases in the collection of data and in the capability to analyze data are creating previously unimaginable opportunities to improve performance in educational practice. Educators are beginning to have opportunities to use analytics not just to sort and select, but also to: (a) identify and ameliorate risk factors rather than avoid them; and (b) analyze the learning process in order to improve its effectiveness.

Institutional researchers in colleges and universities have begun to employ data from their instructional and administrative data systems to identify events or patterns that signal student disengagement or personal problems correlated with withdrawal or academic failure. Linda Baer and John Campbell described the emergence of these efforts in the Educause book *Game Changers: Education and Information Technologies*.[47] Some commercial vendors, such as Civitas Learning (www.civitaslearning.com) have developed platforms to assist institutions in using predictive analytics with some promising results.[48] The Tennessee Board of Regents is analyzing its past data on student achievement to give students information to help them identify an efficient pathway toward successfully meeting degree requirements.[49]

Another promising development is the use of analytics to learn from the interactions of students with content on computer-assisted instructional platforms. A chapter in *Game Changers* describing the Open Learning Initiative at Carnegie Mellon University explains how computer-assisted instruction can become personalized and adaptive to individual learners, even more so than traditional instructional delivery methods in all but the smallest classes.[50] Because much learning is occurring in a digital environment, course designers and instructors can use analysis to gain useful insights into student understanding, obstacles to learning, and the effectiveness or ineffectiveness of the presentation of learning materials. A newly formed professional association of educators, the Society for Learning Analytics Research (http://sola research.org/about), has been created to advance this work, and interesting research findings and practical applications are beginning to accumulate.[51]

Less high tech, but operating on the same principles of real-time data collection and utilization, are the very brief practical measurement surveys employed by the Carnegie Foundation's Community College Pathways initiatives (see Chapter 5). These surveys are used to monitor student perceptions and experiences during the learning process. All these approaches employ technology as a tool to improve the timely delivery of information that can be used to improve student learning. These are not silver bullets, but if they realize their potential, these approaches will enhance, rather than displace, the role of high-quality human relationships and interaction in teaching and learning.

As suggested by these examples, the depth of data being collected on individuals has great potential to improve the effectiveness of policy and practice. The expansion and greater utilization of data on individuals also creates potential for harmful abuse. The Asilomar Convention on Learning Research in Higher Education, held in June 2014, proposed principles to guide ethical practice as researchers and practitioners explore these uncharted waters. As its organizers recognize, the principles developed at this convening[52] will likely need to be revisited continuously as this field grows and matures.

Employing Financial Supports, Incentives, and Sanctions

A political leader deeply involved in education policy once told me, "Money changes behavior, and a lot of money changes a lot of behavior!" His straightforward logic is the justification for bonus targets in business, performance funding in higher education, merit salary increases, and merit-based financial assistance. In fact, most policy initiatives targeted on social problems employ money as a primary tool. But money is limited. Although money serves many essential purposes, neither the amount of money provided nor the way it is distributed is a panacea.

Money is both a resource and an incentive. If the capability exists to achieve a policy objective, money can enable and motivate people to do the necessary work. If the capability to do the necessary work is absent or in short supply, achieving the policy goal will require investing in capacity building, as well as investing directly in production. The essential conditions for the successful use of money to achieve a policy objective include

- supporting the expansion of existing capabilities, or developing capabilities where they do not exist in sufficient supply;
- motivating people with incentives and enabling them with necessary final resources to achieve goals;
- avoiding perverse incentives and unproductive expenditures; and
- monitoring outcomes and adapting policy to improve.

The past successes and missteps of the United States in increasing postsecondary educational attainment illustrate both effective and ineffective attempts to meet these conditions.

At the end of World War II, some forward-thinking political leaders recognized that increasing postsecondary educational attainment and investments in research and development were becoming increasingly important to the nation.[53] Although a policy consensus around this goal was slow to develop, the GI Bill, with the immediate purpose of achieving a gradual reintegration of veterans into the workforce, provided the necessary incentives and resources to achieve an immediate increase in postsecondary attainment.

The federal government relied on established accreditors as a means of avoiding perverse incentives for the creation of low-quality educational institutions to meet this need. This generally worked well; most of the surge in postsecondary attainment was achieved by the expansion of existing public and private colleges and universities to accommodate the enrollment of veterans.

The launching of Sputnik by the former Soviet Union in 1957 dramatically accelerated the development of a national policy consensus favoring more widespread educational attainment. At that moment, baby boomers were crowding elementary schools. The National Defense Education Act signed in 1958 provided additional federal funding to education at every level. It provided student loans, some of which were forgivable, to students who became educators. It supported grants to the states to improve instruction and laboratory facilities in science, math, and foreign languages. It supported graduate fellowships that would increase the supply of faculty. It supported the training of counselors. It supported research and experimentation in educational television.

In response to federal initiatives and driven by their own sense of urgency, states expanded existing colleges and universities and built new ones, including community colleges to accommodate enrollment demand. The 1965

Higher Education Act established a direct federal role in supporting higher education that by the 1970s included Pell Grants and a massive guaranteed loan program.

During the entire 70-year period from World War II to the present, fueled by these governmental policies, postsecondary educational attainment grew in the United States. As shown in Figure 7.1, the early growth was rapid, especially in the 1960s when the baby boom entered college. The rate of growth slowed considerably after 1975, but it continued at a modest pace with steadily larger fractions of the population enrolling and graduating from colleges and universities into the early twenty-first century.

In 2015, however, it is evident that many policy makers are dissatisfied with the nation's performance in postsecondary education. Some common concerns: Too many students who enroll fail to complete degrees and certificates; an inadequate supply of well-trained workers is available to meet the demands of business and industry; and higher education is becoming too expensive for students and families.

This dissatisfaction is not rooted in the failure of the educational system to meet the needs of the nation in the last third of the twentieth century. It is rooted in the inability of that system to meet the growing demands of the twenty-first century. Figure 7.2, developed by the Georgetown Center on Education and the Economy, shows nearly 80% of jobs in 1964 were held

Figure 7.1 Postsecondary Enrollment as Percentage of U.S. Population

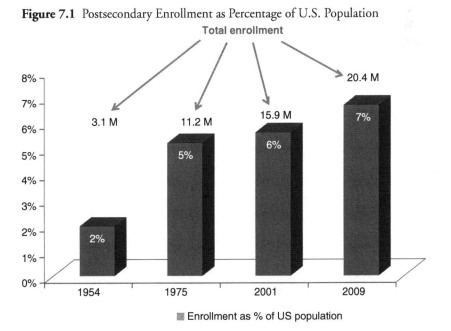

■ Enrollment as % of US population

Figure 7.2 Percentage of the Workforce by Educational Level

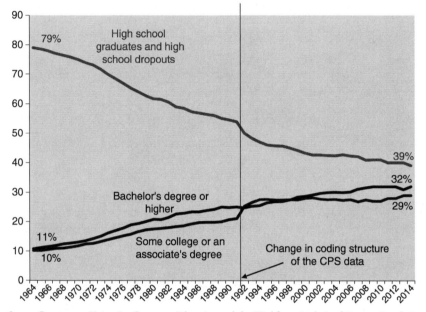

Source: Georgetown University Center on Education and the Workforce Analysis of Current Population Survey, microdata 1964–2014.

by people with a high school education or less. By 2014, that percentage shrank to 39%. The number of jobs in the U.S. economy grew from 91 million in 1973 to 155 million in 2009; virtually all of the new jobs have been filled by workers with postsecondary training. The percentage of all jobs held by workers with a bachelor's degree or higher grew from 16% in 1973 to 32% in 2007.[54] Whereas 20 years ago the United States led the world in the percentage of the young adult (25 to 34 years old) workforce with an associate's degree or higher, by 2012 it ranked fourteenth among Organisation for Economic Co-operation and Development (OECD) countries.[55]

The constantly growing demands from students and employers for more postsecondary attainment during this period has clearly become a challenge for policy makers, as well as for educators. The GI Bill, the National Defense Education Act, the Higher Education Act (through its various reauthorizations), and the substantial state investments during the last half of the twentieth century in postsecondary education all have provided supports and financial incentives to students and to institutions leading to more postsecondary attainment. The size of these coarse-grained incentives (institutional support, student financial assistance programs, etc.) has almost certainly been primarily responsible for the scope, scale, and considerable successes of postsecondary education in the United States. But in the first decade of the twenty-first century, the inadequate level of postsecondary educational attainment has become a policy issue. Educational finance policy is part of the problem. Let's take a look at each essential component in turn.

Supporting Existing Capabilities and Developing Capabilities

The past successes in expanding educational attainment in the United States involved the expansion of an educational system that was primarily designed to generate a postsecondary attainment rate of 20% to 40% of the adult population. This expansion achieved its successes by expanding postsecondary institutional capacity and making higher education affordable for a much wider fraction of the population. It did not increase the capability of the elementary and secondary educational system to prepare a larger fraction of the population to succeed in postsecondary education. And it did not increase the capability of postsecondary educators to help a larger fraction of the population acquire the knowledge and skills associated with a postsecondary degree.

Wide gaps exist among the states on the dimensions of preparation and completion as measured by the Measuring Up initiative described in Chapter 3. Even the best-performing states on those (admittedly crude) measures of preparation enroll many students in college who require remedial instruction. Increasing postsecondary attainment in the future will require new investments or more productive use of existing revenues to increase the effectiveness of instruction both in K–12 and postsecondary education.

Motivating With Incentives and Enabling With Necessary Financial Resources

Postsecondary attainment is a joint product of students, faculty, and educational institutions. The obvious economic and noneconomic incentives for seeking postsecondary education, combined with state and federal financial policies, have been sufficient to motivate millions of students to enroll and to motivate thousands of institutions to enroll them. The adequacy of the financial resources provided is more questionable.

It is difficult to generalize about financial adequacy because the level of spending per student spans such an enormous range in American higher education. More selective institutions, especially in the independent, non-profit sector, may spend $30,000 to $50,000 per full-time equivalent (FTE) student for instruction, student services, and overheads. Most students attend public institutions, and the greatest number of students who enroll but fail to complete a postsecondary credential attend community colleges and for-profit institutions. Community colleges typically have $8,000 to

$12,000 in revenues per FTE student, possibly not enough to serve their students well.

Another dimension of resource adequacy is the relative share of the cost of higher education borne by students and the public. In inflation-adjusted dollars, public colleges and universities have had essentially the same level of revenues per student for the past 25 years. Student tuition and fees plus state and local support per FTE student now average $11,500 in public 2-year and 4-year institutions. These two key revenue sources that finance virtually all instruction have never totaled much more than $12,000 per student in constant dollars. But 25 years ago the states provided about 75% of those revenues, and students and their families paid 25%. Today the states cover about 53% and student tuition and fees provide 47%.[56]

In the context of this shift of funding burden to students, the level of financial assistance available to low- and moderate-income students is a serious concern. Although both the states and the federal government have financed quite substantial student assistance programs, these programs increasingly fall short of providing the assistance a low-income student would need to enroll in a full-time program of study. Many students enroll part time, and there is a large correlation between extensive part-time enrollment and failure to complete a degree or certificate.[57]

Avoiding Perverse Incentives and Unproductive Expenditures

While it seemed perfectly logical to finance higher education by providing funding based on student enrollment, policy makers at both the state and federal levels have learned that paying for enrollments alone at open admissions institutions is a perverse incentive. If student enrollment, not course completion or ultimate graduation, drives institutional revenues, there is a powerful incentive to enroll students who are unlikely to be successful.

This became especially evident in the 1990s when large numbers of students defaulted on student loans after failing to complete academic programs and finding they could not acquire adequately well-paying jobs to pay their student loans. This has occurred and continues to occur most frequently at community colleges and for-profit, open enrollment institutions, but due to higher costs, the rate of loan defaults is much higher at the for-profit institutions.

Of course, low admission standards would not be a problem if institutions were effective in retaining and helping the students they admit complete a degree or certificate. But the incidence of open admissions institutions that also have a high rate of completion is quite low.

Although policy makers have responded to this problem several times (among other things, creating a graduation rate survey that was well intentioned but incapable of accounting for part-time or mobile students), they face conflicting priorities. Their responses have been restrained because of a desire to provide broad access to higher education, especially for students who might not enroll without encouragement and financial support. On the political left, policy options that would erect higher academic barriers for eligibility for federal assistance were opposed because they would likely restrict opportunity. On the political right, the preference for market-based strategies and the inclination to support private sector, for-profit providers of education has generated resistance to policies that target these providers. Postsecondary education institutions have generally been united in resisting all policies to address perverse incentives that would add to administrative regulatory burdens.

The Obama administration's proposal for a college rating scheme, announced in 2014, is the most recent effort to attack this problem. After struggling to solve the technical and political problems involved, the administration decided to provide more consumer information without actually ranking individual colleges based on that information. Although pressures to increase college completion could actually lead to improved preparation and better instruction of disadvantaged students, policy makers run the risk of another perverse incentive—to dilute academic standards.

Inadequate preparation and the admission of underprepared students without the ability to successfully educate them is not the only unproductive expenditure in relation to the goal of increasing attainment. The competition for students among institutions, especially those institutions who are able to be selective in admissions, tends to generate spending that makes institutions more attractive in comparison to their competitors, often without contributing materially to the quality or breadth of educational attainment. Outraged news stories about luxurious athletic facilities periodically appear, but students keep paying (sometimes with borrowed funds) to support them. Institutions also compete to have prestigious program offerings, especially law schools, medical schools, and graduate programs, that might not be justified in terms of cost and benefit.

Concerns about the cost of higher education also have led to substantial subsidies to higher-income students and families, whose participation in postsecondary education is virtually certain regardless of the amount of subsidy. Some states have very large scholarship programs based entirely on academic achievement, regardless of financial need. Other subsidies, such as tax benefits for contributing to college savings plans, are less visible but still material. (In Colorado, any contributions to a 529 college savings plan for children or grandchildren results in a reduction of gross taxable income for state tax purposes. In addition to tax-free investment income for the life of the plan, contributors receive an immediate tax savings of 4.6% of the contribution. Recently, a proposal to eliminate this benefit for taxpayers with an annual income above $500,000 and to double the benefit for taxpayers earning under $150,000 was defeated in a Senate Committee.)[58]

Monitoring Outcomes and Adapting Policy to Improve

Public policy makers have limited control over practice, even in authoritarian regimes. They have only blunt instruments—appropriations, laws, and regulatory authority—at their disposal. The checks and balances in the U.S. federal system, whose effects are compounded by active participation in democratic decision making, further limit the agility, responsiveness, and potency of public policy.

Policy makers find it difficult to make nonincremental changes in appropriations, despite ambitious efforts to make policy more rational and responsive to performance. Aaron Wildavsky's classic analysis of the federal budget process in *The Politics of the Budgetary Process*[59] brilliantly describes the organizational and interpersonal dynamics that make nonincremental change difficult. In 1974, I studied 10 years of appropriations for higher education in three states, Illinois, Michigan, and Wisconsin, that on the surface had very different structures for decision making. In Wisconsin and Illinois, these structures were especially intended to increase rational planning and budgeting. From year to year, all of these states made quite incremental budget decisions, even though over longer periods of time some perceptible evidence of nonincremental planning and budgeting became evident.[60]

Given these realities, policy makers often resort to strategies that might shape outcomes on the margin. Such fine-grained financial incentives (performance funding for institutions, closely targeted scholarship or loan forgiveness programs, etc.) have generally produced disappointing results. The impact of a fine-grained policy incentive is typically overwhelmed or limited by other priorities of the people and organizations involved. Regulatory burden and transaction costs frequently outweigh policy impact.

As Howard Bowen famously observed, an institution's highest priority is normally to protect and expand its financial resources.[61] One can easily imagine institutions being quite responsive to particular financial incentives if the stakes are large and the institution can readily improve performance in ways that will generate substantially more revenue. Typically, however, neither condition is present. When automatic performance factors have been introduced into budgetary formulas, institutions have worked vigorously and generally successfully to make the formulas multifaceted and complicated enough to avert any substantial reduction in their share of the budgetary pie.[62]

This is not to say that the discussion of performance and efforts to introduce performance measures into the budgetary process have no effect at all. Emphasizing priorities and measuring performance (especially, but not only, in the context of budget allocations) usually does have an impact on institutional behavior. One excellent outcome is to draw attention to relatively easy fixes: Are there policies that discourage timely degree completion? Is academic advising weak? Are some courses turning out to be insurmountable barriers to many students? Another positive outcome has been the increasing sophistication of data systems to measure dimensions of performance.

But after easy improvements are found, some risks appear. When the stakes are high and the budget mechanisms are formulaic, there is a risk of gaming the data, cheating, or degrading standards. Also, if the institution has inadequate capability, it may need additional resources, rather than fewer, in order to improve. A budget mechanism that requires improvement before resources are provided could easily be self-defeating.

If nothing else, the history of efforts to increase educational attainment in the United States makes clear the complexity of the task. Public policy investments are essential, but practical challenges beyond the control of blunt policy instruments and the conflicting interests of public policy stakeholders make it difficult for public policy to achieve optimal efficiency. These problems have not been recently discovered. Alice Rivlin's *Systematic Thinking for Social Action* cogently laid them out in 1971 based on the experience of the PPBS movement of the 1960s.[63] Policy analysis and research is needed to make the dynamics and tradeoffs more clear, but it seems to take a lot of compelling evidence or perhaps a clear external threat to overcome policy inertia.

Aligning Policy and Practice in Partnership

Policy establishes the general rules and background parameters for practice and provides resources and incentives for practical action. But policy is a blunt instrument. Policy is not self-executing; capable practitioners must execute policy whether the objective is national defense, building and maintaining a transportation system, education, or health care. Policy will be ineffective in achieving its objectives if practitioners lack the knowledge and skill required to execute policy, if resources are not allocated to appropriate and essential functions, or if the resources are inadequate to do the job. Policy will also be ineffective if it overreaches by intruding too deeply into the realm of practice with its blunt instruments of hierarchy and bureaucracy.

The practice side of the partnership can also contribute to policy failure. If practitioners fail to develop and perform the necessary capabilities, if they do not use available resources effectively and efficiently, and if they fail to assemble good policy advice and deliver it persuasively to policy makers, the partnership cannot succeed. Perhaps the strongest partnerships between policy and practice emerge when practitioners recognize a need, mobilize their resources to address it, and successfully enlist the support of policy makers. The successful alignment of policy and practice must include the development of practical capabilities; the adequate and effective allocation of resources; and disciplined, reflective, and continuously improving practice.

Policy and practice never perform flawlessly, but their performance separately and collectively can be assessed and improved. This chapter's review of the policy goal of achieving widespread postsecondary attainment in the United States, although far short of a comprehensive analysis, sketches a transition from alignment and successful pursuit of a goal, followed by increasingly ambitious goals with failures of both policy and practice. These failures have been compounded by a deteriorating partnership between policy makers and practitioners.

In the 1950s, the United States enjoyed substantial advantages over virtually every other country on the globe. It was victorious in World War II, without suffering the damage to its infrastructure and economy experienced in Europe, Russia, and Japan. It first focused attention on the education of its veterans and strengthened both its economy and its military through research and development. When the 1957 launching of Sputnik aroused fears of losing competitive ground to the Soviet Union, the nation quickly mobilized both policy and practice to increase educational attainment at every level. New goals were established, and new resources were invested in building both the capabilities and capacity of the educational system. The increased focus on education coincided with a large increase in the population of young people, and the U.S. baby boom generation became the best educated in the world.

In addition to investments to increase educational attainment, the nation also made investments to increase the equality of educational opportunity in 1965 through the Higher Education Act, and especially Title I of the Elementary and Secondary Education Act. These acts have produced some success in broadening participation and reducing gaps in postsecondary success among racial minorities and economically disadvantaged students, but these achievements were far less dramatic than the broad increase in educational attainment of the population as a whole.[64]

By 1980 the rapid gains in postsecondary participation and attainment of the 1960s and early 1970s subsided to a steady state of modest, incremental growth. Financial investments were incremental and stable in constant dollars, with some variation in response to economic downturns and recovery. Concern with the quality of elementary and secondary education grew dramatically, but it was focused largely on high-poverty urban schools. The report *A Nation At Risk*,[65] released in 1983, sounded an alarm and launched a flurry of policy and practice initiatives that continue to this day.

The U.S. educational reform initiatives of the past quarter century have certainly not achieved their aspirations, even though one could argue that educational attainment in the United States is marginally better and likely no worse than it was before. Why has progress fallen short of our aspirations?

A straightforward, simple answer to that question would violate most of the premises of this book; the problem is complicated, with many, many moving parts. But a major factor may be that both practitioners and policy makers have been slow to recognize the extent of change and innovation required for more widespread educational achievement. And they have not worked together effectively to make those changes.

Educators often respond to policy criticism with requests for additional financial resources. Policy makers usually respond with calls for greater efficiency and cost-effectiveness. Increasingly, policy makers have sought improvement by changing the practitioners—placing leaders from business, government, or the military into positions of educational leadership; providing incentives and subsidies for for-profit enterprises to manage schools or develop new educational delivery mechanisms, and recruiting teachers from other professions or alternative pathways, such as Teach for America. These strategies have made contributions, especially in overcoming inertia and introducing different ideas and approaches, but they have not yielded dramatic improvements consistently or at scale.

Educators have been told by policy leaders that they cannot rely simply on "new money" to solve problems, and "the most important money is the money you have." Improvement must come primarily from using current resources differently and more effectively. Policy leaders similarly must recognize that problems cannot be solved simply with new practitioners. Existing human resources must be more effectively utilized. In a massive social enterprise, large numbers of practitioners cannot be replaced at scale. Policy makers must work with the practitioners they have.

Both educational and policy leaders striving for improvement are often stymied by political inertia. Established interests resist change. For example, beginning in 2012 the Council of Chief State School Officers (CCSSO) and the Council for the Accreditation of Educator Preparation (CAEP) developed thoughtful, synergistic strategies to improve the training and licensing of teachers and school principals.[66] The level of common purpose and consensus on strategic directions created an opportunity for significant progress. The process of implementation continues 3 years later, but it is painfully slow in the face of passivity or active resistance in both the communities of policy and practice.

In the policy arena, it is very difficult to reallocate resources and political support to more urgent priorities from established, arguably lower-priority purposes. Higher education finance, as discussed previously, is one well-documented example of many. The implementation of well-considered, carefully crafted policy strategies, such as the teacher education initiative discussed previously and the development of Common Core Standards for mathematics and English Language Arts, are subject to political inertia as well as professional inertia, perhaps more so.

Further increases in educational attainment in the United States are essential, and they are possible. Perhaps, because they are essential, they may be inevitable. The seeds of improvement are constantly being planted. But these seeds are unlikely to germinate and flourish without building increased capabilities in the profession of education. Nor are they likely to germinate until policy makers make educational attainment a more urgent priority and find ways to work collaboratively with practicing, professional educators who have developed the necessary capabilities.

In Conclusion

This book has considered how evidence and research can help solve problems and improve human lives. Although I have never doubted the potential of evidence and research to make useful contributions, this book was conceived in frustration: Why is so much research inconclusive and inconsequential? Why do policy makers fail to respond to evidence of need, or fail to allocate or reallocate resources to urgent priorities? Why is it so difficult to improve practice? Why are so many efforts to address serious problems more contentious than productive? What dangers should be recognized and avoided? What actually does work?

Inevitably, the conclusion of such a book cannot be conclusive. These questions are far too large and too difficult for one book or one person to master. But the attempt has refined my hunches (or *heuristics*, to use the scholarly term) in response to these questions. Let me conclude with a brief reprise of this book's argument.

Much of the research on policy and practice is inconclusive because human beings, human agency, and human interactions are extremely complex. In the face of this reality, the usual methods of reductionist science do not yield conclusive results. It is unrealistic to expect research findings to give authoritative guidance to policy and practice in the complex, adaptive systems of human society.

Because of this complexity, experimental studies with random assignment to treatment and control groups have generally been inconclusive and much less productive than hoped 50 years ago. Experiments are most useful, and conclusive, when the presenting problem is not very complicated and the intervention is simple and easy to replicate with fidelity. (Reducing barriers to filling out a student financial aid application with the help of tax preparers is an excellent example of such a study.) The evolution of evaluation science into a diverse profession with various subfields and approaches occurred partially in response to the inadequacy of experimentation for analyzing complex problems and interventions.

These limitations notwithstanding, reliable, valid measurement of both social outcomes and the factors associated with outcomes is crucial for the improvement of policy and practice. Much important work has occurred in the measurement domain, but more is needed. The development of useful metrics and robust data on educational and social issues warrants more attention and scholarly prestige than it is normally given.

Although measurement is clearly the foundation for improvement, the field is littered with landmines. Practitioners and policy makers need to be sophisticated and cautious in the uses of measurement. Different purposes require different measurement instruments. Many vitally important outcomes are difficult to measure precisely. Even the best measures are subject to error and the risk of misguided inference. Individuals and institutions have rights to privacy that must be acknowledged and scrupulously observed. Used wisely, measurement can help make things better, but allocating unwarranted precision or validity to any single measure can be problematic, even harmful. The risk of harm grows if measurement plays a direct, unbuffered role in decisions of consequence. Fine-grained measurement is crucial for improving practice where the context is accessible and small interventions and rapid adaptation are feasible. When fine-grained measurement is employed to guide policy dangers abound.

Improving practice requires an appreciation of complexity, the wise use of measurement, an understanding of the surrounding systems and context of practice, and respect, not unqualified deference, for practitioner wisdom and judgment. Practice, in education and other complex professions, has improved and continues to improve. Some of the most dramatic improvements in business and in medicine have occurred through improvement science, a disciplined analysis of systems, process interactions, and outcomes in order to find pathways for improvement. Such approaches, combined with efforts to gain deeper understanding of fundamental issues, are more promising than searches for silver bullets or easy victories.

The pathway toward improved policy includes a similar appreciation of complexity and the wise use of measurement. In the policy environment, however, the stakes are higher and decisions must emerge out of the interplay of different interests and views about how the world works. Although the interests and views at play in the policy environment sometimes seem to be categorically different and irreconcilable, they vary among influential policy shapers and evolve over time. Interests and views overlap, and evidence and research can help policy makers focus on priority problems and discover common interests and pathways to improvement. Scholars and analysts can contribute by providing good measurement over time of social conditions, by learning more about fundamental systems and factors that shape outcomes, and by helping policy makers and practitioners understand and appreciate their mutual interdependence.

In a MacArthur Foundation Board of Directors meeting, the physicist Murray Gell-Mann once commented, "Ah! We are making a list. This is what we do in philanthropy as a substitute for thinking." Gell-Mann's caution against oversimplification notwithstanding, a summary listing of pitfalls and ways to realize the potential of evidence to improve education seems to be an appropriate way to conclude this effort.

Pitfalls to Avoid

- Assuming what "works"—the effectiveness of complex interventions—can be proven through the experimental method or some other analytical means, and employing such methods to judge *all* interventions (Chapters 1 and 2).
- Expecting that extensive measurement can, in itself, yield control over outcomes or prescribe effective pathways to control outcomes (Chapter 3).
- Failing to tailor measurement to purpose and use. Coarse-grained measures are appropriate and necessary for policy, inappropriate for practice; fine-grained measures are essential for practice, inappropriate for policy (Chapter 4).
- Attempting to collect and use measures for policy interventions that are likely to be perceived as threatening or an invasion of privacy (Chapter 4).
- Collecting more data than can be productively used on the assumption that more data inevitably leads to greater understanding and influence over outcomes (Chapter 4).
- Falling prey to the allures of *high modernism*—efforts to engineer "ideal" outcomes for complex processes through formal planning and processes controlled by hierarchy and bureaucracy, without providing space for the exercise of practical wisdom. One consequence of high modernism is restrictive work rules that prevent problem solving and eventually work against the interests of all stakeholders (Chapters 4 and 7).

- Seeking to determine the "effects" of broad structural conditions (e.g., a governance system) that are either beyond the control of policy makers or, for practical reasons, highly unlikely to attract their commitment to change (Chapter 6).
- Seeking to influence policy or practice in a particular setting with general or abstract information or with studies that are incomprehensible to nonspecialists (Chapter 6).
- Assuming that evidence can successfully alter world views, or disprove or prove the effects of very complex interventions (markets, charter schools, etc.; Chapters 6 and 7).
- Attaching direct, high-stakes consequences to data employed for accountability; perverse incentives are unavoidable (Chapter 7).
- Employing Theory X management as a general strategy for improving results, rather than addressing the exceptional cases of poor performance with appropriately exceptional remedies (Chapter 7).
- Attempting to improve practice with blunt policy instruments (Chapter 7).

Unlocking the Potential of Evidence for Improvement

- Conducting experimental research on straightforward interventions to address simple problems, where relatively strong, positive effect sizes are likely and implementation at scale is feasible (Chapter 2).
- Relentlessly measuring over time what both policy makers and practitioners value (Chapters 3, 4, 5, and 7).
- Improving the quality of information related to what practitioners and policy-makers value (Chapters 3, 4, 6, and 7).
- Giving policy makers and practitioners locally relevant data that speak to their questions and priorities, instill ownership in solving problems, and lead to action (Chapters 5 and 6).
- Creating and testing theories of action for improvement by employing short learning cycles in the context of practice (Chapter 5).
- Employing simple, efficient surveys (measurement in the flow of practice) to monitor progress in addressing issues relevant to improvement (Chapter 5).
- Developing communities of practitioners who employ disciplined approaches for improving outcomes and share learning, as in Success for All and the Carnegie Networked Improvement Communities (Chapters 2 and 5).
- Employing plural methods—mixed, quantitative, and qualitative inquiries—to understand what contributes to a problem, and to

develop and test interventions designed to solve it (Chapters 5, 6, and 7).

- Analyzing complex interactions in situational context (including data analytics) in order to develop practical, testable interventions from the examination of what is associated with positive and negative outcomes (Chapters 5 and 7).
- Using evidence to identify strengths and weaknesses in current policy and practice, while avoiding counterproductive attacks on world views that are unlikely to change (Chapters 6 and 7).
- Using evidence to harness human agency and build relationships of mutual respect in an appropriate division of labor between policy makers and practitioners (Chapters 5 and 7).

Although progress on complex problems is typically laborious and slow, complexity is not an insurmountable obstacle. The limited progress we can observe in the time span of an individual life is often discouraging. But multifaceted strategies, with continuous testing of theories and adaptation based on empirical results, have successfully solved many complex human problems. The global increases in educational attainment, in agricultural productivity, and in human health over the past century are clear evidence of what can be achieved. Avoiding superficial strategies and increasing the wise and judicious use of evidence and research can accelerate future progress.

Notes

1. Curry, T. (2014, April 2). Representative Paul Ryan: The War on Poverty has "failed miserably." *In Plain Sight*. Retrieved from http://www.nbcnews.com /feature/in-plain-sight/rep-paul-ryan-war-poverty-has-failed-miserably-v19681085

2. Mohn, S. (2014, March 19). Poverty: Laziness or lack of opportunity? *Huffington Post*. Retrieved from http://www.huffingtonpost.com/sid-mohn/poverty -laziness-or-lack-_b_4994213.html

The source of Moen's assertion is: Fox, L., Garfinkel, I., Kaushal, N., Waldfogel, J., & Wimer, C. (2014). *Waging war on poverty: Historical trends in poverty using the supplemental poverty measure*. National Bureau of Economic Research, Working Paper 19789. Retrieved from http://www.nber.org/papers/w19789

3. A very nice discussion of the various important, but limited roles of evidence and research in policy making appears in the chapter "Alternatives to Authoritativeness" in Lindblom, C. E., & Cohen, D. K. (1979). *Usable knowledge: Social science and social problem solving* (pp. 72–85). New Haven, CT: Yale University Press.

4. Stone, D. A. (1988). *Policy paradox and political reason*. Glenview, IL: Scott, Foresman and Company, p. 306.

5. Ibid., p. 301.

6. Cohen, D. K., & Moffitt, S. L. (2009). *The ordeal of equality: Did federal regulation fix the schools?* Cambridge, MA: Harvard University Press, p. 38.

7. Bensimon, E. M., & Malcom, L. (Eds.). (2012). *Confronting equity issues on campus: Implementing the equity scorecard in theory and practice.* Sterling, VA: Stylus.

8. Kuh, G. D. (2007 , September/October). Risky business: Promises and pitfalls of institutional transparency. *Change Magazine,* 31–35. See also: Ewell, P. T. (1999). Linking performance measures to resource allocation: Exploring unmapped terrain. *Quality in Higher Education, 5*(3), 191–209.

9. Baseball offers a good example of moderate stakes. If you strike out, you sit down until your next turn at bat. The stakes become high (being cut from the team) only if you persistently strike out and fail to improve.

10. OECD's studies of educational attainment (PISA and PIAAC), and TIMSS and PIRLS, independent international studies of mathematics and reading attainment, have stimulated enormous interest among policy makers and educators.

Organization for Economic Cooperation and Development. (2015, March 24). *OECD programme for international student assessment.* Retrieved from http://www.oecd-ilibrary.org/education/pisa_19963777

Organization for Economic Cooperation and Development. (2015, March 24). *OECD skills studies.* Retrieved from http://www.oecd-ilibrary.org/education/oecd-skills-studies_23078731

TIMSS & PIRLS. (2015, March 24). *TIMSS & PIRLS.* Retrieved from http://timssandpirls.bc.edu/home/pdf/TP_About.pdf

11. U.S. Chamber of Commerce Foundation. (2014). *Leaders and laggards.* Retrieved from http://www.leadersandlaggards.org/sites/default/files/Leaders%20and%20Laggards%20A%20State-by-State%20Report%20Card%20on%20K-12%20Educational%20Effectiveness.pdf

Leaders and Laggards rates the states, not only on measured educational outcomes, but also on policies judged by the Chamber of Commerce to be desirable, such as school choice, teacher education practices, and data systems. Measuring Up and Quality Counts are more circumspect about avoiding judgments and inferences not based on hard data.

12. Jefferson, T. (1785). *Notes on the state of Virginia.* The Federalist Papers Project (pp., 167–168). Retrieved from http://www.thefederalistpapers.org/wp-content/uploads/2012/12/Thomas-Jefferson-Notes-On-The-State-Of-Virginia.pdf

13. Lemann, N. (1999). *The big test: The secret history of the American meritocracy.* New York, NY: Farrar, Straus and Giroux.

14. Katzman, J. (2015, March 31). *Secrets of the SAT:* Frontline *interview.* Retrieved from http://www.pbs.org/wgbh/pages/frontline/shows/sats/interviews/katzman.html

15. Deciding what to measure is difficult for all organizations whose mission is not simply generating economic returns. Sawhill and Williamson used the example of the Nature Conservancy to suggest approaches for tackling this problem in nonprofits.

Sawhill, J., & Williamson, D. (2001, May). Measuring what matters in nonprofits. *McKinsey Quarterly.* Retrieved from http://www.mckinsey.com/insights/social_sector/measuring_what_matters_in_nonprofits

16. Chickering, A. W., & Gamson, Z. F. (1987, March). Seven principles for good practice in undergraduate education. *AAHE Bulletin,* 3–7. Retrieved from http://files.eric.ed.gov/fulltext/ED282491.pdf

17. Astin, A. W. (1977). *Four critical years: Effects of college on beliefs, attitudes, and knowledge.* San Francisco, CA: Jossey-Bass.

Astin, A. W. (1993). *What matters in college: Four critical years revisited.* San Francisco, CA: Jossey-Bass.

Astin, A. W. (1984). Student involvement: A developmental theory for higher education. *Journal of College Student Development, 25*(4), 297–308.

Pace, C. R. (1980). Measuring the quality of student effort. *Current Issues in Higher Education,* 2, 10–16.

Pace, C. R. (1984). *Measuring the quality of college student experiences: An account of the development and use of the college student experiences questionnaire.* Los Angeles, CA: Higher Education Research Institute.

Pace, C. R. (1990). *The undergraduate: A report of their activities and college experiences in the 1980s.* Los Angeles, CA: Center for the Study of Evaluation.

18. National Survey of Student Engagement. (2015, March 8). *About NSSE.* Retrieved from wehttp://nsse.iub.edu/html/about.cfm

19. High School Survey of Student Engagement. (2015). *High school survey of student engagement.* Retrieved from http://ceep.indiana.edu/hssse/about/survey.shtml

20. Council for Aid to Education. (2015, April 14). *CLA-overview.* Retrieved from http://cae.org/participating-institutions/cla-overview

21. Tennessee Tech University. (2015, April 14). *Critical thinking assessment test.* Retrieved from https://www.tntech.edu/cat

22. Association of American Colleges and Universities. (2015). *VALUE rubric development project.* Retrieved from http://www.aacu.org/value/rubrics

23. Kuh, G. D., Ikenberry, S. O., Jankowski, N. A., Cain, T. R., Ewell, P. T., Hutchings, P., & Kinzie, J. (2014). *Using evidence of student learning to improve higher education.* San Francisco, CA: Jossey-Bass.

24. Bryk, A. S., Sebring, P. B., Allensworth, E., Luppescu, S., & Easton, J. Q. (2010). *Organizing schools for improvement: Lessons from Chicago.* Chicago: University of Chicago Press, p. 45.

25. Ibid., pp. 29–41.

26. Ibid., pp. 42–78.

27. Ibid., pp. 77, 79–96.

28. Ibid., pp. 135–157.

29. The MacArthur Foundation Project on Human Development in Chicago Neighborhoods generated a multiyear, interdisciplinary analysis of these factors among Chicago neighborhoods. See: Sampson, R. J., Raudenbush, S. W., and Earls, F. (1997). Neighborhoods and violent crime: A multilevel study of collective efficacy. *Science, 277*(5328), 918–924.

30. Bryk et al. (2010), pp. 158–196.

31. McGregor, D. (1985). *The human side of enterprise.* New York, NY: McGraw-Hill, pp. 33–57.

32. Hill, P. T., & Celio, M. B. (1998). *Fixing urban schools.* Washington, DC: Brookings Institution Press, pp. 34–37.

33. State Higher Education Executive Officers. (2005). *Accountability for better results: A national imperative for higher education.* Retrieved from http://www.sheeo.org/sites/default/files/publications/Accountability%20for%20Better%20Results.pdf

34. U.S. Department of Education. (2006). *A test of leadership: Charting the future of U.S. higher education.* Retrieved from http://www2.ed.gov/about/bdscomm/list/hiedfuture/reports/final-report.pdf

For an analysis of these two reports, see: Lingenfelter, P. E. (2007). How should states respond to *A test of leadership? Change Magazine, 39*(1) doi:10.3200/CHNG.39.1.13-19

35. Barber, M., Moffitt, A., & Kihn, P. (2011). *Deliverology 101: A field guide for educational leaders.* Thousand Oaks, CA: Corwin Press.

36. Ewell, P. T. (2009, November). *Assessment, accountability, and improvement: Revisiting the tension.* Retrieved from http://www.learningoutcomeassessment.org/documents/PeterEwell_005.pdf

37. Ariely, D. (2011). *The upside of irrationality.* New York, NY: Harper Perennial, pp. 17–52.

38. Pfeffer, J. (2005). Changing mental models: HR's most important task. *Human Resource Management, 44*(2), 123–128, especially p. 126. doi:10.1002/hrm.20053.

39. Simon, H. A. (1981). *The sciences of the artificial.* Cambridge, MA: MIT Press.

40. Ibid., pp. 195–196.

41. Ibid., pp. 195–208.

42. Pareto principle. (2015, March 17). In *Wikipedia.* Retrieved from http://en.wikipedia.org/wiki/Pareto_principle

43. Kuh, G. D. (2008). *High-impact educational practices: What they are, who has access to them, and why they matter.* Washington, DC: AAC&U.

44. Bryk et al. (2010).

45. Bowen, W. G., Chingos, M. M., & McPherson, M. S. (2011). *Crossing the finish line: Completing college at America's public universities.* Princeton, NJ: Princeton University Press.

46. Peurach, D. (2011). *Seeing complexity in public education: Problems, possibilities, and success for all.* Oxford Scholarship Online. New York: Oxford University Press, p. 239. doi:10.1093/acprof:oso/9780199736539.001.0001

47. Baer, L., & Campbell, J. (2012). From metrics to analytics, reporting to action: Analytics' role in changing the learning environment. In Oblinger, D. G. (Ed.), *Game changers: Education and information technologies* (pp. 53–65). Washington, DC: Educause.

48. Milliron, M. D., Malcolm, L., & Kil, D. (2014). Insight and action analytics: Three case studies to consider. *Research and Practice in Assessment, 9:* 70–89. Retrieved from http://www.rpajournal.com/dev/wp-content/uploads/2014/10/A7.pdf

49. Denley, T. (2014). How predictive analysis and choice architecture can improve student success. *Research and Practice in Assessment,* 61–69. Retrieved from http://www.rpajournal.com/dev/wp-content/uploads/2014/10/A6.pdf

50. Strader, R., & Thille, C. (2012). The open learning initiative: Enacting instruction online. In Oblinger, D. G. (Ed.), *Game changers: Education and information technologies* (pp. 201–213). Washington, DC: Educause.

51. Thille, C., Schneider, E., Kizilcec, R. F., Piech, C., Halawa, S. A., & Greene, D. K. (2014). The future of data-enriched assessment. *Research and Practice in Assessment*, *9*, 5–16. Retrieved from http://www.rpajournal.com/dev/wp-content/uploads/2014/10/A1.pdf

52. Asilomar Convention for Learning Research in Higher Education [website]. (2015, March 12). Retrieved from http://asilomar-highered.info

53. The Truman Commission Report, *Higher Education for American Democracy, A Report* set forth a vision for the subsequent growth of postsecondary education in the United States. John Dale Russell, who was the director of the Division of Higher Education in the Office of Higher Education at that time, later became a spokesperson for the Truman Commission and the founder of the association of State Higher Education Executive Officers. See:

United States President's Commission on Higher Education, & Zook, G. F. (1947). *Higher education for American democracy, a report.* Retrieved from http://catalog.hathitrust.org/Record/001117586.

Lingenfelter, P. E., & Mingle, J. R. (2014). *Public policy for higher education in the United States: A brief history of state leadership.* Retrieved from http://www.sheeo.org/sites/default/files/History_Web.pdf

54. Carnevale, A. P., Smith, N., & Strohl, J. (2010). *Help wanted: Projections of jobs and education requirements through 2018*, p. 14. Retrieved from https://cew.georgetown.edu/wp-content/uploads/2014/12/fullreport.pdf

55. Organization for Economic Cooperation and Development. (2013, September 11). *United States country note—Education at a glance 2012: OECD indicators.* Retrieved from http://www.oecd.org/unitedstates/CN%20-%20United%20States.pdf

56. State Higher Education Executive Officers. (2015). *State higher education finance, fiscal year 2013,* p. 22. Retrieved from http://www.sheeo.org/resources/publications/shef——-state-higher-education-finance-fy13

57. Shapiro, D., Dundar, A., Wakhunga, P. K., Yuan, X., & Harrell, A. T. (VA). (2015) *Completing college: A state-level view of student attainment rates.* Retrieved from http://nscresearchcenter.org/wp-content/uploads/NSC_Signature_Report_8_StateSupp.pdf

58. Bartels, L. (2015, March 16). Clash over college savings. *The Denver Post,* pp. 4A–5A.

59. Wildavsky, A. (1974). *The politics of the budgetary process* (2nd ed.). Boston, MA: Little, Brown.

60. Lingenfelter, P. E. (1974). *The politics of higher education appropriations in three Midwestern states* (Unpublished doctoral dissertation). University of Michigan, Ann Arbor.

61. Bowen, H. R. (1980). *The costs of higher education.* San Francisco, CA: Jossey-Bass.

62. For different perspectives on performance funding see:

Burke, J. C. (2005). Reinventing accountability: From bureaucratic rules to performance results. In J. C. Burke and Associates (Eds.), *Achieving accountability in higher education: Balancing public, academic, and market demands* (pp. 216–245). San Francisco, CA: Jossey-Bass.

Lingenfelter, P. E. (2008). Financing public colleges and universities in the United States. In H. F. Ladd & E. B. Fiske (Eds.), *Handbook of research in education finance and policy* (pp. 651–670). New York, NY: Routledge.

Jones, D. P. (2011). *Performance funding: From idea to action.* Retrieved from http://www.nchems.org/pubs/docs/Performance%20Funding%20121411.pdf

Snyder, M. (2015). *Driving better outcomes: Typology and principles to inform outcomes-based funding models.* Retrieved from http://hcmstrategists.com/driving outcomes/wp-content/themes/hcm/pdf/Driving%20Outcomes.pdf

Tandberg, D., & Hillman, N. W. (2015). *State performance funding for higher education: Silver bullet or red herring?* Retrieved from http://www.wiscape.wisc.edu/ docs/WebDispenser/wiscapedocuments/pb018.pdf?sfvrsn=4

63. Rivlin, A. (1971). *Systematic thinking for social action.* Washington, DC: Brookings Institution Press.

64. The persistence of racial gaps in opportunity and attainment is well documented. See especially: Orfield, G., Marin, P., Horn, C. L. (Eds.). (2005). *Higher education and the color line: College access racial equity, and social change.* Cambridge, MA: Harvard Education Press.

65. National Commission on Excellence in Education (1983). *A nation at risk: An imperative for educational reform.* Retrieved from http://www2.ed.gov/pubs/ NatAtRisk/index.html

66. Council of Chief State School Officers. (2012). *Our responsibility, our promise: Transforming educator preparation and entry into the profession.* Retrieved from http://ccsso.org/Documents/2012/Our%20Responsibility%20Our%20Prom ise_2012.pdf and

Council for the Accreditation of Educator Preparation. (2013). *CAEP 2013 standards for the accreditation of educator preparation.* Retrieved from https://caepnet .files.wordpress.com/2015/02/final_board_amended_20150213.pdf

BIBLIOGRAPHY

Adams, K. B., Matto, H. C., & LeCroy, C. W. (2009). Limitations of evidence-based practice for social work education: Unpacking the complexity. *Journal of Social Work Education*, *45*(2), 165–186.

Ahmed-Ullah, N. S., & Byrne, J. (2014, August 27). Chicago public schools reports graduation rate up. *Chicago Tribune*. Retrieved from http://www.chicagotribune.com/news/ct-cps-graduation-rate-met-0827-20140827-story.html

Altruism (ethics). (2014, September 24). In *Wikipedia*. Retrieved from http://en.wikipedia.org/wiki/Altruism_(ethics)

American Council on Education. (2014, April 7). *American college application campaign*. Retrieved from https://www.acenet.edu/about-ace/special-initiatives/Pages/ACAC.aspx

Apple, M. W. (1996). *Cultural politics and education*. New York, NY: Teachers College Press.

Ariely, D. (2011). *The upside of irrationality*. New York, NY: Harper Perennial.

Asilomar Convention for Learning Research in Higher Education [website]. (2015, March 12). Retrieved from http://asilomar-highered.info

Association of American Colleges and Universities. (2015). *VALUE rubric development project*. Retrieved from http://www.aacu.org/value/rubrics

Astin, A. W. (1977). *Four critical years: Effects of college on beliefs, attitudes, and knowledge*. San Francisco, CA: Jossey-Bass.

———. (1984). Student involvement: A developmental theory for higher education. *Journal of College Student Development*, *25*(4), 297–308.

———. (1993). *What matters in college: Four critical years revisited*. San Francisco, CA: Jossey-Bass.

Baer, L., & Campbell, J. (2012). From metrics to analytics, reporting to action: Analytics' role in changing the learning environment. In Oblinger, D. G. (Ed.), *Game changers: Education and information technologies* (pp. 53–65). Washington, DC: Educause.

Bailey, M. J., & Danziger, S. (Eds.). (2013). *Legacies of the war on poverty*. New York, NY: Russell Sage Foundation.

Ball, D. L., & Cohen, D. K. (1999). Developing practice, developing practitioners: Toward a practice-based theory of professional education. In L. Darling-Hammond & G. Sykes (Eds.), *Teaching as the learning profession: Handbook of policy and practice* (pp. 3–32). San Francisco, CA: Jossey-Bass.

Ball, D. L., & Forzani, F. M. (2007). 2007 Wallace foundation distinguished lecture—what makes education research "educational"? *Educational Researcher*, *36*(9), 529–540. Retrieved from http://edr.sagepub.com/content/36/9/529

Barber, M., Moffitt, A., & Kihn, P. (2011). *Deliverology 101: A field guide for educational leaders*. Thousand Oaks, CA: Corwin Press.

Bartels, L. (2015, March 16). Clash over college savings. *Denver Post*, pp. 4A–5A.

Bell, J. (2007). *Transforming higher education: National imperative—state responsibility*. Denver, CO: National Conference of State Legislatures.

Bennett, B. (2014, October 23). The standardization paradox [website]. *Carnegie Commons*. Retrieved from http://commons.carnegiefoundation.org/what-we-are-learning/2014/the-standardization-paradox/

Bensimon, E. M., & Malcom, L. (Eds.). (2012). *Confronting equity issues on campus: Implementing the equity scorecard in theory and practice*. Sterling, VA: Stylus.

Berwick, D. M. (2008). The science of improvement. *Journal of the American Medical Association, 299*(10), 1182–1184.

Bettinger, E. P., Long, B. T., Oreopoulos, P., & Sanbonmatsu, L. (2009). *The role of simplification and information in college decisions: Results from the H&R Block FAFSA experiment*. NBER Working Paper Series, 15361. Retrieved from http://www.nber.org/papers/w15361.pdf

Betts, J. R., & Tang, Y. E. (2014, August). *A meta-analysis of the literature on the effect of charter schools on student achievement*. CRPE Working Paper. Retrieved from http://www.crpe.org/sites/default/files/CRPE_meta-analysis_charter-schools-effect-student-achievement_workingpaper.pdf

———. (2014, November 3). *Setting the record straight on charter schools and achievement: A reply to Francesca Lopez*. CRPE Working Paper. Retrieved from http://www.crpe.org/sites/default/files/crpe.response_to_lopez_review.11.3.2014.pdf

Bowen, H. R. (1980). *The costs of higher education*. San Francisco, CA: Jossey-Bass.

Bowen, W. G., Chingos, M. M., & McPherson, M. S. (2011). *Crossing the finish line: Completing college at America's public universities*. Princeton, NJ: Princeton University Press.

Bryk, A. S., Gomez, L. M., & Grunow, A. (2010). Getting ideas into action: Building networked improvement communities in education. *Carnegie Perspective*. Retrieved from http://www.carnegiefoundation.org/spotlight/webinar-bryk-gomez-building-networked-improvement-communities-in-education

Bryk, A. S., Gomez, L. M., Grunow, A., & LeMahieu, P. (in press). *Improving: How America's schools can get better at getting better*. Cambridge, MA: Harvard Education Publishing.

Bryk, A. S., Sebring, P. B., Allensworth, E., Luppescu, S., & Easton, J. Q. (2010). *Organizing schools for improvement: Lessons from Chicago*. Chicago, IL: University of Chicago Press.

Burke, J. C. (2005). Reinventing accountability: From bureaucratic rules to performance results. In J. C. Burke & Associates (Eds.), *Achieving accountability in higher education: Balancing public, academic, and market demands* (pp. 216–245). San Francisco, CA: Jossey-Bass.

Buros Center for Testing. (2014, January 19). *Mental measurement yearbooks*. Retrieved from http://buros.org/mental-measurements-yearbook

Bureau of Labor Statistics. (2014, February 12). In *Wikipedia*. Retrieved from http://en.wikipedia.org/wiki/Bureau_of_Labor_Statistics

Bush, V. (1945). *Science, the endless frontier: A report to the president* (Report OCLC 1594001). Retrieved from https://www.nsf.gov/od/lpa/nsf50/vbush1945.htm#transmittal

Business-Higher Education Forum. (2004). *Public accountability for student learning in higher education*. Retrieved from http://www.bhef.com/sites/g/files/g829556/f/report_2004_public_accountability.pdf

Cacio, E., & Reber, S. (2013). The K–12 education battle. In M. J. Bailey, & S. Danziger (Eds.), *Legacies of the war on poverty* (pp. 66–92). New York, NY: Russell Sage Foundation.

Campbell, D. L., & Stanley, J. C. (1963). *Experimental and quasi-experimental designs for research*. Chicago, IL: Rand McNally.

Carnegie Foundation for the Advancement of Teaching. (2014, November 18). *The six core principles of improvement*. Retrieved from http://www.carnegiefoundation.org/our-ideas/six-core-principles-improvement/

Carnevale, A. P., Smith, N., & Strohl, J. (2010). *Help wanted: Projections of jobs and education requirements through 2018*. Retrieved from https://cew.georgetown.edu/wp-content/uploads/2014/12/fullreport.pdf

Centers for Disease Control and Prevention. (2013, December 22). *Who should not get vaccinated with these vaccines?* Retrieved from http://www.cdc.gov/vaccines/vpd-vac/should-not-vacc.htm

Chickering, A. W., & Gamson, Z. F. (1987, March). Seven principles for good practice in undergraduate education. *AAHE Bulletin*, 3–7. Retrieved from http://files.eric.ed.gov/fulltext/ED282491.pdf

Chui, M., Farrell, D., & Jackson, K. (2014, April 7). *How government can promote open data and help unleash over $3 trillion in economic value*. Retrieved from http://www.mckinsey.com/Insights/public_sector/how_government_can_promote_open_data?cid=other-eml-alt-mip-mck-oth-1404

Coalition for Evidence-Based Policy. (2013, December 10). *Our mission*. Retrieved from http://coalition4evidence.org

Coalition for Evidence-Based Policy. (2014, January 14). *Top tier evidence: Success for All for grades K–2*. Retrieved from http://evidencebasedprograms.org/1366-2/success-forall

Coburn, C. E., & Stein, M. K. (Eds.). (2013). *Research and practice in education: Building alliances, bridging the divide*. Lanham, MD: Rowman & Littlefield.

Cohen, D. K., & Moffitt, S. L. (2009). *The ordeal of equality: Did federal regulation fix the schools?* Cambridge, MA: Harvard University Press.

Collins, F. S., Hudson, K. L., Briggs, J. P., & Lauer, M. S. (2014). PCORnet: Turning a dream into reality. *Journal of the American Medical Informatics Association: JAMIA, 21*(4), 576–577. doi:10.1136/amiajnl-2014-002864

Common Core State Standards Initiative. (2014, February 21). *In the states*. Retrieved from http://www.corestandards.org/in-the-states

———. (2015, July 6). *Standards-setting criteria*. Retrieved from http://www.corestandards.org/assets/Criteria.pdf

Common Education Data Standards. (2014). *What is CEDS?* Retrieved from https://ceds.ed.gov/whatIsCEDS.aspx

Complete College America. (2014, April 7). *Complete College America.* Retrieved from http://completecollege.org

Cook, T. D. (1985). Post-positivist critical multiplism. In R. L. Shotland & M. M. Mark (Eds.), *Social science and social policy* (pp. 21–62). Beverly Hills, CA: SAGE Publications.

Cook, T. D., Scriven, M., Coryn, C. L., & Evergreen, S. D. (2010). Contemporary thinking about causation in evaluation: A dialogue with Tom Cook and Michael Scriven. *American Journal of Evaluation, 31*(1), 105–117.

Council for the Accreditation of Educator Preparation. (2013). *CAEP 2013 standards for the accreditation of educator preparation.* Retrieved from https://caepnet.files.wordpress.com/2015/02/final_board_amended_20150213.pdf

Council for Aid to Education. (2015, April 14). *CLA-overview.* Retrieved from http://cae.org/participating-institutions/cla-overview

Council of Chief State School Officers. (2012). *Our responsibility, our promise: Transforming educator preparation and entry into the profession.* Retrieved from http://ccsso.org/Documents/2012/Our%20Responsibility%20Our%20Promise_2012.pdf

Cunningham, A. F., & Wellman, J. V. (2001, November). *Beneath the surface: A statistical analysis of the major variable associated with state grades in measuring up 2000.* Retrieved from http://www.highereducation.org/reports/wellman/wellman.pdf

Curry, T. (2014, April 2). Representative Paul Ryan: The War on Poverty has "failed miserably." *In Plain Sight.* Retrieved from http://www.nbcnews.com/feature/in-plain-sight/rep-paul-ryan-war-poverty-has-failed-miserably-v19681085

Dahl, R. A., & Lindblom, C. E. (1953). *Politics, economics, and welfare: Planning and politico-economic systems resolved into basic social processes.* New York, NY: Harper & Row.

Darling-Hammond, L. (2010). *The flat world and education: How America's commitment to equity will determine our future.* New York, NY: Teachers College Press.

Darwin, C. (1859). *On the Origin of Species by Means of Natural Selection, or the Preservation of Favoured Races in the Struggle for Life.* Retrieved from https://en.wikisource.org/wiki/On_the_Origin_of_Species_(1859)

Data Quality Campaign. (2014, February 12). *10 essential elements.* Retrieved from http://www.dataqualitycampaign.org/your-states-progress/10-essential-elements

Datnow, A., & Park, V. (2010). Success for All: Using tools to transport research-based practices to the classroom. In C. E. Coburn & M. K. Stein (Eds.), *Research and practice in education: Building alliances, bridging the divide* (pp. 77–91). Lanham, MD: Rowman & Littlefield.

de Tocqueville, A. (1997). *Democracy in America* (Vol. 1). New York, NY: Alfred A. Knopf.

Denley, T. (2014). How predictive analysis and choice architecture can improve student success. *Research and Practice in Assessment,* 61–69. Retrieved from http://www.rpajournal.com/dev/wp-content/uploads/2014/10/A6.pdf

Downs, A. (1957). *An economic theory of democracy.* New York, NY: Harper & Row.

Drucker, P. F. (1978). *Adventures of a bystander.* New York, NY: Harper & Row.

Dynarski, S. (2000). Hope for whom? Financial aid for the middle class and its impact on college attendance. *National Tax Journal, 53*(3), 2.

Elmore, R. F. (2015, January 5). The future is learning, but what about schooling. *Inside Higher Ed.* Retrieved from https://www.insidehighered.com/blogs/higher-ed-beta/future-learning-what-about-schooling

Ewell, P. T. (1999). Linking performance measures to resource allocation: Exploring unmapped terrain. *Quality in Higher Education, 5*(3), 191–209.

———. (2005). Power in numbers: The values in our metrics. *Change, 37*(4), 10–16

———. (2009, November). *Assessment, accountability, and improvement: Revisiting the tension.* Retrieved from http://www.learningoutcomeassessment.org/documents/PeterEwell_005.pdf

Ewell, P., & L'Orange H. P. (2009, September 14). *The ideal state postsecondary data system: 15 essential characteristics and required functionality.* Retrieved from http://www.sheeo.org/sites/default/files/publications/ideal_data_system.pdf

Fisher, R. A. (1925). *Statistical methods for research workers.* London, England: Oliver & Boyd.

———. (1935). *The design of experiments.* London, England: Oliver & Boyd.

Fisse, J., & Braithwaite, J. (1983). *The Impact of Publicity on Corporate Offenders.* Albany, NY: SUNY Press.

Fox, L., Garfinkel, I., Kaushal, N., Waldfogel, J., & Wimer, C. (2014). *Waging war on poverty: Historical trends in poverty using the supplemental poverty measure.* National Bureau of Economic Research, Working Paper 19789. Retrieved from http://www.nber.org/papers/w19789

Friedman, T. L. (2007). *The world is flat: A brief history of the twenty-first century.* New York, NY: Picador.

Gage, N. L. (1963). *Handbook of research on teaching.* Chicago, IL: Rand McNally.

Gawande, A. (2004, December 6). The bell curve. *New Yorker.* Retrieved from http://www.newyorker.com/magazine/2004/12/06/the-bell-curve

———. (2007). *Better: A surgeon's notes on performance.* New York, NY: Henry Holt & Company.

———. (2009). *Checklist manifesto: How to get things right.* New York, NY: Metropolitan Books.

———. (2014, May 5). *Atul Gawande* [website]. Retrieved from http://atulgawande.com

Gibbs, C., Ludwig, J., & Miller, D. L. (2013). Head Start origins and impacts. In M. J. Bailey, & S. Danziger (Eds.), *Legacies of the war on poverty* (pp. 39–65). New York, NY: Russell Sage Foundation.

Gill, J. I., & Saunders, L. (Eds.). (1992). *Developing effective policy analysis in higher education.* San Francisco, CA: Jossey-Bass.

Given, L. M. (Ed.). (2008). *The SAGE encyclopedia of qualitative research methods.* Los Angeles, CA: SAGE.

Graham, P. A. (2005). *Schooling America: How the public schools meet the nation's changing needs.* New York, NY: Oxford University Press.

Granger, R. C., and Maynard, R. (2015). Unlocking the potential of the "What Works" approach to policymaking and practice: Improving impact evaluations. *American Journal of Evaluation*, 1–12.

Grove, M. (2014, October 11). The new school rules. *The Economist*. Retrieved from http://www.economist.com/news/britain/21623766-academies-programme-has-transformed-englands-educational-landscape-new-school-rules?zid=316&ah=2f6fb672faf113fdd3b11cd1b1bf8a77

Haley Will, K. (2006, July 23). Big Brother on campus. *Washington Post*, p. B07.

Havelock, R. G. (1971). *Planning for innovation through dissemination and utilization of knowledge*. Center for Research on the Utilization of Scientific Knowledge, University of Michigan: Ann Arbor.

High School Survey of Student Engagement. (2015). *High school survey of student engagement*. Retrieved from http://ceep.indiana.edu/hssse/about/survey.shtml

Hill, P. T., & Celio, M. B. (1998). *Fixing urban schools*. Washington, DC: Brookings Institution Press.

Hitch, C. J. (1996). Management problems of large organizations. *Operations Research, 44*, 257–264.

Hodas, S. (2015, January 15). *Clash of cultures: Blue collar, white collar, and school reform*. Retrieved from http://www.crpe.org/thelens/clash-cultures-blue-collar-white-collar-and-school-reform

Holzer, H. J. (2013). Workforce development programs. In M. J. Bailey, & S. Danziger (Eds.), *Legacies of the war on poverty* (pp. 121–150). New York, NY: Russell Sage Foundation.

Hubbard, L., Mehan, H., & Stein, M. K. (2006). *Reform as learning: School reform, organizational culture, and community politics in San Diego*. New York, NY: Routledge.

Hutchings, P., Kinzie, J., & Kuh, G. D. (2014). Evidence of student learning: What counts and what matters for improvement. In G. D. Kuh, S. O. Ikenberry, N. A. Jankowski, T. R. Cain, P. T. Ewell, P. Hutchings, & J. Kinzie (Eds.), *Using evidence of student learning to improve higher education* (pp. 52–83). San Francisco, CA: Jossey-Bass.

Information Management. (2014, September 26). In *Wikipedia*. Retrieved from http://en.wikipedia.org/wiki/Information_management

Institute of Education Sciences. (2014, January 08). *Find what works*. Retrieved from http://ies.ed.gov/ncee/wwc/findwhatworks.aspx

———. (2014, January 14). *Find what works, literacy*. Retrieved from http://ies.ed.gov/ncee/wwc/FindWhatWorks.aspx

———. (2014, February 17). *Statewide longitudinal date systems grant program*. Retrieved from http://nces.ed.gov/programs/slds/stateinfo.asp

———. (2015, July 03). *Find what works*. Retrieved from http://ies.ed.gov/ncee/wwc/Publications_Reviews.aspx?f=All%20Publication%20and%20Product%20Types,3;#pubsearch

Institute of Medicine. (2013). Crossing the quality chasm: The Institute of Medicine's Health Care Quality initiative. *Institute of Medicine of the National Academies*. Retrieved from http://www.iom.edu/Global/News%20Announcements/Crossing-the-Quality-Chasm-The-IOM-Health-Care-Quality-Initiative.aspx

Institute of Medicine of the National Academies. (2015, July 15). *Crossing the quality chasm: The institute of medicine's health care quality initiative.* Retrieved from http://iom.nationalacademies.org/Reports/2001/Crossing-the-Quality-Chasm-ANew-Health-System-for-the-21st-Century.aspx

Jacobs, J. (1961). *The Death and Life of Great American Cities.* New York, NY: Vintage Books.

Jefferson, T. (1785). *Notes on the state of Virginia.* The Federalist Papers Project. Retrieved from http://www.thefederalistpapers.org/wp-content/uploads/2012/12/Thomas-Jefferson-Notes-On-The-State-Of-Virginia.pdf

Johnson, R., Onwuegbuzie, A. J., & Turner, L. A. (2007). Toward a definition of mixed methods research. *Journal of Mixed Methods Research, 1,* 112–133. doi:10.1177/1558689806298224

Jones, D. P. (1982). *Data and information for executive decisions in higher education.* Boulder, CO: NCHEMS.

———. (2011). *Performance funding: From idea to action.* Retrieved from http://www.nchems.org/pubs/docs/Performance%20Funding%20121411.pdf

Kamisar, B. (2014, January 8). InBloom sputters amid concerns about privacy of student data. *Education Week,* pp. 1, 13.

Katzman, J. (2015, March 31). *Secrets of the SAT:* Frontline *interview.* Retrieved from http://www.pbs.org/wgbh/pages/frontline/shows/sats/interviews/katzman.html

King, M. (2014). Why data is education's "killer app." *Education Week, 33*(27), 28–29. Retrieved from http://www.edweek.org/ew/articles/2014/04/02/27king.h33.html?tkn=MXRFBsdCGluvqL5nPvU7iMuIaxIgqOgBy1p7&cmp=ENL-II-NEWS2&print=1

Kissinger, H. (1994). *Diplomacy.* New York, NY: Simon & Schuster.

Knowledge Management. (2014, September 26). In *Wikipedia.* Retrieved from http://en.wikipedia.org/wiki/Knowledge_management

Knowles, T. (2014, April 25). Pushing Chicago's graduation rates to new heights. *Chicago Tribune.* Retrieved from http://articles.chicagotribune.com/2014-04-25/opinion/ct-dropout-crisis-chicago-solution-perspec-0425-20140425_1_school-graduation-graduation-rate-new-heights

Koretz, D. (2008). *Measuring up: What educational testing really tells us.* Cambridge, MA: Harvard University Press.

Kuh, G. D. (2007, September/October). Risky business: Promises and pitfalls of institutional transparency. *Change Magazine,* 31–35.

———. (2008). *High-impact educational practices: What they are, who has access to them, and why they matter.* Washington, DC: AAC&U.

Kuh, G. D., Ikenberry, S. O., Jankowski, N. A., Cain, T. R., Ewell, P. T., Hutchings, P., & Kinzie, J. (2014). *Using evidence of student learning to improve higher education.* San Francisco, CA: Jossey-Bass.

Langley, G. J., Moen, R. D., Nolan, K. M., Nolan, T. W., Norman, C. L., & Provost, L. P. (2000). *The improvement guide: A practical approach to enhancing organizational performance.* San Francisco, CA: Jossey-Bass.

Lasswell, H. D. (1950). *Who gets what, when, and how.* New York, NY: Peter Smith.

Layton, L. (2014, February 9). Teachers union head calls for core "course correction." *Washington Post.* Retrieved from http://www.washingtonpost.com/local/edu cation/teachers-union-head-calls-for-core-course-correction/2014/02/19/0f 6b2222-99b8-11e3-80ac-63a8ba7f7942_story.html

Layzell, D. T. (1990, October 24). Most research on higher education is stale, irrelevant, and of little use to policy makers. *Chronicle of Higher Education,* pp. B1–B3.

Lazer, S., Mazzeo, J., Twing, J. S., Way, W. D., Camara, W., & Sweeney, K. (2014, February 28). *Thoughts on an assessment of common core standards.* Retrieved from http://images.pearsonassessments.com/images/tmrs/tmrs_rg/Thoughtona CommonCoreAssessmentSystem.pdf

Lemann, N. (1999). *The big test: The secret history of the American meritocracy.* New York, NY: Farrar, Straus and Giroux.

Lindblom, C. E., & Cohen, D. K. (1979). *Usable knowledge: Social science and social problem solving.* New Haven, CT: Yale University Press.

Lingenfelter, P. E. (1974). *The politics of higher education appropriations in three Midwestern states* (Unpublished doctoral dissertation). University of Michigan, Ann Arbor.

———. (2007). How should states respond to *A test of leadership? Change Magazine, 39*(1). doi:10.3200/CHNG.39.1.13-19

———. (2007, January 19). *K–12 and higher education: Cultural differences and consequences.* Retrieved from http://archive.sheeo.org/about/paulpres/AAC&U%20 January%202007.pdf

———. (2008). Financing public colleges and universities in the United States. In H. F. Ladd & E. B. Fiske (Eds.), *Handbook of research in education finance and policy* (pp. 651–670). New York, NY: Routledge.

———. (2010, November 22). *Why SHEEO supports the common core state standards.* Retrieved from http://www.sheeo.org/sites/default/files/20101216-Why-SHEEO-supports-the-Common-Core-State-Standards.pdf.

———. (2011, May). Evidence and impact: How scholarship can improve policy and practice. *Change Magazine, 43*(3). doi:10.1080/00091383.2011.569260

Lingenfelter, P. E., & Mingle, J. R. (2014). *Public policy for higher education in the United States: A brief history of state leadership.* Retrieved from http://www.sheeo .org/sites/default/files/History_Web.pdf

Long, B. T. (2013). Supporting access to higher education. In M. J. Bailey, & S. Danziger (Eds.), *Legacies of the war on poverty* (pp. 93–120). New York, NY: Russell Sage Foundation.

Lopez, F. (2014, September 30). *Review of a meta-analysis of the literature of the effect of charter schools on student achievement.* Think Tank Reviews. Retrieved from http://nepc.colorado.edu/thinktank/review-meta-analysis-effect-charter

Loshin, D. (2003, March 1). Who owns data? *Information Management.* Retrieved from http://www.information-management.com/issues/20030301/6389-1.html ?zkPrintable=1&nopagination=1

Madaus, G. (2001). *A brief history of attempts to monitor testing.* Retrieved from http://www.bc.edu/research/nbetpp/publications/v2n2.html

Mayer-Schönberger, V., & Cukier, K. (2013). *Big data: A revolution that will transform how we live, work, and think.* New York, NY: Houghton Mifflin Harcourt.

McCann, C., & Laitinen, A. (2014, March). *College blackout: How the higher education lobby fought to keep students in the dark.* Retrieved from http://education.newamerica.net/sites/newamerica.net/files/policydocs/CollegeBlackoutFINAL.pdf

McGregor, D. (1985). *The human side of enterprise.* New York, NY: McGraw-Hill

MDRC. (2013, December 10). *About MRDC.* Retrieved from http://www.mdrc.org/about/about-mdrc-overview-0

Mehta, J., Gomez, L. M., & Bryk, A. S. (2012). Building on practical knowledge. In Mehta, J., Schwartz, R. B. & Hess, F. M. (Eds.), *The futures of school reform* (pp. 35–64). Cambridge, MA: Harvard Education Press.

Mehta, J., Schwartz, R. B., & Hess, F. M. (Eds.). (2012). *The futures of school reform.* Cambridge, MA: Harvard Education Press.

Messick, S. (1990). Validity of test interpretation and use. *Educational Testing Service research report* RR-90(11). Princeton, NJ: Educational Testing Service.

Milliron, M. D., Malcolm, L., & Kil, D. (2014). Insight and action analytics: Three case studies to consider. *Research and Practice in Assessment, 9,* 70–89. Retrieved from http://www.rpajournal.com/dev/wp-content/uploads/2014/10/A7.pdf.

Mitchell, S. D. (2009). *Unsimple truths: Science, complexity, and policy.* Chicago: University Of Chicago Press.

Mohn, S. (2014, March 19). Poverty: Laziness or lack of opportunity. *Huffington Post online.* Retrieved from http://www.huffingtonpost.com/sid-mohn/poverty-laziness-or-lack-_b_4994213.html.

Moore, W. (1970). *The professions.* New York, NY: Russell Sage Foundation.

Morgan, D. L. (2007, January). Paradigms lost and pragmatism regained: Methodological implications of combining qualitative and quantitative methods. *Journal of Mixed Methods Research, 1,* 48–76. doi: 10.1177/2345678906292462

Mortensen, T. (2014, February 17). *Public high school graduation rates by state, 1981 to 2010.* Retrieved from http://www.postsecondary.org/spreadslist.asp

National Association of College and University Attorneys. (2014, March 20). *Higher Education Opportunity Act.* Retrieved from http://www.nacua.org/documents/heoa.pdf

National Forum on College Level Learning. (2014, February 17). *National forum on college level learning.* Retrieved from http://www.collegelevellearning.org

National Center for Education Statistics. (2014, February 8). In *Wikipedia.* Retrieved from http://en.wikipedia.org/wiki/National_Center_for_Education_Statistics

————. (2014, February 17). *Statewide longitudinal date systems grant program.* Retrieved from http://nces.ed.gov/programs/slds/stateinfo.asp

————. (2014, March 20). *Graduate rate survey.* Retrieved from http://nces.ed.gov/ipeds/glossary/index.asp?id=812

National Commission on Excellence in Education (1983). *A nation at risk: An imperative for educational reform.* Retrieved from http://www2.ed.gov/pubs/NatAtRisk/index.html

National Governors Association. (2005, July 16). *Governors sign compact on graduation rates*. Retrieved from http://www.nga.org/cms/home/news-room/news-releases/page_2005/col2-content/main-content-list/title_governors-sign-compact-on-high-school-graduation-rate-at-annual-meeting.html

National Research Council and Institute of Medicine. (2013, December 10). *Preventing mental, emotional, and behavioral disorders among young people: Progress and possibilities*. Retrieved from http://www.nap.edu/openbook.php?record_id=12480&page=373

National Survey of Student Engagement. (2015, March 8). *About NSSE*. Retrieved from http://nsse.iub.edu/html/about.cfm

Newman, J. (2014, February 14). What experts on college-rating system mean by "we need better data." *Chronicle of Higher Education*. Retrieved from http://chronicle.com/blogs/data/2014/02/14/what-experts-on-college-ratings-system-mean-by-we-need-better-data/

No Child Left Behind (NCLB) Act of 2001, 20 U.S.C.A. § 6301 et seq.

Nussbaum, M. C. (2004). *Hiding from humanity: Disgust, shame, and the law*. Princeton, NJ: Princeton University Press.

Nutting, P. A., Beasley, J. W., & Werner, J. J. (1999). Practice-based research networks answer primary care questions. *JAMA, 281*(8), 686–688. doi:10.1001/jama.281.8.686

Objectivism (Ayn Rand). (2014, September 24). In *Wikipedia*. Retrieved from http://en.wikipedia.org/wiki/Objectivism_(Ayn_Rand)

Open Learning Initiative. (2014, April 9). *Open Learning Initiative*. Retrieved from https://oli.cmu.edu

Orfield, G., Marin, P., Horn, C. L. (Eds.). (2005). *Higher education and the color line: College access racial equity, and social change*. Cambridge, MA: Harvard Education Press.

Organization for Economic Cooperation and Development. (2013, September 11). *United States country note—Education at a glance 2012:* OECD indicators. Retrieved from http://www.oecd.org/unitedstates/CN%20-%20United%20States.pdf

———. (2014, January). *AHELO feasibility study report, Volume 1: Design and implementation*. Retrieved from http://www.oecd.org/edu/skills-beyond-school/AHELOFSReportVolume1.pdf

———. (2014, April 10). *OECD skills surveys*. Retrieved from http://www.oecd.org/site/piaac

———. (2014, January). *AHELO feasibility study report, Volume 2: Data analysis and national experiences*. Retrieved from http://www.oecd.org/edu/skills-beyond-school/AHELOFSReportVolume2.pdf

———. (2014, February 25). *Testing student and university performance globally: OECD's AHELO*. Retrieved from http://www.oecd.org/edu/skills-beyond-school/testingstudentanduniversityperformancegloballyoecdsahelo.htm

———. (2014, February 28). *Countries participating in the AHELO feasibility study*. Retrieved from http://www.oecd.org/edu/skills-beyond-school/countriesparticipatingintheahelofeasibilitystudy.htm

————. (2015, March 24). *OECD programme for international student assessment.* Retrieved from http://www.oecd-ilibrary.org/education/pisa_19963777

————. (2015, March 24). *OECD skills studies.* Retrieved from http://www.oecd-ilibrary.org/education/oecd-skills-studies_23078731

Orszag, P., & Bridgeland, J. (2013). Can government play moneyball? *The Atlantic, 312*(1), 63–66.

Osborne, D., & Gabler, T. (1992). *Reinventing government: How the entrepreneurial spirit is transforming the public sector.* Reading, MA: Addison-Wesley.

Pace, C. R. (1980). Measuring the quality of student effort. *Current Issues in Higher Education, 2,* 10–16.

————. (1984). *Measuring the quality of college student experiences: An account of the development and use of the college student experiences questionnaire.* Los Angeles, CA: Higher Education Research Institute.

————. (1990). *The undergraduate: A report of their activities and college experiences in the 1980s.* Los Angeles, CA: Center for the Study of Evaluation.

Pareto principle. (2015, March 17). In *Wikipedia.* Retrieved from http://en.wikipedia.org/wiki/Pareto_principle

Parsons, B. A. (2002). *Evaluative inquiry: Using evaluation to promote student success.* Thousand Oaks, CA: Corwin Press.

Partnership for Assessment of Readiness for College and Careers. (2014, February 21). *About PARCC.* Retrieved from https://www.parcconline.org/aboutparcc

Pawson, R. (2002). Evidence and policy and naming and shaming. *Policy Studies, 23*(3/4), 211–230.

————. (2006). *Evidence-based policy: A realist perspective.* London, England: SAGE Publications.

Pawson, R., & Tilley, N. (1997). *Realistic evaluation.* London, England: SAGE Publications.

Pellegrino, J. W., Chudowsky, N., & Glaser, R. (Eds.). (2001). *Knowing what students know: The science and design of educational assessment.* Washington, DC: National Academy Press.

Perna, L.W., & Finney, J. E. (2014). *The attainment agenda: State policy leadership in higher education.* Baltimore, MD: Johns Hopkins University Press.

Peterson, R. T. (2008). *Peterson field guide to birds of North America.* Boston, MA: Houghton Mifflin Harcourt.

Peurach, D. (2011). *Seeing complexity in public education: Problems, possibilities, and success for all.* Oxford Scholarship Online. New York, NY: Oxford University Press. doi:10.1093/acprof:oso/9780199736539.001.0001

Pfeffer, J. (2005). Changing mental models: HR's most important task. *Human Resource Management, 44*(2), 123–128. doi:10.1002/hrm.20053.

Piety, P. J. (2013). *Assessing the educational data movement.* New York, NY: Teachers College Press.

Quality Counts. (1997). *Education Week.* Retrieved from http://www.edweek.org/ew/qc/

Quint, J. C., Balu, R., DeLaurentis, M., Rappaport, S., Smith, T. J., & Zhu, P. (2013). *The Success for All model of school reform: Early findings from the Investing in Innovation (i3) scale-up.* Retrieved from http://www.mdrc.org/publication/success-all-model-school-reform

Ranking of world universities. (2014, April 10). In *Wikipedia.* Retrieved from http://en.wikipedia.org/wiki/Academic_Ranking_of_World_Universities

Raudenbush, S., and Bloom, H. (2015, April). *Learning about and from variation in program impacts using multisite trials.* MDRC.

Ravitch, D. (2000). *Left back: A century of battles over school reform.* New York, NY: Simon & Schuster.

Reason, P., & Bradbury, H. (2008). *The SAGE handbook of action research: Participative inquiry and practice* (2nd ed.). London, England: SAGE Publications.

Rivlin, A. M. (1971) *Systematic thinking for social action.* Washington, DC: Brookings Institution.

Rossi, P. H., & Freeman, H. E. (1989). *Evaluation: A systematic approach* (4th ed.). Newbury Park, CA: SAGE Publications.

Sampson, R. J., Raudenbush, S. W., & Earls, F. (1997). Neighborhoods and violent crime: A multilevel study of collective efficacy. *Science, 277*(5328), 918–924.

Sawhill, J., & Williamson, D. (2001, May). Measuring what matters in nonprofits. *McKinsey Quarterly.* Retrieved from http://www.mckinsey.com/insights/social_sector/measuring_what_matters_in_nonprofits

Schein, E. (1973). *Professional education.* New York, NY: McGraw-Hill.

Schön, D. A. (1983). *The reflective practitioner: How professionals think in action.* New York, NY: Basic Books.

———. (1995). Causality and causal inference in the study of organizations. In R. F. Goodmann & W. R. Fisher (Eds.), *Rethinking knowledge: Reflections across the disciplines* (pp. 69–100). Albany, NY: SUNY Press.

Schools in Chicago are called the worst by education chief. (1987, November 8). *The New York Times.* Retrieved from http://www.nytimes.com/1987/11/08/us/schools-in-chicago-are-called-the-worst-by-education-chief.html

Scott, J. C. (1998). *Seeing like a state: How certain schemes to improve the human condition have failed.* New Haven, CT: Yale University Press.

Senge, P. (1990). *The fifth discipline.* New York, NY: Doubleday/Currency.

Senge, P., Cambron-McCage, N., Lucas, T., Smith, B., Dutton, J., & Kliner, A. (2000). *Schools that learn: A fifth discipline fieldbook for educators, parents, and everyone who cares about education.* New York, NY: Doubleday/Currency.

Shadish, W. R., Cook, T. D., & Leviton, L. C. (1991). *Foundations of program evaluation: Theories of practice.* Newbury Park, CA: SAGE Publications.

Shapiro, D., Dundar, A., Wakhunga, P. K., Yuan, X., & Harrell, A. T. (VA). (2015). *Completing college: A state-level view of student attainment rates.* Retrieved from http://nscresearchcenter.org/wp-content/uploads/NSC_Signature_Report_8_StateSupp.pdf.

Shapiro, D., Dundar, A., Ziskin, M., Yuan, X., & Harrell, A. (2013, December 16). *Completing college: A national view of student attainment rates—Fall 2007 cohort.* Retrieved from http://nscresearchcenter.org/signaturereport6/

Shick, A. (1969). Systems, politics, and systems budgeting. *Public Administration Review, 29,* 137–151.

Shulman, L. S. (2004). *The wisdom of practice: Essays on teaching, learning, and learning to teach.* San Francisco, CA: Jossey-Bass.

Simon, H. A. (1981). *The sciences of the artificial.* Cambridge, MA: MIT Press

Slavin, R. E., Madden, N. A., Chambers, B., & Haxby, B. (2009). *2 million children: Success for All.* Thousand Oak, CA: Corwin Press.

Smith, R. V., Densmore, L., & Lener, E. (press, 2015). *Graduate research: A guide for students in the sciences* (4th ed.). Seattle, WA: University of Washington Press.

Snyder, M. (2015). *Driving better outcomes: Typology and principles to inform outcomes-based funding models.* Retrieved from http://hcmstrategists.com/driving outcomes/wp-content/themes/hcm/pdf/Driving%20Outcomes.pdf

Solberg, L., Mosser, G., & McDonald, S. (1997, March). The three faces of performance measurement: Improvement, accountability, and research. *Journal on Quality Improvement, 23*(3), 135–147.

Sowell, T. (2014, December 16). *Thomas Sowell archives.* Retrieved from http://www.jewishworldreview.com/cols/sowell1.asp

Soydan, H., & Palinkas, L. A. (2014). *Evidence-based practice in social work: Development of a new professional culture.* London, England: Routledge.

Spencer Foundation Strategic Initiatives. (2015, April 14). *Data use and educational improvement.* Retrieved from http://www.spencer.org/content.cfm/data-use-and-educational-improvement-activities

Standard-setting study. (n.d.). In *Wikipedia.* Retrieved from http://en.wikipedia.org/wiki/Standard-setting_study

State Higher Education Executive Officers. (2005). *Accountability for better results: A national imperative for higher education.* Retrieved from http://www.sheeo.org/sites/default/files/publications/Accountability%20for%20Better%20Results.pdf

———. (2015). *State higher education finance, fiscal year 2013.* Retrieved from http://www.sheeo.org/resources/publications/shef——-state-higher-education-finance-fy13

Stokes, D. E. (1997). *Pasteur's quadrant: Basic science and technological innovation.* Washington DC: Brookings Institution Press.

Stone, D. A. (1988). *Policy paradox and political reason.* Glenview, IL: Scott, Foresman and Company.

Strader, R., & Thille, C. (2012). The open learning initiative: Enacting instruction online. In Oblinger, D. G. (Ed.), *Game changers: Education and information technologies* (pp. 201–213). Washington, DC: Educause.

Swanson, C. B., & Barlage, J. (2006, December). *Influence: A study of the factors shaping education policy.* Retrieved from http://www.edweek.org/media/influence_study.pdf

Tan, E. J., McGill, S., Tanner, E. K., Carlson, M. C., Rebok, G. W., Seeman, T. E., & Fried, L. P. (2014). The evolution of an academic-community partnership in the design, implementation, and evaluation of Experience Corps. Baltimore City: A courtship model. *The Gerontologist, 54*(2), 314–321.

Tandberg, D., & Hillman, N. W. (2015). *State performance funding for higher education: Silver bullet or red herring?* Retrieved from http://www.wiscape.wisc.edu/docs/WebDispenser/wiscapedocuments/pb018.pdf?sfvrsn=4

Tennessee Tech University. (2015, April 14). *Critical thinking assessment test.* Retrieved from https://www.tntech.edu/cat

Thernstrom, A., & Thernstrom, S. (2003). *No excuses: Closing the racial gap in learning.* New York, NY: Simon & Schuster.

Thille, C., Schneider, E., Kizilcec, R. F., Piech, C., Halawa, S. A., & Greene, D. K. (2014). The future of data-enriched assessment. *Research and Practice in Assessment, 9,* 5–16. Retrieved from http://www.rpajournal.com/dev/wp-content/uploads/2014/10/A1.pdf

Thyer, B. A. (2004). What is evidence-based practice? *Brief Treatment and Crisis Intervention, 4*(2), 167–176.

TIMSS & PIRLS. (2015, March 24). *TIMSS & PIRLS.* Retrieved from http://timssandpirls.bc.edu/home/pdf/TP_About.pdf

U.S. Chamber of Commerce Foundation. (2014). *Leaders and laggards.* Retrieved from http://www.leadersandlaggards.org/sites/default/files/Leaders%20and%20Laggards%20A%20State-by-State%20Report%20Card%20on%20K-12%20Educational%20Effectiveness.pdf

U.S. Department of Education. (2006). *A test of leadership: Charting the future of U.S. higher education.* Retrieved from http://www2.ed.gov/about/bdscomm/list/hiedfuture/reports/final-report.pdf

———. (2014, March 22). *FERPA general guidance for students.* Retrieved from https://www2.ed.gov/policy/gen/guid/fpco/ferpa/students.html

United States President's Commission on Higher Education, & Zook, G. F. (1947). *Higher education for American democracy, a report.* Retrieved from http://catalog.hathitrust.org/Record/001117586

Van Voorhis, F. L., Maier, M., Epstein, J. L., & Lloyd, C. M. (2014, January 8). *The impact of family involvement on the education of children ages 3 to 8: A focus on literacy and math achievement outcomes and social-emotional skills.* Retrieved from http://www.mdrc.org/publication/impact-family-involvement-education-children-ages-3-8

Walker, J. S., Bruns, E. J., Conlan, L., & LaForce, C. (2011). The national wraparound initiative: A community of practice approach to building knowledge in the field of children's mental health. *Best Practices in Mental Health, 7*(1), 26–46.

Walters, P. B., & Lareau, A. (2009). Education research that matters: Influence, scientific rigor, and policymaking. In P. B. Walters, A. Lareau, S. Ranis (Eds.), *Education research on trial: Policy reform and the call for scientific rigor* (pp. 197–220). New York, NY: Routledge.

Weaver, W. (1948). Science and complexity. *American Scientist, 36*(4), 536–544.

Weiss, M. J., Bloom, H. S., & Brock, T. (2014, January 8). *A conceptual framework for studying the sources of variation in program effects.* Retrieved from http://www.mdrc.org/sites/default/files/a-conceptual_framework_for_studying_the_sources.pdf

Westfall, J. M., Mold, J., & Fagnan, L. (2007). Practice-based research—"blue highways" on the NIH roadmap. *JAMA, 297*(4), 403–406. doi:10.1001/jama.297.4.403

Western Interstate Commission for Higher Education. (2014, March 25). *Facilitating development of a multistate longitudinal data exchange.* Retrieved from http://www.wiche.edu/longitudinalDataExchange

Wildavsky, A. (1969). Rescuing policy analysis from PPBS. *Public Administration Review, 29*, 189–202.

———. (1974). *The politics of the budgetary process* (2nd ed.). Boston, MA: Little, Brown.

Wilson, E. O. (1999). *Consilience: The unity of knowledge.* New York, NY: Random House Digital.

Yeager, D., Bryk, A., Muhich, J., Hausman, H., & Morales, L. (2014). *Practical measurement.* Retrieved from http://cdn.carnegiefoundation.org/wp-content/uploads/2014/09/Practical_Measurement_Yeager-Bryk1.pdf

ABOUT THE AUTHOR

Paul E. Lingenfelter served as CEO and president of the State Higher Education Executive Officers (SHEEO) from 2000 to 2013. During this time, Lingenfelter staffed the National Commission on Accountability in Higher Education, created the annual State Higher Education Finance study, and worked to improve data systems and build stronger relationships between K–12 and higher education.

Previously, Lingenfelter was vice president of the program on human and community development at the John D. and Catherine T. MacArthur Foundation, which supported research and practice in economics; mental health; and human development, education, and community development.

He is now a senior scholar at the National Institute for Learning Outcomes Assessment at the University of Illinois and an adjunct professor at the University of Colorado-Denver School of Public Affairs.

Lingenfelter has been a frequent participant in international meetings on higher education issues including governance, budgeting, quality assurance, and the assessment of student learning. He has published widely on issues in higher education and philanthropy and served on numerous education boards and commissions.

(Continued from preceding page)

Intersectionality in Educational Research

Edited by Dannielle Joy Davis, Rachelle Brunn-Bevel, and James L. Olive

Foreword by Susan Jones

"This book offers a comprehensive, complex, and well-organized overview of intersectionality as a tool for critical inquiry and analysis and highlights its usefulness as a theoretical perspective and a qualitative and quantitative methodology. Incorporating examples relevant to a variety of disciplines and considering educational issues that range in relevance from K–12 to higher education, this book is a must-read for policy makers, researchers, educators, administrators, practitioners, advocates, and others vested in understanding the intersections of social disparities such as race, class, and gender, and the ways in which such intersections shape the educational experiences and outcomes of marginalized populations. Whether your knowledge of intersectionality reflects that of a novice or seasoned scholar, you will find this book enthralling and the reflective questions at the end of each chapter thought provoking."—*Yvette Murphy-Erby*, *Associate Dean, Fulbright College of Arts and Sciences, University of Arkansas*

Sty/us

22883 Quicksilver Drive
Sterling, VA 20166-2102   Subscribe to our e-mail alerts: www.Styluspub.com

Also available from Stylus

Research, Actionable Knowledge, and Social Change
Reclaiming Social Responsibility Through Research Partnerships

Edward P. St. John

Foreword by Penny A. Pasque

"St. John's book offers hope for practitioners, researchers, and policy makers interested in moving past studying problems and moving toward addressing them. He provides both theoretical and practical guidance for individuals designing and engaging with actionable research. This book serves as a useful tool for graduate students, seasoned scholars, and those outside the academy who are interested in building partnerships."—**Ronald Hallett**, *Assistant Professor, Director, Creating Opportunities Via Education, Benerd School of Education, University of the Pacific*

"St. John has spent his career studying the intersections of policy, practice, and research. He has struggled with how those of us concerned with social justice might move away from entrenched notions of research and measurement and instead infuse our work in more direct ways to achieve ends aimed at improving the public good. This book summarizes his ideas and suggests that actionable research has the potential of promoting social justice and fairness in education and social systems. The book will appeal to educational and social researchers interested in collaborating with practitioners committed to improving equity."—**William G. Tierney**, *Wilbur-Kieffer Professor of Higher Education, University of Southern California*

(Continues on previous page)